Authorship Contested

> Drawing on a range of both print and online situations and cases, such as forgeries, exclusions, silences, deceptive online personas, and denied authorship, this exciting new collection offers us engaging and complex perspectives on the concept of contested authorship.
> —*Chris Anson, North Carolina State University, U.S.A.*

This volume explores a dimension of authorship not given its due in the critical discourse to this point—authorship contested. Much of the existing critical literature begins with a text and the proposition that the text has an author. The debates move from here to questions about who the author is, whether or not the author's identity is even relevant, and what relationship she or he does and does not have to the text. The authors contributing to this collection, however, ask about circumstances surrounding efforts to prevent authors from even being allowed to have these questions asked of them, from even being identified as authors. They ask about the political, cultural, economic, and social circumstances that motivate a prospective audience to resist an author's efforts to have a text published, read, and discussed. Particularly noteworthy is the range of everyday rhetorical situations in which contesting authorship occurs—from the production of a corporate document to the publication of fan fiction. Each chapter also focuses on particular instances in which authorship has been contested, demonstrating how theories about various forms of contested authorship play out in a range of events, from the complex issues surrounding peer review to authorship in the age of intelligent machines.

Amy E. Robillard is Associate Professor of Rhetoric and Composition at Illinois State University, U.S.A.

Ron Fortune is Professor Emeritus of English at Illinois State University, U.S.A.

Routledge Studies in Rhetoric and Communication

1. Rhetorics, Literacies, and Narratives of Sustainability
   Edited by Peter Goggin

2. Queer Temporalities in Gay Male Representation
   Tragedy, Normativity, and Futurity
   Dustin Bradley Goltz

3. The Rhetoric of Intellectual Property
   Copyright Law and the Regulation of Digital Culture
   Jessica Reyman

4. Media Representations of Gender and Torture Post-9/11
   Marita Gronnvoll

5. Rhetoric, Remembrance, and Visual Form
   Sighting Memory
   Anne Teresa Demo and Bradford Vivian (editors)

6. Reading, Writing, and the Rhetorics of Whiteness
   Wendy Ryden and Ian Marshall

7. Radical Pedagogies of Socrates and Freire
   Ancient Rhetoric/Radical Praxis
   S.G. Brown

8. Ecology, Writing Theory, and New Media
   Writing Ecology
   Edited by Sidney I. Dobrin

9. The Rhetoric of Food
   Discourse, Materiality, and Power
   Edited by Joshua J. Frye and Michael S. Bruner

10. The Multimediated Rhetoric of the Internet
    Digital Fusion
    Carolyn Handa

11. Communicating Marginalized Masculinities
    Identity Politics in TV, Film, and New Media
    Edited by Ronald L. Jackson II and Jamie E. Moshin

12. Perspectives on Human-Animal Communication
    International Communication
    Edited by Emily Plec

13. Rhetoric and Discourse in Supreme Court Oral Arguments
    Sensemaking in Judicial Decisions
    Ryan A. Malphurs

14. Rhetoric, History, and Women's Oratorical Education
    American Women Learn to Speak
    Edited by David Gold and Catherine L. Hobbs

15. Cultivating Cosmopolitanism for Intercultural Communication
    Communicating as Global Citizens
    Miriam Sobré-Denton and Nilanjana Bardhan

16 Environmental Rhetoric and Ecologies of Place
 Edited by Peter N. Goggin

17 Rhetoric and Ethics in the Cybernetic Age
 The Transhuman Condition
 Jeff Pruchnic

18 Communication, Public Opinion, and Globalization in Urban China
 Francis L.F. Lee, Chin-Chuan Lee, Mike Z. Yao, Tsan-Kuo Chang, Fen Jennifer Lin, and Chris Fei Shen

19 Adaptive Rhetoric
 Evolution, Culture, and the Art of Persuasion
 Alex C. Parrish

20 Communication, Public Discourse, and Road Safety Campaigns
 Persuading People to Be Safer
 Nurit Guttman

21 Mapping Christian Rhetorics
 Connecting Conversations, Charting New Territories
 Edited by Michael-John DePalma and Jeffrey M. Ringer

22 Identity and Power in Narratives of Displacement
 Katrina M. Powell

23 Pedagogies of Public Memory
 Teaching Writing and Rhetoric at Museums, Archives, and Memorials
 Edited by Jane Greer and Laurie Grobman

24 Authorship Contested
 Cultural Challenges to the Authentic, Autonomous Author
 Edited by Amy E. Robillard and Ron Fortune

Authorship Contested
Cultural Challenges to the Authentic, Autonomous Author

Edited by Amy E. Robillard
and Ron Fortune

LONDON AND NEW YORK

First published 2016 by Routledge

2 Park Square, Milton Park, Abingdon, Oxfordshire OX14 4RN
711 Third Avenue, New York, NY 10017

Routledge is an imprint of the Taylor & Francis Group, an informa business

First issued in paperback 2017

Copyright © 2016 Taylor & Francis

The right of the editors to be identified as the author of the editorial material, and of the authors for their individual chapters, has been asserted in accordance with sections 77 and 78 of the Copyright, Designs and Patents Act 1988.

All rights reserved. No part of this book may be reprinted or reproduced or utilised in any form or by any electronic, mechanical, or other means, now known or hereafter invented, including photocopying and recording, or in any information storage or retrieval system, without permission in writing from the publishers.

Notice:
Product or corporate names may be trademarks or registered trademarks, and are used only for identification and explanation without intent to infringe.

Library of Congress Cataloging in Publication Data

Authorship contested : cultural challenges to the authentic, autonomous author / edited by Amy E. Robillard and Ron Fortune.
  pages cm — (Routledge studies in rhetoric and communication)
  Includes bibliographical references and index.
  1. Authorship. 2. Creation (Literary, artistic, etc.) I. Robillard, Amy E., editor. II. Fortune, Ron, 1948- editor.
PN145.A975 2015
808.02—dc23   2015007294

ISBN: 978-1-138-91172-7 (hbk)
ISBN: 978-0-8153-9639-0 (pbk)

Typeset in Sabon
by codeMantra

Contents

Foreword ix
REBECCA MOORE HOWARD
Acknowledgements xiii

Introduction 1
AMY E. ROBILLARD AND RON FORTUNE

PART I
Contrived Authorship

1 *A Gay Girl in Damascus*: Multi-vocal Construction
   and Refutation of Authorial Ethos 21
   JULIA MARIE SMITH

2 Writing in the Dead Zone: Authorship in the
   Age of Intelligent Machines 40
   KYLE JENSEN

3 Writers Who Forge: Forgery as a Response to
   Contested Authorship 55
   RON FORTUNE

PART II
Distributed Authorship

4 Authorial Ethos as Location: How Technical Manuals
   Embody Authorial Ethos without Authors 71
   ERIN A. FROST AND KELLIE SHARP-HOSKINS

5 The *Kairos* of Authorship in Activist Rhetoric 89
   SETH KAHN AND KEVIN MAHONEY

6   In the Author's Hands: Contesting Authorship and
    Ownership in Fan Fiction   107
    RACHEL PARISH

PART III
Excluded Authorship

7   Writing after Stonewall: The Lost Forms of Gay Authorship   121
    JAMES ZEBROSKI

8   The Sound of Silence: Defense of Marriage, Don't Ask,
    Don't Tell, and Post-Authorship Theory   135
    PAUL BUTLER

9   The Emotional Contests of Peer Review   148
    AMY E. ROBILLARD

PART IV
Nascent Authorship

10 "I Feel Like This Is Fake": Spontaneous Mediocrity
    and Studied Genius   161
    VAL PERRY RENDEL

11 Student Authorship in the Age of Permissions:
    Fostering a Gift Economy in First-Year Writing Programs   172
    MATT HOLLRAH

12 Authorizing Plagiarism   192
    JOSEPH HARRIS

    Contributors   207
    Index   211

Foreword

Rebecca Moore Howard

People who inquire about my scholarly field look askance when I say it's authorship studies. Most are not brazen enough to respond, "What's that?" So I kindly step in and try to define it. Even though I work in the field, I don't find the definition easy: "plagiarism, intellectual property, cultural constructions of the author." Just a list; not really a definition, and each of the subfields demands its own definition.

When people then discover that my sub-speciality is plagiarism, they leer uneasily, no doubt wondering whether I can see in their expression the history of their own transgressions. Next they want to know what percentage of students plagiarize, and whether the Internet has increased plagiarism. When I explain that's not what I study—that my focus is on analyzing the importance that our culture attaches to the notion of plagiarism—I can often see the shades being drawn, as I am silently written off as one of those not-to-be-trusted ivory-tower college professors who needs to get a *real* job.

At the beginning of fall semester 2014, however, a colleague asked me to address our new Ph.D. students and talk about transformative moments in my teaching. I described my first semester in front of a college classroom, when I realized that none of the thousands of international students on my campus was in my class, because they were being taught grammar in separate composition classes designed "just for them." Meanwhile, the monolingual U.S. students were learning rhetoric in mine. My doctoral dissertation grew out of my indignation.

I also described a moment ten years later when I realized that the conservative white men in the required general education course I was teaching utterly distrusted me. I was teaching French feminist high theory, and they believed I was teaching it *against* them, positioning them as oppressors. I worked hard to revise my syllabus and my presentation of the materials so that all my students understood that my objective was to examine the naturalized structures—in this case, binary, hierarchized gender—that keep *all* of us in neat boxes, contained and limited.

To the assembled Ph.D. students I also described the moment a decade after that when I had absorbed enough of Pierre Bourdieu's research and analyses to understand that the institutional structures within which I work are positioned to reinforce and naturalize existing social hierarchy, so that learners believe their social immobility is a result of their own academic shortcomings. I said to the assembled group that I now live within these contradictions—my persistent pedagogic hope banging up against my understanding of the hegemonic function of college instruction.

Then I said, "You may be wondering where all this went. This fall I'm teaching undergraduate and graduate authorship seminars. What does authorship have to do with what we once called liberatory pedagogy?" I went on to explain that authorship studies is all about who is and is not positioned to claim the status of "author"; whose voice is and isn't heard; and what circumstances enable or prevent the claim.

I like that definition. I'm sticking with it. Really, when one looks closely, isn't *all* authorship contested?

Not enough of the scholarship of writing and rhetorical studies addresses these concerns. Joseph Harris offers an ideal: "What composition contests ... is a division of the universe of discourse into authors and non-authors" 204. The list of works cited in *Authorship Contested* includes quite a lot of sources. How many, though, are from the field of writing and rhetorical studies? Precious few, actually. In my field, thousands study writing in its cultural context, and hordes teach freshman English, now known as first-year composition. How many of these teachers, though, think about whether the students in their classrooms will ever feel themselves empowered as *authors*? How many of those classrooms instead, 150 years after the invention of college composition, continue the battle (a deliberately chosen noun) to clean up students' prose so that they fit more neatly into their roles as obedient non-authors?

Before such questions can be answered in the positive, the scholarship of writing and rhetorical studies must recognize and explore the notion that authorship is not a natural category but a naturalized one: It is a category that seems normal and thus not subject to contestation. The scholarship of writing and rhetorical studies must recognize and explore the range of rhetorical situations in which the contestation of authorship will actually help scholars and practitioners of writing and rhetorical studies develop more useful practices.

This volume gathers essays that speak from a fresh angle: Instead of focusing on the identity of the author—which is ultimately an individualist perspective—they attend to the *contests over* the identity of the author. This takes us, I believe, to the heart of authorship. It is not a quality that inheres in a body or a text, or in a reader, but in the rhetorical situation itself.

The notion that these elements—writer, text, reader—are freestanding components of discourse is inherent in James Kinneavy's "communication triangle," more commonly known as "the rhetorical triangle." Kinneavy's *Theory of Discourse*, which derives from psycholinguistics and pragmatics as much as it does rhetoric, was published in 1971 and was very much a piece of, rather than a departure from, the intellectual conversations of its historical period. The same is true of Roland Barthes's 1967 "Death of the Author" and Michel Foucault's 1969 "What Is an Author?"—both central texts in authorship theory.

Kinneavy's *Theory of Discourse* was published four years after Barthes placed an essay in the U.S. avant-garde, multimedia *Aspen: The Magazine in a Box*, to which cultural agents such as Andy Warhol and John Lennon also contributed. As John Logie carefully details, Barthes's essay was republished in a French journal in 1968 and then translated back into English in the 1977 *Image—Music—Text*, an important collection of Barthes's essays. Logie explains that the invisibility of the first publication of "Death" has resulted in scholars' misinterpreting the cultural situation in which it was intended to participate. Scholarship that dates the original publication of "Death" in a 1968 French journal typically contextualizes the essay in the political upheaval of May 1968 Paris, when in fact its first publication took place a year earlier, in the U.S., and as an invited piece for a boxed arts journal that also included mazes, phonograph recordings, musical scores, films, and poetry. In short, "The Death of the Author" is a case in which the writer, the text, the publisher, the reader, and the rhetorical situation are all in flux and are, in Logie's telling, contested.

The French publication of the essay gave rise to Foucault's famous rejoinder. At contest in the exchange was not the death of the author, for in a sense, both theorists agreed on that fact. The question was where authorship "lived." In Barthes' account, it was in the reader; in Foucault's, in a culturally constructed "author function" independent of the person(s) who actually produced the text.

Kinneavy's communication triangle appeared two years later, in the 1971 *Theory of Discourse*, and it, too, pulls apart the writer, reader, and text—or, in Kinneavy's lexicon, the encoder, decoder, and signal. All three writers were working in the aftermath of the New Criticism that located all meaning in the text, to be extracted by the trained, vanguard reader through applications of the research method known as "close reading." The New Critical focus on the text was itself a corrective to earlier biographical criticism that posited all textual meaning in authorial intention. In an important sense, Barthes and Foucault make their own contributions to the New Critical challenge to the hegemony of authorial intention—theirs just one demonstration of the extent to which poststructuralism is implicated in the modernism it putatively corrects and replaces.

My point here, though, is the easy separability of the components of author, reader, and text at the time when Barthes, Foucault, and Kinneavy are writing. Current histories of the scholarly field of authorship may reach back, as does Seán Burke's, to include figures from Plato to T.S. Eliot. These are, however, background material for the contemporary field of authorship studies, which begins in earnest, according to most accounts, with Barthes and Foucault. Just as their influence has persisted in and dominated the interdisciplinary field of authorship studies, so Kinneavy's communications triangle had longstanding traction in the field of writing and rhetorical studies, albeit with successive challenges and corrections.

Those challenges and corrections, which are usefully limned in Jenny Edbauer's 2005 "Unframing Models of Public Distribution: From Rhetorical Situation to Rhetorical Ecologies," demonstrate an emerging scholarly concern that is very much of a piece with the collective perspective being advanced in *Authorship Contested*. A look at Edbauer's contribution to writing and rhetorical studies helps unveil, I believe, the contribution that *Authorship Contested* makes to the field of authorship studies. Edbauer's challenge to longstanding scholarly notions of the rhetorical situation draws on Barbara Biesecker to correct a representation of "rhetoric as a totality of discrete elements: audience, rhetor, exigence, constraints, and text." Such representations, Edbauer argues, treat rhetoric as "*elemental conglomerations*" (7). As an improvement, Edbauer offers a notion of rhetoric as interactive, always in motion, instable.

Just as Barthes, Foucault, and Kinneavy were part of their cultural milieu, so Edbauer's essay and *Authorship Contested* resonate with contemporary thought and letters. Both Edbauer's essay and *Authorship Contested* approach rhetoric and writing as instable, dynamic sites of always-shifting relationships. Can we still talk about the "elements" of that ecological scene? Of course. But no longer can we think that one element can be isolated from the others and analyzed out of its context, to produce a silver-bullet explanation of the entire scene. Gone is the structuralist or even poststructuralist pulling-apart of separable pieces, separate "elements." Gone is the notion of an explanatory mechanism of authorship that transcends cultural and rhetorical context. Here in this volume we enter *contests* of authorship populated by multiple and often unpredictable agents. *Authorship Contested* offers perspectives on authorship that answer a contemporary desire to honor and enter into the ecologies of authorship.

WORKS CITED

Barthes, Roland. "The death of the author." *Aspen: The Magazine in a Box* 5+6. *ubu.com*. UbuWeb, 1967.

———. "The Death of the Author." *Image—Music—Text*. Stephen Heath (Trans. and ed) New York: Hill, 1977: 142–48.

Bitzer, Lloyd F. "The Rhetorical Situation." *Philosophy and Rhetoric* 1.1 (1968): 1–14.

Burke, Seán, ed. *Authorship: From Plato to the Postmodern*. Edinburgh: Edinburgh UP, 1995.

Edbauer, Jenny. "Unframing Models of Public Distribution: From Rhetorical Situation to Rhetorical Ecologies." *Rhetoric Society Quarterly* 35 (2005): 5–24.

Foucault, Michel. "What Is an Author?" *Bulletin de la Societe Française de Philosophie* 63.3 (1969): 73–104. Rpt. *Language, Countermemory, Practice: Selected Essays and Interviews*. Donald F. Bouchard (ed.). Donald F. Bouchard and Sherry Simon (Trans.). Ithaca: Cornell UP, 1977. 113–38.

Kinneavy, James L. *A Theory of Discourse*. New York: W.W. Norton, 1971.

Logie, John. "1967: The Birth of 'The Death of the Author.'" *College English* 75.5 (May 2013): 493–512.

Acknowledgements

Amy would like to thank the graduate students in the Fall 2010 and Fall 2013 sections of English 496 at Illinois State University for their insights into and enthusiasm for the concept of contested authorship. It was in those courses that it became clear that contested authorship was a concept that needed to be approached from so many more angles and perspectives than I'd initially anticipated.

Introduction
Amy E. Robillard and Ron Fortune

In 2001, renowned African-American scholar and historian Henry Louis Gates, Jr. purchased a manuscript called *The Bondwoman's Narrative* by Hannah Crafts and set out to investigate the circumstances of its authorship, its provenance, and the identity of its author. Gates believed *The Bondwoman's Narrative* to be the first novel written by a female fugitive slave, a designation that promises to complicate further an already complex history of slave authorship in this country. Contested by a nation eager to disown its shameful past, slave authorship, largely autobiographical, has withstood challenges to former slaves' intelligence, literacy, veracity, motive, and identity. Many such challenges derive from the well-known fact that former slaves often received editorial and publishing assistance from white abolitionists; in Crafts's *Bondwoman's Narrative*, a new generation of scholars gains access to a manuscript "unedited, unaffected, unglossed, unaided by even the most well-intentioned or unobtrusive editorial hand," which allows access to "the mind of a slave in an unmediated fashion heretofore not possible" (Gates xxxv). The possibilities afforded by this discovery necessitate careful authentication, a process Gates details in his introduction to Crafts's work, published in 2002.

The irony, of course, comes in the form of renowned scholar Henry Louis Gates, Jr. characterizing the work of Hannah Crafts as "unmediated," even as he is introducing her work to the world. Pointing to such irony is not, though, an attempt to contest Gates's work or his enthusiasm about *The Bondwoman's Narrative*, but instead to call attention to Crafts's manuscript as a form of contested authorship that has, indeed, received a great deal of attention because of the very uncontested authorial identity of Henry Louis Gates, Jr. Gates's recovery of Hannah Crafts's manuscript points, too, to the consequences of authorship's contestations; for decades, scholars of African-American literature had been deprived of the opportunity to study what is now widely understood to be the first novel written by an American slave. Scholars had never been able to be "absolutely certain that [they] have enjoyed the pleasure of reading a text in the exact order of wording in which a fugitive slave constructed it" (Gates xxxvi). The costs of Crafts's manuscript's invisibility can never be fully understood, just as the costs of the suppression of so many works by women writers, black writers, writers from the working classes can never be known.

The challenges to Crafts's work that Gates anticipated are akin to the challenges to authorship experienced today, in a culture unsure about the value of authorship, uncomfortable with attribution, collaboration, and the limitations of memory. For five decades now scholars have been debating authorship—what it is, who can claim it, how attribution works or is supposed to work, why it matters—and this collection contributes to these debates a layered and multi-disciplinary consideration of contested authorship, or challenges to others' claims of authorship. This shift in perspective from definitions and distribution of authorship to contested authorship, we believe, expands the reach of authorship studies in significant and exciting ways. Beginning with the concept of contested authorship, scholars might approach accusations of plagiarism or forgery, of false identity or embellishment, of dishonesty or collaboration, with a rhetorical rather than a punitive disposition. Rather than dismissing out of hand the work of fan fiction or automated writing, we might instead begin from the concept of contested authorship, asking ourselves what we risk when we rush to judgment rather than analysis. What rhetorical work does contestation accomplish? What story does contestation tell about us?

This book's attention to contested authorship builds on the work of scholars who have spent the last several decades unpacking the concept of authorship. One line of inquiry has explored the multiplicity of authorship as a response to the problematic notion of the author as an isolated, God-like creator. Martha Woodmansee, in her essay, "On the Author Effect: Recovering Collectivity," demonstrates the ways in which the modernist conceptualization of the autonomous author obfuscates the historical complexities of writing and publishing. Noting that the idea of the author working alone began with late eighteenth- and early nineteenth-century studies such as Young's *Conjectures on Original Composition* and Wordsworth's *Essay, Supplementary to the Preface*, she stresses how much such a view of authorship departs from the work of writing as practiced across the centuries. Her analysis of the parallels between the Renaissance commonplace book and contemporary hyperdocuments, for example, suggests the persistence over time of authorship as a collective effort in which a writer participates in the production of a document that necessarily bears the prints of multiple hands. Jack Stillinger's *Multiple Authorship and the Myth of Solitary Genius* illustrates the irony underlying the Romantic view of authorship that projects the author as a solitary genius. This study documents how, in practice, the Romantic writers, whose isolated efforts were celebrated in the essays Woodmansee cites, themselves practiced the collective authorship that ideas of writing at the time dismissed. This disjunction between what we have long held authorship to be and what scholarship has shown actual writing practices to entail invites questions that remained hidden under the cloak of a misguided view of the author, including questions regarding contested authorship.

While Woodmansee and others look at all contributors to the production of a text as contributing craftsmen, Lisa Ede and Andrea Lunsford respond to the prevailing "commonsensical view [in composition studies] of writing as an individual act" by documenting, through case citations and data-driven research, how common co- and group-authorship is across academic disciplines among professional writers (7). Their work ultimately moves toward offering a "pedagogy of collaboration" designed to make available to students instruction in writing practices that reflect how commonly writers work together. It is interesting to note that a factor precipitating their own investigation into collaborative writing and its place in writing instruction was the response they received to their interest in writing collaboratively themselves. After working together on an article for a volume of essays and discovering how productive it proved, they were advised that continuing to collaborate could be problematic: "What seemed natural to us, however, seemed anything but natural to our English Department colleagues" (6). Some colleagues feared for how their collaborative work would fare in tenure or promotion decisions, decisions driven by an underlying assumption that all worthwhile writing is produced by a single writer working alone. The resistance they recount parallels a phenomenon evident in a number of the essays collected here. In many instances contestation amounts to an effort to deny authorship because the writing in question upsets a set of assumptions about authorship that an audience brings to the documents in question. It may be a matter of how the writing is composed or the form it takes or the social or economic or literary status of the writer(s)—if it goes against the assumptions that audiences hold dear about who legitimate writers are and how they work, contestation results.

Andrew Bennett has argued that all postmodern conceptions of authorship have defined themselves in terms of their resistance to one or more aspects of the modern notion of authorship. This notion "involves the idea of an individual (singular) who is responsible for or who originates, who writes or composes, a ... text and who is thereby considered an inventor or founder and who is associated with the inventor or founder of all of nature, with God (God-the-father), and is thought to have certain ownership rights over the text as well as a certain authority over its interpretation" (7). For scholars working on plagiarism, an author's ownership of a text and control over its interpretation is a vexed proposition. Lise Buranen and Alice M. Roy's collection *Perspectives on Plagiarism and Intellectual Property in a Postmodern World* examines the consequences of postmodern theories of language and writing on stable conceptions of plagiarism that assume the thing-ness of words and ideas. Recognizing that no author works in a vacuum but instead draws on works that have gone before, they pose the central paradox of plagiarism: "Why condemn an author for borrowing from another if such borrowing is inevitable and even fundamental to the creative process?"(6). They resolve the apparent paradox by asserting the borrowing author's responsibility to transform the borrowed material in the creation of a new work. Their discussion of plagiarism compromises the idea of absolute ownership of a text of the kind that Bennett describes since ownership extends to all writers implicated in the creation of any text as the author of that text borrows from and transforms works that have gone before. As authors use writers and texts that have preceded them and, in turn, get used by those who follow, the concept of authorship becomes more diffuse and open to constructions that in the past were either never articulated or, if articulated, found problematic.

One way in which writing instruction at the post-secondary level reflects this shift to a diffusive concept of authorship based on shared ownership of a text is through its evolving treatment of plagiarism. This shift is particularly evident in the application of patchwriting to discussions of student plagiarism in colleges and universities. Rebecca Moore Howard defines patchwriting as "copying from a source text and then deleting some words, altering grammatical structures, or plugging in one-for-one synonyms" ("Pentimento" 233). Rather than treating patchwriting exclusively as a feebly disguised effort to steal someone else's writing and claim it as one's own, writing instructors need to allow for the possibility that it represents a stage in the student writer's effort to join a discourse community and to learn the discourse alternatives common in the texts encountered in an academic career. In their recommendations regarding the institutional policies that govern the treatment of plagiarism, scholars such as Howard do not encourage institutions to dismiss the possibility of plagiarism but rather urge them to allow for forms of writing that have been mistaken for plagiarism. In this, they call on these entities to replace the impulse to contest authorship with an openness to legitimate forms of writing that productively play into students' efforts to learn.

Not far from the efforts to develop policies on plagiarism in colleges and universities is the effort in legal studies to resolve the tension between the singular author with ownership rights and the recognition of the complexities of authorship, complexities that don't easily fit within the strict frames that laws attempt to establish. In *Authors and Owners: The Invention of Copyright*, Mark Rose locates the beginning of the dilemma with the Statute of Anne (1710), which established copyright and construed the literary product as a property to which an author could lay claim just as a landowner could lay claim to an estate. Significantly, Rose notes the simultaneous emergence of the legal concept of text as an author's property and "the representation of originality as a central value in cultural production" (6). Historically, as later generations have problematized the notion of authorial originality, copyright law has continued to maintain the strict frame that insists on a constricting view of author as originator and owner. Writing in response to the 1991 Supreme Court decision that made authorial originality the primary criterion by which ownership (and by extension the legal protection of copyright law) could be established, Peter Jaszi notes, "That Romantic 'authorship' is alive and well in late twentieth-century American legal culture has consequences for the law's engagement with (or failure to engage) the realities of contemporary polyvocal writing practice—which increasingly is collective, corporate, and collaborative" (38). While Jaszi puzzles over the apparent incompatibility between the law and collective authorship, others begin with the idea of postmodern, destabilized authorship and wonder how the law and postmodern writing practice can be reconciled. Elton Fukumoto, in "The Author Effect After the 'Death of the Author': Copyright in a Postmodern Age," looks at the literary concept of pastiche and an expansion of the fair use law as bases for creating a place for postmodern authorship in copyright law. Fukumoto explores what might be a useful bridge between alternate views of the work of writing, though the sense persists that underlying philosophical differences will not yield easily to reconciliation.

The commotion surrounding policies and writing practices at postsecondary institutions and copyright law and notions of postmodern authorship creates an environment conducive to exploring contested authorship because both involve various instances where authors come up against structures indifferent to or actively set against their efforts as writers. Our purpose here is not to argue for any particular resolutions to the concomitant problems but rather to see the commotion as an invitation to explore the circumstances surrounding a range of rhetorical occasions in which authors are silenced or discouraged or simply ignored for reasons not wholly related to the writing itself.

Of the extraneous reasons used to contest authorship, the most widely studied include class, gender, race, ethnicity, and religion. All of these conditions are difference markers, and as many authors affected by these differences have learned, difference breeds contestation. The example with which we begin this discussion, Hannah Crafts's authorship of *The Bondwoman's Narrative*, exemplifies two of these bases for contestation simultaneously. Crafts was a female and a black slave. In his introduction to the manuscript facsimile of this work, Gates explores at length why Hannah Crafts never published her novel. He begins his analysis by noting, "Publishing at any time is extraordinarily difficult, and was especially so for a woman in the nineteenth century. For an African American woman, publishing a book was virtually a miraculous event. ..." (lx–lxi). That Crafts was a woman situated her in a long tradition of authorial contestation. From the earliest days of printing in the West, women were marked for exclusion by their gender. In *The Imprint of Gender*, Wendy Wall describes how aspiring women writers in the Renaissance found themselves at a disadvantage: "Constrained by the norms of acceptable feminine behavior, women were specifically discouraged from tapping into the newly popular channel of print; to do so threatened the cornerstone of their moral and social well-being" (280). It is true that, during the Renaissance and since, through various strategies and accommodations, women have succeeded as authors; yet, for many, gender proved to be a marker they couldn't readily circumvent. Even if they did succeed in getting their writing published, they published a fraction of what men did, they likely wrote for much smaller audiences, and their works had a much shorter shelf life than the works of their male counterparts. In his introduction to an anthology of women's writing, 1560–1700, Paul Salzman writes, "It has now become evident, as manuscript sources as well as printed books are uncovered, that while far fewer women wrote than men (it has been estimated that an average of 1 per cent of all published writing in the seventeenth century was produced by women), a bibliography of published and unpublished writing from [Isabella] Whitney to [Aphra] Behn would still run to thousands of items" (ix). That Salzman includes in his bibliography unpublished writing, that the bibliography is a product of efforts to "uncover" lost works, and that the total is a small fraction of men's literary productivity over the same period – all of these factors suggest the presence of forms of contestation based on gender. More recently, the organization Women in Literary Arts (VIDA) instituted its VIDA Count, an annual tally of the number of women writers represented in top-tier journals, publications, and press outlets, as well as the number of women writers winning the most prestigious writing awards. The results evidence a deep imbalance between male and female writers, demonstrating that contestation based on gender prevents much writing from being published even today.

In most if not all of the situations we've described so far, bases for contestation derive from characteristics of the contested authors or from the social, economic, and cultural environments in which they are writing. With technology daily changing the means and mechanisms through which writers pursue authorship, we are seeing increasing evidence of the role that technology is playing in precipitating an audience's resistance to an author's efforts. Computer technology so readily allows for, and some would even say invites, textual manipulation and disguise that, for many, it provides a fertile ground for authorial deception. In "The Roles of Trust in Cyberspace," David Clark observes that we are coming "to grips with the painful fact that not everyone on the internet is trustworthy," and he proceeds to describe two trends he sees emerging in communication on the Internet. The first is that we are adding "restraints and restrictions in the patterns of communication to try to prevent bad things from happening" and the second is "a gradual drawing back from the optimistic position that anyone should be able to communicate with us at will" (19). Both trends are evident in the publication of books designed to advise those who use the Internet on the precautions they should take in engaging the documents they encounter. Anne P. Mintz's *Web of Deception: Misinformation on the Internet* notes the emerging "industry" of resources designed to assist "Internet nomads [who] often lack the background and training to evaluate or criticize basic information sources" in developing the abilities they need to protect themselves from the deceptions that await them on the Web (xviii). Authors of Internet documents are advised to be on their guard regarding the suspicions that attend the medium and to be prepared to write with these suspicions in mind.

Beyond the ways in which audiences have learned to anticipate how digital documents can be manipulated, technology has also introduced new kinds of discourses and documents, which has some audiences unsure of what to do with the resulting digital materials. Just as difference breeds authorial contestation, textual novelty can surprise audiences, and with surprise can come suspicion. Many academic institutions have been reluctant to accept online publications as the equivalent of print documents in personnel evaluations. This hesitation is evident even when the print and digital documents are identical. That these institutions are still in the process of establishing guidelines for assessing digital documents attests to a continuing uncertainty about how to evaluate authors who offer these documents for review. James Richardson argues that "the predominant attitude in the academy is that digital projects are inferior to publications in peer-reviewed scholarly journals, and should be viewed with some skepticism as to their merit as scholarship." As new forms of digital documents continue to proliferate, the prospect of continued contestation seems likely. Indeed, as Carolyn Guertin's *Digital Prohibition: Piracy and Authorship in New Media Art* explores new authorial and publishing models made available through the emergence of digital technology, she also describes the attendant forms of resistance that these models evoke.

As this overview suggests, contested authorship takes various forms based on an audience's concept of what it means to be an author and what texts should be. Given this variety, we have organized the essays collected here according to what we see as some of the most common patterns associated with efforts to cancel an author's work. The essays in the first section, "Contrived Authorship," explore situations in which authors manufacture artificial authorship and encounter resistance to what they have created. In some cases, this resistance has an almost moral dimension as the defiant public responds as if a principled understanding that must exist between author and reader has been violated. Resistance in the second category of essays, "Distributed Authorship," extends from the reading public's expectations that authorship is limited in scope and precisely assignable. Rhetorical situations where authorial attribution is distributed and imprecise can confuse and frustrate an audience to the point that they dismiss the work entirely or futilely try to make the work fit within their *a priori* concept of authorship. The third section, "Excluded Authorship," focuses on occasions in which contesting authorship is most extreme, occasions in which authorship is denied less for the circumstances involved in composition and more for who the authors are and what they represent. The resistance often reflects a reading public's disposition to limit who has a right to authorship and who doesn't, and this disposition creates a class of excluded authors whose work is rejected without due consideration. The essays in the final section examine writers whose authorship is challenged because they are students, and as such are assumed not to have reached a stage where their writing can be regarded as "real" writing. The students' perceived nascent state as writers evokes a condescension that refuses to allow them an identity as authors.

What remains true in all cases of contested authorship is that contestation derives in large part from a cultural discomfort with shifting conceptions of what it means to write and what it means to be an author. As Howard points out, authorship becomes a site of contest "when the circumstances of writing are in transition as they were in the West in the shift from manuscript to print culture in the Renaissance—and as they are today in the shift from print to electronic literacy" (*Standing* 71). As our categories become increasingly unstable—author, writer, book, text, source—so too do our efforts to stabilize those categories by excluding those who just don't belong.

CONTRIVED AUTHORSHIP

As he worked to theorize the "empty space left by the author's disappearance" (121), Foucault observed that the relationship between a proper name and the author's name remains significant, for while the proper name refers to the individual person, the author's name functions to categorize a body of work. Though Foucault suggests that the author function is only one way to categorize the circulation of discourses that we identify as worth our attention, and he writes that "we can easily imagine a culture where discourse would circulate without any need for an author" (138), history has not borne out any such indifference to who's speaking. If anything, scholarship in rhetoric and composition has demonstrated a simultaneous willingness to theorize about the consequences of the author's disappearance and a hesitance to put into practice such indifference. If the academy still insists on a single identifiable author in works of scholarship (Ede and Lunsford), lay readers take for granted a one-to-one correspondence between an author's name and the living embodiment of that name. The vehemence with which transgressions against authorship are greeted in the popular press—witness the avalanche of angry responses to James Frey—suggests that instances of authorship in which the author claims to be someone—or some *thing*—that he is not challenges cultural values related to authorship that remain fixed in place more than fifty years after Foucault's suggestion that we approach such issues with indifference. It *matters* who's speaking, and the essays in the opening section reveal most blatantly the anxiety and suspicion that accompany the manipulation of authors' identities.

In cases of contrived authorship, a category we created to describe authorship that others have come to see as deceptive and characterized by careful planning, even scheming, the authors under consideration invent authorship in ways that make readers anxious, as their ingenuity and cleverness threaten readers' identities as intelligent and discerning. They toy with our faith in the one-to-one correspondence between author's name and identifiable person and in so doing expose the values that undergird our attributions of authorship. That we value individuality, autonomy, and authenticity goes without saying. What these cases of contrived authorship also reveal is our discomfort with the extent to which an author's persona is created, fashioned, *contrived*. When a writer claims to be someone he's not for the purposes of distributing his work in ways he could not otherwise accomplish, he (and sometimes she) calls attention to the many players participating in the creation of the symbolic value of a work. Contesting such forms of contrived authorship is motivated by a collective desire to distance ourselves from the experience of having been duped; what becomes clear in these instances of contested authorship is the extent to which our conceptualizations of identity as fixed often blind us to the complexities of cultural production.

The contrived authorship behind the blog *A Gay Girl in Damascus* is the subject of Julia Marie Smith's contribution. On June 7, 2011, the audience of the blog launched a campaign through petitions, news articles, and Twitter, to rescue the blog's author, Amina Abdallah Arraf al Omaril, a self-described lesbian Syrian-American activist, from Syrian security forces. The publicity that followed the campaign led to the disclosure that Tom MacMasters, a heterosexual American man, had created Amina and had been writing under her identity the entire time. In "*A Gay Girl in Damascus*: Multi-vocal Construction and Refutation of Authorial Ethos," Smith argues that, while MacMasters successfully created Amina's persona, he alone did not create her ethos. To explain the functions of the many voices in creating, sustaining, and ultimately deconstructing Amina and her accompanying agenda, Smith employs the concept of a *rhetorical chorus*. Drawing on the language of musical texture, Smith's work challenges the rush to judgment that assigns blame to the autonomous author. Just as no author works alone, neither can a forger succeed alone. Moreover, Smith's analysis demonstrates what life-writing scholars have observed about life writing hoaxes: They tend to cross gender and ethnic lines in ways that raise questions about whose stories are judged to be worth publishing.

In "Writing in the Dead Zone: Authorship in the Age of Intelligent Machines," Kyle Jensen examines the relationship between automated authorship and human anxiety, suggesting that anxiety is in fact a reasonable response to the problem of algorithmic writing. Pointing to the fact that anxiety about machines taking over humanity has animated the popular imagination for decades, Jensen takes a different route, suggesting that algorithmic writing reminds us that writing and humans are not coextensive with one another and that the concept of *authorship* can be understood as a bridging device that redresses the anxiety that results from that fact. An important contribution to conversations about the dangers of automatic writing, Jensen's work reminds us that such anxiety is not new but it reemerges with greater velocity in an age of artificial reasoning. Contesting such contrived authorship is our attempt to ward off the overwhelming sense of dislocation resulting from the prospect of automated writing.

In "Writers Who Forge: Forgery as a Response to Contested Authorship," Ron Fortune describes patterns in the work of serious writers who turn to forgery as a means of responding to the resistance they encounter in their efforts to be authors. While James Macpherson and Thomas Chatterton exhibit how some writers react to authorial contestation by realizing their purposes as writers through forgery, James Whitcomb Riley demonstrates a more aggressively defiant reaction to those who would contest his authorship. An emerging poet with some local success in his own right, Riley was driven by a desire to demonstrate that the primary difference between his writing, which had suffered a succession of rejections from national magazines, and the poetry of a uniformly acknowledged master, was reputation rather than the quality of the writing itself. Fortune's analysis of the Riley/Poe forgery highlights the persistent problems forgers have negotiating, on the one hand, an insistence that the work belongs to the writers whose identities they have assumed and, on the other, a desire for recognition of their own writing ability, an ability put in doubt by an audience's initial resistance to what an author has written.

DISTRIBUTED AUTHORSHIP

As we noted earlier in this Introduction, Jack Stillinger, in *Multiple Authorship and the Myth of Solitary Genius*, responds to what he perceives as a mistaken but predominant "romantic notion of single authorship." He pursues a "more realistic account" of the ways in which texts actually come together, an account that embraces the "social, cultural, and material conditions in which [texts are] produced" (183). His account sets against the "myth of solitary genius" a view of writing as multiple and distributed. While the reading public might derive some comfort from being able to assign one text to one author, writing is a messy process and this messiness entails a multiplicity of hands involved in the creation of any text, with the various hands contributing indirectly and directly to what the text becomes in its published form. Scholars in rhetoric and composition, most notably Andrea Lunsford and Lisa Ede in *Singular Texts/Plural Authors*, have written extensively about the realities of collaborative writing and have called on teachers and scholars to challenge the academy's insistence on autonomous authorship by enacting collaboration both in our writing and our teaching ("Collaboration"). The essays in this section examine a range of rhetorical situations in which distributed authorship connects with various forms of contestation that authors must engage as they compose their texts. Texts whose authors are distributed over time and space might be challenged for the ways in which such authorial distribution obfuscates what many might consider to be the *original* author. As the essays in this section suggest, distributed authorship stokes our anxieties regarding attribution of texts for which there is no author function.

Erin Frost and Kellie Sharp-Hoskins, in "Authorial Ethos as Location: How Technical Manuals Embody Authorial Ethos without Authors," analyze a situation in which contested authorship is at the core of how a corporation chooses to present its technical documents to its clients. They examine technical documents written in corporate settings in which the corporation expects rhetorical advantages to accrue from the refusal to name the actual authors who write the corporation's technical documents. Instead, the corporation claims authorship and effectively removes the actual writers from view. There is a distributed authorship here in the sense that the writer(s) lay claim to authorship as the individuals who are responsible for its composition. The corporation is responsible for articulating the rhetorical need for the document and the goals that the successful document will meet when completed. The essay explores the dynamic of a process that seeks to remove an audience's opportunity to contest a document by eliminating the subjectivity associated with individual authorship and replacing it with an objectivity and neutrality perceived to be characteristic of corporate documents. Arguing that this rhetorical maneuver manifests a "masculinist economy of authorship," Frost and Sharp-Hoskins discuss its implications for the concept of authorship itself.

In Seth Kahn and Kevin Mahoney's "The *Kairos* of Authorship in Activist Rhetoric," distributed authorship involves group composing dedicated to the advancement of the activist causes that join the authors to one another. That activist authors produce documents designed to resist conditions these authors find problematic necessarily invites contestation and efforts to resist the writing they produce. Investigating the rhetoric surrounding the Occupy Wall Street movement, Kahn and Mahoney demonstrate how a deliberate decision to refuse to name the authors of the documents associated with the movement reflects a commitment to the collective voice of the community. While documents presented as the writing of the group strengthens the sense of collectivity, the absence of named individual authors can also evoke contestation from a public audience seeking to critique the writing and the activist arguments it embodies. At the same time, the activist writing associated with Raging Chicken Press highlights writer identities attempting to gain access to and resist the public discourses supporting the political, social, and economic values that these activists consider so problematic. The Press itself offers a gathering place where these like-minded authors gather to advocate for causes that face efforts to silence them before the ink is dry on the page.

Rachel Parish, in "In the Author's Hands: Contesting Authorship and Ownership in Fan Fiction," identifies the distributed authorship that defines fan fiction as the source of its contestation. Some readers find in fan fiction not only a means for appreciative readers to extend the life of a text into texts that the original authors might never have envisioned but also an opportunity for these readers to participate actively in the text in ways not available to them as readers only. As they add the texts they have created to the original text on which they are building, they become co-creators in a material way that gives substantive expression to the abstract co-creation they experience as readers. Still, many find the resulting documents objectionable, arguing that adding material texts to the original text and expecting these addenda to be received as legitimate extensions of the original violates the authority and prerogatives of the original author. As the discussion here argues for the benefits of fan fiction in spite of the objections it faces, it examines the ways in which the very definition of "author" requires new ways of thinking about reading, writing, and the life of a text.

EXCLUDED AUTHORSHIP

The metaphor of intellectual property is based in, and was founded on, the concept of real property, and of ownership of such property. An author, Mark Rose explains in *Authors and Owners*, came to be understood as one who both originated and owned the product of his intellectual labor. "All forms of property," Rose writes, "are socially constructed and, like copyright, bear in their lineaments the traces of the struggles in which they were fabricated" (8). It makes sense, then, that one of the ways in which authorship has historically been contested is based in the question of who can be legitimately understood to have a claim to ownership. Minority groups have long been excluded from participating in a culture of ownership, and as the essays in this section show, contestation based on exclusion from a dominant group remains commonplace.

Feminist scholars have noted that the author died/disappeared right around the same time women and scholars of color began publishing, thus posing a different challenge to Foucault's indifference to who's speaking. Efforts to reclaim the authorship of those who have been silenced are extensive in the humanities; indeed, the category of excluded authorship is perhaps the one with which most scholars in the humanities are familiar, pointing as it does to the circumstances that motivate so much recovery work in, for instance, women's literatures, African-American literatures, working-class literatures, Chicana/o literatures, and queer literatures. Before these writers' authorship can be complicated by theories of multiple or collaborative authorship, they must first be recovered and designated authors in their own right. As the example of Hannah Crafts's recovered manuscript illustrates, a kind of authorial sponsorship is often necessary to draw attention to marginalized authors' status as excluded.

We characterize these authors as excluded rather than silenced to highlight their efforts to resist being silenced; the authors under examination in this section recognize to some degree that their writing may be contested, but they continue to write from their marginalized positions. They face efforts to exclude them from authorship because of their lifestyles, their political beliefs, their gender, their race, their stance within the group to which they address themselves, or their perceived relationship to the material about which they choose to write. A sense of not belonging characterizes the authors under consideration in this section, whether that not belonging is an effect of one's sexual orientation or one's status as not-yet-published. Contestation based on exclusion reveals a great deal about not just what we value but *who* we value.

James Zebroski's "Writing after Stonewall: The Lost Forms of Gay Authorship" examines the history of gay writing with particular attention to debates over recognized forms of gay authorship since the appearance of Samuel Steward's work in the mid- to late twentieth-century. Specifically he examines how, above and beyond the difficulty that gay writers faced in getting their work published for a good portion of the century, Steward's life and diversified art resisted the neat categories that were available for classifying work by gay authors and, in the process, precipitated a new variety in the forms of art that gay authors produced. Perhaps predictably, this new variety faced a new resistance both inside and outside the gay community and led to the development of "a creative writer ideology." This ideology fixed what would be acceptable within the publishing and educational establishments, resulting in the exclusion of most forms of gay authorship. Throughout the history of gay authorship in the twentieth century, exclusion seems to be ever-present, even to the point where frameworks for recognizing gay authors and their work have built within them arguments for exclusion.

In his contribution, "The Sound of Silence: Defense of Marriage, Don't Ask, Don't Tell, and Post-Authorship Theory," Paul Butler explores the strategies a marginalized group uses to overcome its exclusion. Specifically, he examines the counter-discourse developed by those faced with the exclusion implicit in policies such as the Defense of Marriage Act and Don't Ask, Don't Tell. Interestingly, he argues that one way to inclusion is to use the rhetoric of those who would exclude marginalized groups against the dominant group. By co-opting this rhetoric, the subordinate group is able to persuade the opposition to accept them almost without knowing that this is what they are doing. The successful response to the forces of exclusion, in effect, involves persuading the dominant group that the sense of difference that drives their efforts to exclude is insubstantial and that they have more in common with the group they would silence than they had thought.

In "The Emotional Contests of Peer Review," Amy E. Robillard sees a sense of exclusion among reviewers in a double-blind review process precipitating their own exclusionary, gate-keeping disposition toward the authors whose works they review. In the lack of academic recognition that reviewers receive for their work she sees seeds of resistance to authors who have submitted work for their consideration. Analyzing two layered forms of contested authorship that result from a rhetorical situation that itself has a built-in expectation of rejection, Robillard points to the crucial role of the academic editor in ensuring the proper functioning of the norm of attribution upon which all academic writing is based.

NASCENT AUTHORSHIP

Perhaps the most frequently addressed form of authorial exclusion in rhetoric and composition is that of the student author. In response to widespread contestation of students' authorship based in students' presumed nascence, Tracy Hamler Carrick and Rebecca Moore Howard's collection, *Authorship in Composition Studies*, includes a number of chapters devoted to recognizing the status of students as authors. Perhaps more importantly, Carrick and Howard address the disconnect at work in the field between asking students to compose original works and asking them to read the work of canonical authors understood to be autonomous authorial geniuses. As Robillard points out in her chapter in Carrick and Howard's collection, the study of student writing defines the early work of composition studies (42). It didn't take long before the study of student writing led the field to consider the complexities of plagiarism, posing as it did problems that challenged the field's desire to champion student writing. With the concept of "patchwriting"—the process by which students imitate the structure and syntax of established authors, substituting synonyms without really changing the meaning—Howard distinguished from plagiarism a middle stage of academic authorship and jumpstarted an enduring interest in the cultural work performed by the concept of plagiarism (*Standing*).

The essays in the last section address both the need to share with students the writing processes of writers we might otherwise assume to be originary geniuses and the possibilities that accompany combining the study of student writing with attention to plagiarism as a form of authorship with a complex history. We developed the category of nascent authorship for this section out of our understanding not that students *are* nascent but that the rhetorical strategies contesting their status as authors position them as nascent. Contestation of student authorship relies on an understanding of authorship as a product of expertise and autonomy; student writing can be so easily contested because its authors are generally young and dependent on the scaffolding of teachers, assignments, and coursework. Students are excluded from authorship because they are conceptualized as novices. By contrast, we recognize and celebrate students as authors and enact such recognition in our teaching and scholarship; indeed, the very concept of contested authorship grows out of our continued engagement with the punitive and criminal rhetoric surrounding plagiarism. And so this collection ends where the concept of contested authorship originated: in student authorship.

In her chapter, "'I Feel Like This Is Fake': Spontaneous Mediocrity and Studied Genius," Val Perry Rendel describes a course in which she asked students to examine cases of contested authorship in order to problematize the commonplace understanding of an author as one who gets it right the first time. Students study the erased processes of authors across genres (e.g., fiction, drama, diaries, journalism, nonfiction) and work together to determine the extent to which they believe that making authors' writing processes visible delegitimizes their status as authors. Rendel emphasizes cases in which the contested author also happens to be one whose ethos students understand to be beyond reproach (e.g., Shakespeare, Martin Luther King, Jr.) in order to help students see that cases of plagiarism are rarely black and white. Crucial to students' development as authors themselves is a more complex understanding of the factors outside a text that contribute to an author's ethos, and Rendel's work in this chapter suggests that one way to help students conceptualize themselves as authors is to upset their beliefs about the relationship between process and authors.

In his contribution, "Student Intellectual Property in an Age of Permissions: Fostering a Gift Economy in First-Year Writing Programs," Matt Hollrah builds on Jonathan Lethem's provocative 2007 *Harper's* essay, "The Ecstasy of Influence: A Plagiarism." Lethem enacts the very argument he's making as he composes a case for the necessity and value of drawing on the work of others in ways that extend, repurpose, revise, and honor that work. Composed entirely of passages taken verbatim from his more than twenty-five sources, "The Ecstasy of Influence" demonstrates that writers and artists have always borrowed from the work of others and argues for the value of a gift economy over a punitive approach to textual influence. Hollrah's contribution examines the court case *A.V. et al, v. iParadigms* as a particularly rich example of the ways in which student authorship is regularly contested in both our educational and legal systems. Arguing that plagiarism accusations ultimately deny a student control over her text and its reproduction, Hollrah suggests that recategorizing intellectual property as a gift rather than a commodity can go a long way toward fostering students' necessary sense of ownership and control over their work. Celebrating student writing as gifts circulating in a gift economy brings into stark relief the extent to which student writing is so often contested before it is even written.

Also influenced by Lethem's essay, Joseph Harris's contribution describes a teaching experiment modeled after Lethem's essay; asking students to "work in the mode of Lethem" to "compose an original plagiarism" of their own, Harris asks students to consider what it means to draw on the work of others to create a work they can paradoxically call their own. Harris found himself surprised at the range and quality of students' responses to the assignment: Students composed screenplays, political speeches, brochures, short stories, fairy tales, advice columns, elegies, song mash-ups, and video remixes. Harris shows us that many students came to view "originality" as the stance a writer takes toward sources and materials, rather than as expressions of utterly new ideas or sincere feelings. Ultimately, Harris argues that writing plagiarisms of this curiously open and inventive sort seemed to teach many of them more about the ethics of working with sources than trying to avoid plagiarism ever had.

When we consider the ways in which authorship is so frequently contested, we come face to face with the realities of writing, of human memory, of collaboration, of influence. Through an analysis of authorial contestation, we have an opportunity to explore not only the expectations writers have of their writing and of the audiences to which this writing is offered but also the complications that play into how audiences receive what the writer has written. In some instances writers anticipate contestation and write accordingly; in others, the contestation is the last response they expect. Sometimes contestation is a condition of the rhetorical context in which the writer writes, while at other times, it is a function of how readers choose to engage what the author has written. Regardless of its source and of how it develops, examining instances in which authorial contestation figures prominently into the exchange between writers and their readers adds substantially to the various perspectives on authorship and reception that have been percolating in the critical literature over the past decades.

WORKS CITED

Bennett, Andrew. *The Author.* New York: Routledge, 2005.
Bourdieu, Pierre. *Distinction: The Social Critique of the Judgement of Taste.* Cambridge: Harvard UP, 1984.
Buranen, Lise, and Alice M. Roy, eds. *Perspectives on Plagiarism and Intellectual Property in a Postmodern World.* Albany: SUNY P, 1999.
Carrick, Tracy Hamler, and Rebecca Moore Howard, eds. *Authorship in Composition Studies.* Boston: Thomson Wadsworth, 2006.
Clark, David. "The Roles of Trust in Cyberspace." In *Trust, Computing, and Society.* Ed. Richard H.R. Harper. Cambridge: Cambridge UP, 2014: 17–37.
Ede, Lisa, and Andrea A. Lunsford. "Collaboration and Concepts of Authorship." *PMLA* 116.2 (2001): 354–69.
Eisner, Caroline, and Martha Vicinus, eds. *Originality, Imitation, and Plagiarism: Teaching Writing in the Digital Age.* Ann Arbor: U of Michigan P, 2008.
Foucault, Michel. "What Is an Author?" *Language, Counter-Memory, Practice: Selected Essays and Interviews.* Ed. Donald Bouchard. Ithaca: Cornell UP, 1977.
Frey, James. *A Million Little Pieces.* New York: Doubleday, 2003.
Fukomoto, Elton. "The Author Effect After the 'Death of the Author': Copyright in a Postmodern Age." *Washington Law Review* 72.3 (1997): 903–934.
Gates, Henry Louis, Jr. "Introduction." *The Bondwoman's Narrative: Facsimile Edition.* Hannah Crafts. Ed. and Intro. Henry Louis Gates, Jr. New York: Warner Books, 2002.
Guertin, Carolyn. *Digital Prohibition: Piracy and Authorship in New Media Art.* New York: Continuum, 2012.
Horner, Bruce. "Students, Authorship, and the Work of Composition." *College English* 59.5 (1997): 505–529.
Howard, Rebecca Moore. "A Plagiarism Pentimento." *Journal of Teaching Writing* 11.3 (Summer 1993): 233–46.
———. *Standing in the Shadow of Giants: Plagiarists, Authors, Collaborators.* Stamford, CT: Ablex, 1999.
Jaszi, Peter. "On the Author Effect: Contemporary Copyright and Collective Creativity." *The Construction of Authorship: Textual Appropriation in Law and Literature.* Ed. Martha Woodmansee and Peter Jaszi. Durham: Duke UP, 1994: 29–56.

Lethem, Jonathan. "The Ecstasy of Influence: A Plagiarism." *Harper's* Feb 2007: 59–71.

Lunsford, Andrea, and Lisa Ede. *Singular Texts/Plural Authors: Perspectives on Collaborative Writing.* Carbondale: Southern Illinois UP, 1990.

Mintz, Anne P. *Web of Deception: Misinformation on the Internet.* Medford: Information Today, 2002.

Richardson, James. "Establishing a New Paradigm: The Call To Reform the Tenure and Promotion Standards for Digital Media Faculty." *JITP: The Journal of Interactive Technology and Pedagogy.* Issue 3. Web. 2 Jan. 2014.

Robillard, Amy E. "Students and Authors in Composition Scholarship." *Authorship in Composition Studies.* Ed. Tracy Hamler Carrick and Rebecca Moore Howard. Boston: Thomson Wadsworth, 2006: 41–56.

Rose, Mark. *Authors and Owners: The Invention of Copyright.* Cambridge: Harvard UP, 1993.

Salzman, Paul. *Early Modern Women's Writing: An Anthology 1560–1700.* New York: Oxford World Classics, 2000.

Stillinger, Jack. *Multiple Authorship and the Myth of Solitary Genius.* New York: Oxford UP, 1991.

Wall, Wendy. *The Imprint of Gender: Authorship and Publication in the English Renaissance.* Ithaca: Cornell UP, 1993.

Williams, Susan S. *Reclaiming Authorship: Literary Women in America, 1850–1900.* Philadelphia: U of Pennsylvania P, 2006.

Woodmansee, Martha. "On the Author Effect: Recovering Collectivity." *The Construction of Authorship: Textual Appropriation in Law and Literature.* Durham: Duke UP, 1994.

Woodmansee, Martha, and Peter Jaszi, eds. *The Construction of Authorship: Textual Appropriation in Law and Literature.* Durham: Duke UP, 1994.

Part I
Contrived Authorship

1 *A Gay Girl in Damascus*
Multi-vocal Construction and Refutation of Authorial Ethos

Julia Marie Smith

On June 7, 2011, the audience of the blog *A Gay Girl in Damascus* launched a sincere and urgent campaign through petitions, news articles, and Twitter to rescue the blog's author, Amina Abdallah Arraf al Omaril, a self-described lesbian Syrian-American activist, from Syrian security forces. As a result, *The Washington Post*, NPR, and Palestinian news site *Electronic Intifada* investigated Amina. They soon came to the startling conclusion that no one had actually seen Amina in person (including her Canadian girlfriend). By June 9, it was revealed that Amina, A Gay Girl in Damascus, was the pseudonym of Tom MacMaster, a straight American man who created the persona in order to shed light on the Syrian situation, present his arguments, and practice his creative writing ability ("Apology to Readers," June 13, 2011). The author's audience was confronted with the dilemma of whether to view this situation as egregious fraud or as the work of a creative author.

Audiences of literary and online hoaxes such as James Frey's *A Million Little Pieces* and Tom MacMaster's *A Gay Girl in Damascus* often react with anger upon discovering that they have been duped (for example, Oprah Winfrey's public rebuking of Frey on her syndicated network talk show, January 26, 2006). These examples of problematic authorship, which are not marked by plagiarism or financial fraud, raise a fundamental question about the nature of contested authorship and authorship in general. In an example of contested authorship, how is ethos constructed, and how are rhetorical messages distributed? Despite scholarly moves to decenter the author as the single authority over a text, the impulse in these situations is to return sole responsibility back to the speaker, denounce the speaker's choices, and censor the speaker's message.[1] As the events surrounding *A Gay Girl in Damascus* reveal, MacMaster was successful in creating his false persona because he did not create his ethos alone. Early on in the process, MacMaster relied on other people to help validate Amina's existence and message. Later, in response to MacMaster's admission, audiences of the blog and the blog's message either moved to denounce MacMaster or scrambled to protect the rhetorical message even as the ethos of the speaker was shattered. Thus, the unmasking of MacMaster as the author of the *Gay Girl in Damascus* blog offers an example of contested authorship in the digital age, where the breakdown of ethos unmasks cultural assumptions regarding individual authorship and the often ignored interventions of others in producing and disseminating rhetorical messages.

In our typical model of a rhetorical event, a single speaker builds his rhetorical ethos and addresses his rhetorical message to a specific audience, since the practice of speaking begins with "a speaker and a subject on which he speaks and someone addressed, and the objective of the speech relates to the last (I mean the hearer)" (Aristotle *On Rhetoric* I: 3:1). The well-constructed speech reflects "the character [ethos] of the speaker, and some in disposing the listener in some way, and some in the speech [logos]" (Aristotle *On Rhetoric* I: 2: 3). Thus ethos is defined as the character of the speaker or as Barbara Warnick explains in her article "Online Ethos": "to be viewed as credible, the author must be perceived as a person of good will who has the audience's best interest at heart and also as an expert in some sense—one who is qualified to speak on the topic at hand" (258). This definition places the burden of ethos on the speaker, who must demonstrate good character, operate through goodwill, and have an expertise in the topic.

However, the hoax *A Gay Girl in Damascus*, as an example, demonstrates that the ethos of the speaker is not lodged only in the speaker's choices or character. In "Collaboration and Conceptions of Authorship," M. Thomas Inge writes, "there has seldom been a time when someone did not stand between author and audience in the role of a mediator, revisor, or collaborator" (624). These mediators problematize our understanding of ethos in particular since their influence shifts the construction and power of ethos. Here, I examine the relationships between MacMaster and other participants who appropriated and transmitted his message online in order to illuminate how rhetorical ethos comes to be constructed not by one individual, but rather through the direct interventions of multiple people. These participants, who I call the *rhetorical chorus*, are separate from other members of the audience because they specifically use their technical and rhetorical skills to distribute the message and promote or build the speaker's ethos by altering the shape of digital spaces. Principally, in this example, these individuals are other bloggers, but many are also journalists and social activists. This chapter uses the terminology of musical texture and chorus, which allows me to identify and analyze the movements of different members of the ensemble who participated in distributing Amina's message and building her ethos, as well as the later contributors who denounced MacMaster. This group acts as mediators, co-actors with the original speaker, by operating between the original speaker and the audience. However, despite their actions as co-participants in the distribution of rhetoric, the chorus neither participates in the act of invention nor functions as coauthoring collaborators. Instead the ensemble appropriates and disseminates the message of the original speaker with its own authority and agendas. They stand apart from the audience because they have the technical skills to alter and arrange the space of the textual artifact or digital space and the rhetorical *techne*, rhetorical artistry, to contribute their own rhetoric.

ACT I: *A GAY GIRL IN DAMASCUS*

In February 2011, a blogger Amina Abdallah Arraf al Omaril, claiming to be a lesbian Syrian-American activist, began a blog entitled *A Gay Girl in Damascus: An Out Syrian Lesbian's Thoughts on Life, the Universe and So On*. This blog caught the attention of many because of her combination of on-the-spot descriptions of the Syrian uprisings, her Sapphic poetry, and her thoughts as "an out Syrian lesbian." Amina further reinforced her feminine identity by designing her blog with pink lettering and pastel floral backgrounds.[2] Amina built on the audience's preconceived expectations regarding the use of a blog to present autobiographical narratives and the use of external sources and relationships with others to give witness to Amina's existence and her authority as a speaker.

Amina created her false persona by first enacting the traditional role of the individual speaker and establishing her ethos based on personal experiences. She described herself as "a dual-national and I grew up between Damascus, Syria and the American South, neither of which was exactly the easiest place to be struggling with what I considered inappropriate desires" ("Halfway out of the Dark" February 19, 2011). Throughout her blog, she delivered autobiographical anecdotes, which were effective in first building an audience and later distributing ideologies. The blog served as an ideal place for the construction of a speaker's identity because it functioned as a site of self-disclosure and self-expression, which served to enhance "self-awareness" and confirm "already-held beliefs" (Miller and Shepherd). Amina articulated her messages by organizing them according to culturally sanctioned forms of self-disclosure and personal narrative to convey her ethos and build ties to her audience. As an example, Amina shared a story of finding an active lesbian community while going out in Syria: "I went into a hair salon one day and, not long after I arrived, I picked up on something between the women working there; I spoke around in circles and so did they ... and finally learned that the women there were all gay" ("'Halfway out of the Dark'" February 19, 2011). With similar stories, such self-disclosure in her blog functioned as a "rhetorical convention" designed to "gain readers in the blog community" (Rak 172). Statements of disclosure in the blog created credibility because of their apparent authenticity. In addition, these personal anecdotes created the possibility of shared experiences as women, as lesbians, as Muslims. Therefore, the audience could accept Amina as a credible speaker because they were familiar with the authority and authenticity of blogging as a medium to convey personal experiences in order to express ideologies.

Through the authority of personal experience living in Syria, Amina promoted several major arguments, which were taken up by others who would become her rhetorical chorus. First, she posited a positive and optimistic view of the lesbian situation in a Middle Eastern community, such as Amina's pleasant encounter with the women in the hair salon

("Halfway out of the Dark," February 19, 2011). Second, her stories about her family depicted familial relationships within a Muslim family as less patriarchal and homophobic than Western media depicts, and she claimed that she was able to easily balance lesbianism and her Muslim faith ("My Hijab, My Choice," April 10, 2011). For example, in the blog post, "Waiting and Worse," Amina described drinking alcohol with her Muslim father, where he claims, "'Silly girl,' he grins, 'we, your mother and me, were fairly certain you were gay'" (May 3, 2011). Third, Amina often set up scenarios and descriptions of her own sexuality in Syria as evidence that Western media only has a superficial understanding of the Middle East and its policies towards the gay community. For example, she made this argument explicit in her blog entry, "PinkWashing Assad?" She argued that Western culture, especially the media, was pinkwashing the Middle East, using false constructs of how gender and sexuality are treated in the Middle East as justification for invading or compelling Middle Eastern countries to adopt Western ideals (May 28, 2011). As the persona developed, Amina positioned herself as a lead voice by using rhetorical techniques familiar to an audience in order to build credibility and organize the message according to culturally sanctioned conventions that often evoke an emotional response from the audience.

However, Amina's role as the individual speaker was further predicated not only on those traditional rhetorical strategies, but also on how other people responded to her—not just her audience, but a specific group of people who took up Amina's message and distributed it elsewhere for their own purposes. Besides being the speaker of the initial message, Amina cannily made use of digital spaces and connections with other people outside of her blog in order to develop relationships with other speakers and activists who held ideologies similar to her own. Amina had an online presence through the use of a Facebook account and a LinkedIn account, and she developed and maintained contact with activists in Syria and the Middle East through e-mail. This web presence helped to clarify and build Amina's ethos, because these sites provided audience members other aspects of Amina's character to reveal her constructed "authenticity." For example, Amina's Facebook page was for Amina Arraf and claimed her birthday was October 12, 1975. On the Facebook page, Amina described herself as "just your typical Syrian/American Lesbian dilettante, dreaming of being the most successful Muslim female author of SF/Fantasy/AltHistory in the English Language" ("Amina Arraf"). Amina also had made an earlier attempt to develop her ethos online through another blog, which was started in September, 2007, and indicated an interest in writing fiction and her autobiography.[3] In other words, Amina was MacMaster's online persona for as many as six years prior to the revelation of the hoax, and her "life" online can be heavily documented in other locations besides her blog. This online life meant that Amina had relationships with others who could vouch for and reinforce the authenticity of both Amina's message and her existence as a speaker.

In early February, as Amina began posting to her blog, she initiated relationships with early members of her rhetorical chorus, members of the news blog *Lez Get Real*, who would later help to promote her ideas and defend her ethos. *Lez Get Real* "is a blog with 'A Gay Girl's View on the World'" developed by Paula Brooks[4] that continues to function as a site for a lesbian community to report the news. The reporters demonstrated their belief in her ethos as a speaker by deferring to Amina's expertise and knowledge about issues in Syria and the Middle East. For example, the February 7, 2011 post "Syria Protests Story Apology," Linda Carbondell quotes Amina's response to an earlier news posting: "I just stumbled on your blog and, as a Syrian lesbian now living in Damascus, I had to read it ... and comment. A fair number of the facts are actually wrong; the economy here's actually doing pretty good (compared to most of the world and certainly compared to Egypt) which, probably more than anything, has undermined any protest movement here." Later, Brooks asked Amina to write news articles (as was announced on June 1, 2011, in the "Happy Pride Month" posting by Bridgette P. La Victoire). In writing for *Lez Get Real*, Amina had the opportunity to extend her socio-political arguments regarding the Middle East and LGBT rights to a different community and enlist their help in advancing her arguments. The community of *Lez Get Real* perceived Amina to be an expert on Syria because of her experiences living there, and they believed she was working with them in good faith. Because of their trust in her authenticity, they were willing to extend to her the authority of a speaker on their site. This relationship built up Amina's ethos by lending her credibility as a speaker on Syrian affairs through their privileging of her voice on their site. They could testify to Amina's identity because of their continued interactions with her. Through her presence in multiple locations online, Amina was able to act as a site for the intersections of several communities. These relationships and networked connections allowed Amina to be positioned as lead voice, because they opened her arguments to the appropriate production and distribution of her ideas by a rhetorical chorus.

ACT II: GOING VIRAL

On April 26, 2011, Amina's blog posting inspired an emotional response from its audience, and the message of the post was taken up immediately by new members of the rhetorical chorus, other bloggers and news organizations. The blog post entitled "My Father, the Hero" describes a nighttime visit to Amina's house by guards from the Syrian military police who arrived to arrest her for blogging against the Syrian government and for being open about her sexuality. In response, Amina's father lashed out at the men and cowed them, using harsh words, into leaving the house without Amina. She writes,

> "So you come here to take Amina. Let me tell you something though. She is not the one you should fear; you should be heaping praises

on her and on people like her. They are the ones saying alawi, sunni, arabi, kurdi, duruzi, christian, everyone is the same and will be equal in the new Syria; they are the ones who, if the revolution comes, will be saving Your mother and your sisters. They are the ones fighting the wahhabi most seriously. You idiots are, though, serving them by saying 'every sunni is salafi, every protester is salafi, every one of them is an enemy' because when you do that you make it so.

"Your Bashar and your Maher, they will not live forever, they will not rule forever, and you both know that. So, if you want good things for yourselves in the future, you will leave and you will not take Amina with you. You will go back and you will tell the rest of yours that the people like her are the best friends the Alawi could ever have and you will not come for her again.

"And right now, you two will both apologize for waking her and putting her through all this. Do you understand me?"

And time froze when he stopped speaking. Now, they would either smack him down and beat him, rape me, and take us both away ... or. ... the first one nodded, then the second one. "Go back to sleep," he said. "We are sorry for troubling you." And they left! As soon as the gate shut ... I heard clapping; everyone in the house was awake now and had been watching from balconies and doorways and windows all around the courtyard ... and everyone was cheering. ... MY DAD had just defeated them! Not with weapons but with words ... and they had left. ... I hugged him and kissed him; I literally owe him my life now. And everyone came down and hugged and kissed, every member of the family, and the servants and everyone ... we had won ... this time ...

She ends the story by stating that her father will remain in Syria to fight for democracy and so while the rest of the family has left for the safety of Beirut, she will remain to be with her father. Because Amina's story exemplifies the courageousness of both her own actions and those of her father, the posting went viral immediately. At least three different communities took up the message of the blog and distributed it into other locations: the LGBT community, academics and activists interested in Middle Eastern politics (specifically Syria), and a couple of different Western media outlets.

The people who distributed Amina's message online followed a homophonic relationship with Amina positioned in the role of lead voice. According to musical terminology, the homophonic relationship "balances the melodic conduct of the individual parts with the harmonies that result from their interactions, but one part—often but not always the highest— usually dominates the entire texture" (Hyer). The chorus may be picking up on specific inflections determined to be the main thrust of the rhetor's speech. Homophonic relationships act as support for the original message by repeating the message, which amplifies different aspects of Amina's message. This support, in our blog example, takes the form of directly mediating the message to other locations to increase readership, emphasizing particular messages from the text, and further magnifying the speaker's ethos.

On April 29, 2011, Heather Clisby updated *HerBlog*'s *Spotlight Blogger* with an article "A Gay Girl in Damascus: My Brave Father" in which she writes of Amina's blog: "this riveting post will bring the recent events in Syria in glaring reality" and "the bravery of Amina and her amazing father is admirable and her writing, unforgettable." Another blog, *WhenSallymetSally*, added a post describing Amina as a "rising internet star" on May 10, 2011. The posting goes on to state "Amina candidly and humorously describes her experiences as a lesbian in Syria, a country that bans homosexuality" and marvels at "how she sees no conflict in being both gay and Muslim. She prays five times a day, fasts at Ramadan and 'covered' for a decade (i.e., wore clothes concealing her face and body)" ("Rising Star"). These blog descriptions demonstrate homophony by shifting Amina's message virtually unchanged to other locations online and then calling for audiences of *HerBlog* and *WhenSallymetSally* to go to Amina's blog and become audiences there as well. These members of the chorus encouraged readers to view Amina's work as heroic and a strong voice for what they see as an otherwise voiceless group, Middle Eastern lesbians. These posts acting in a homophonic role were quick to repeat and amplify the speaker's ethos as a lesbian woman who is able to balance her sexuality with her religious beliefs even in a location where one's openness about sexuality violates religious codes and could lead to death.

In addition, academics and activists who wanted to promote a different view of the Middle East than what is usually supported by Western media outlets acted as homophonic voices by further distributing Amina's message. Joshua Landis, Director for the Center for Middle East Studies and Associate Professor at the University of Oklahoma, posted "News Round Up" (April 28, 2011) and wrote "a new blogger in Damascus who writes like a dream and gives us a wonderful new voice and perspective on life in Syria. Read Amina about her confrontation with two young Alawite intelligence agents—wonderful account of the successful deployment of 'the Damascus gambit' on Syria's complicated chessboard of religion, class, gender, patriarchy, and national one-upmanship." In addition, *Mondoweiss*, a news website devoted to covering American foreign policy in the Middle East, chiefly from a progressive Jewish perspective, also promoted Amina: "so you come to take Amina—a loving Syrian father saves his gay blogger daughter from the security services (April 29, 2011)" (*Gay Girl in Damascus*). *Mondoweiss* distributed Amina's message by directly cutting and pasting part of her blog entry "My Father, the Hero" to their own site. Because of the actions of the *Mondoweiss* editors and academics such as Joshua Landis, Amina's rhetorical agenda was brought to the attention of entirely new audiences. These organizations authenticated Amina's ethos for their audiences, while emphasizing the specific issues that were important to the chorus and described in Amina's blog post.

AMINA IN THE NEWS

In April and May of 2011, reporters from three news agencies—*The Washington Post, The Guardian*, and CNN—took on homophonic roles by demonstrating their support to the overall message while at the same time promoting Amina's message as a crucial component of their own agendas. According to the news reporters, Amina contacted them by e-mail, and other Syrian activists they were in contact with authenticated her. When members of the mainstream media finally became involved in disseminating Amina's rhetoric, a *Washington Post* article described the dissemination of Amina's rhetorical agenda online: "Wednesday, her voice got out there in a more profound way after a blog post she wrote went viral. In the post, she tells of a visit two security service men, wearing black leather jackets and carrying pistols, made to her house in the middle of the night. They had come to arrest her for her blog, 'A Damascus Gay Girl'" (Flock "Syrian Blogger"). As this case of homophony demonstrates, the voices do not blend together in such a way that one voice disappears. Rather, the voices balance between agreeing and disagreeing with the lead speaker. Through their instrumental role, these news reporters lent further credibility to Amina, since they used her as an authoritative source in their articles and therefore used Amina's message to promote her causes and their own.

On Friday, May 6, 2011, *The Guardian* printed an article entitled "A Gay Girl in Damascus becomes heroine of the Syrian revolt: Blog by half-American 'ultimate outsider' describes dangers of political and sexual dissent." This article by Katherine Marsh, a *Guardian* reporter who lives in Syria, states that Amina is an "unlikely hero of revolt in a conservative country" because her blog "is brutally honest, poking at subjects long considered taboo in Arab culture." The article appears to put Amina forward as an example of the people protesting in Syria, a person with whom Marsh's Western audience can sympathize. The blog, according to Marsh, has "the blend of humour and frankness, frivolity and political *nous* [that] comes from upbringing that straddles Syria and the US." In addition, Marsh highlights the other major theme of Amina's blog and personal experience, her homosexuality, as evidence of her heroism: "despite facing prejudice—in both the US and Syria—Abdullah sees no conflict in being both gay and Muslim." Amina is raised in this article to heroine status especially because she has used her dual citizenship and her influential family in Damascus to empower her to speak. Through this article, Amina's personal experience is appropriated by Marsh and redistributed to a new location online. This personal experience is altered to meet Marsh's rhetorical agenda but at the same time promotes Amina's views on both the social and political situation in Syria and her sexuality. Mostly the article reinforces Amina's ethos as a speaker, because it claims her credibility both as a writer and as someone who heroically faces prejudice.

In the May 27, 2011, article, "Will Gays be 'Sacrificial Lambs' in Arab Spring?" Catriona Davies discusses the prospect that, while bringing the possibility of freedom, the uprisings in the Arab world may also give rise to further persecution of homosexuals, since "homosexuality is illegal in 76 countries worldwide and punishable by death in five, including Yemen, Saudi Arabia, and Iran." The article provides quotes from Sami Hamwi, a journalist from Damascus and the Syrian editor of *Gay Middle East*, and Haider Ala Hamoudi, "an expert on Middle Eastern Islamic law at the University of Pittsburgh School of Law," who both express concerns that political change for gay rights is progressive but hampered because traditional Islamic law bans homosexuality. Hamwi has fears about his own safety and that of other reformers. He also conveys "doubts that any political change could significantly improve gay rights." Hamoudi states that "Sheikhs still emphasize that death penalty is the Islamic punishment for gay men." The article then contrasts both men's positions on gay rights with "a more positive view of the situation" provided by Amina Abdallah and her blog. As quoted in the article, Amina claims that "a whole lot of long time changes are coming suddenly bubbling to the surface and views towards women, gay people, and minorities are rapidly changing." She also claims that the responses to her blog have been "almost entirely positive." The article closes by stating that most people interviewed by CNN (with the exception of Amina) state that gay rights are unlikely to occur anytime soon and that in the meantime, recent social movements in the Middle East have actually made the situation more dangerous for the gay population.[5]

These members of the rhetorical chorus appropriated and distributed Amina's messages to new locations online by articulating the message in virtually the same manner as Amina for their own purposes with the exception of the CNN article. Through these homophonic movements, the members of the chorus often preserved her original messages, but their intentions in growing her audience and promoting certain parts of her message were their own. The Western LGBT communities not only distributed Amina's ideas, but also endorsed them as evidence of a lesbian woman and her father standing up against a repressive government for her human rights. While the LGBT communities were describing Amina and her father as examples of heroic defenders of her sexuality, these other organizations emphasized her father's ability and desire to save Amina from the security services. Social activists working on advocating for different issues within the Middle East used Amina's message as evidence of the authenticity of their own views, because she spoke from the privileged position of personal experience. Lastly, the news reporters first reported on Amina's rise as a blogger worth noting and then reinforced Amina's authority to speak by using her to further their own arguments. In making their own contributions and promoting Amina to their own audiences, the rhetorical chorus helped show their readers that Amina was a credible speaker they should trust by repeating and amplifying her rhetoric.

ACT III: A GAY? GIRL? IN DAMASCUS?

On June 5, 2011, the events on the blog *A Gay Girl in Damascus* reached a climax when, in attempting to extricate himself from his blogging persona, MacMaster created a new pseudonym—Amina's cousin Rania O. Ismail. Ismail posted that Amina had been kidnapped by armed members of Syrian security forces. Immediately, followers of the blog and members of the rhetorical chorus who had been promoting and distributing Amina's message went into action to save the blogger. They flocked to Facebook, Twitter, and online petition sites hoping to raise enough awareness of the captured blogger to help rescue her. Sandra Bagaria, Amina's partner in Canada whom she dated through e-mail, started campaigns on Facebook and Twitter to get the word out to Amnesty International and the U.S. State Department. Facebook alone had at least three separate campaigns designed to advertise Amina's abduction: FreeAminaArraf, Free-Amina-Abdallah, and Amina-Abdallah-Arraf-al-Omari. As the fervor over Amina's kidnapping demonstrated, Amina's rhetoric invoked trust and an emotional response from her audience, because the message adhered to "infrastructures of trust" that the audience recognized (Miller 2). They wanted to support an out lesbian Muslim woman who chose to speak even though she lived in a repressive country. The fervor also showed the depth of the emotional connections made between Amina and her audience. Because Amina was no longer able to speak, her rhetorical chorus set out to authenticate her ethos and promote her rhetorical agenda to a range of locations online.

As blog followers and other contacts across the Internet began to mobilize to rescue Amina, new organizations took up the story in an effort to bring awareness to Amina's plight. As these new organizations did more research, they began to find holes in Amina's story and online history: the earliest to do so were Liz Henry of *HerBlog*, Andy Carver of NPR, Ali Abunimah and Benjamin Doherty of *Electronic Intifada*, and Melissa Bell and Elizabeth Flock of *The Washington Post*.[6] These new members of the chorus acted through polyphonic relationships in which other voices entered into the space later than the original speaker and the homophonic relationships. These polyphonic voices operated separately from the original message and sometimes acted as a counterpoint by moving against the original message. With counterpoint, the voices of the rhetorical chorus balance between agreement and disagreement with the original voice. The contrapuntal voices do not bolster or follow the original message like homophonic voices. These cross movements create a situation in which the contributions of the new voices, new rhetorical messages, move abrasively against the original message. In this case the contradictions wore away at the original message to reveal the fraudulent ethos of the speaker.

Initially, the questions about Amina's existence caused confusion: Did she exist? Was she actually a lesbian? Was she really in Syria? Abunimah and Doherty discovered that Amina's articles for the website *Lez Get Real* were posted from IP addresses associated with the University of Edinburgh.

Because Amina claimed to be writing in Syria, a police state, it was entirely possible that she existed and had to hide her identity to protect herself and her family. However, as the reporters and bloggers listed above researched Amina, they discovered that her online persona's identity was not tied to the material body and experiences of a woman, but to MacMaster instead. On June 8, 2011, Liz Sly of *The Washington Post* reported that while Amina had a Canadian girlfriend who was vouching for her existence, the girlfriend, Sandra Bagaria, had never met or even Skyped with Amina, and the United States State Department could find no evidence to confirm Amina's existence. Each contradiction wore against Amina's constructed identity and the constructedness of the identity became more apparent. The portion of the rhetorical chorus who demonstrated that Amina didn't exist did so by tracing the various ways ethos had been established. They found that all the physical evidence indicated that Amina was only an online persona.

ACT IV: A STRAIGHT? MAN? IN EDINBURGH?

On June 9, 2011, Tom MacMaster outed himself as the real author of *A Gay Girl in Damascus* to news organizations. In his "Apology to Readers" post, MacMaster claims, "While the narrative voice may have been fictional, the facts on this blog are true and not misleading as to the situation on the ground. I do not believe I have harmed anyone" (June 12, 2011). He further states, "I feel that I have created an important voice for issues that I feel strongly about" ("Apology to Readers"). With these claims, MacMaster sought to absolve himself of responsibility for committing any sort of fraud. Although he misrepresented his identity online, he believed himself to be acting in good faith and good will by speaking for those who are otherwise silenced in Western society. His most salient point is that he did not harm anyone. He also did not acquire any financial gain from his behavior, and any plagiarism committed would have been incidental to the creation of his fabricated character.

MacMaster's response to being found out raises some pressing concerns regarding contested authorship. While some people sought to place responsibility and blame for their anger at his door, MacMaster claims he was operating within acceptable social constraints since he did not harm others and he created his false persona online in order to have a safe place and identity from which to speak. Since he operates through good will, claims expertise over the subject of Syria, and follows appropriate rhetorical conventions, he appears to still fit with the traditional definition of ethos, which was proposed earlier. However, in response to the circumstances and MacMaster's own apology, the rhetorical chorus intervened through further polyphonic moves in order to articulate their own complicated responses to the situation. Like a chorus, the rhetorical chorus gathered in groups on the world's stage to argue against or defend different aspects of MacMaster's rhetoric and ethos.

ACT V: DÉNOUEMENT

At this point, some parts of the rhetorical chorus had helped to build Amina's ethos, while others helped to erode the layers of credibility to show the hoax beneath. In this last stage, new groups came forward. One part of the rhetorical chorus sought to reject MacMaster's message as the credibility of the speaker evaporated. The other portion of the rhetorical chorus struggled to protect the ethos of the message from the infamy of the lead voice. The last part wanted to reclaim some part of MacMaster's ethos, by claiming his efforts to be acts of good will and necessary for the preservation of certain ideals.

Rejecting the Speaker/Message

The first part of the chorus to articulate views on the hoax had the not-at-all-surprising reaction of anger and rejection. These chorus members as bloggers had the ability to censor the speaker by displaying "outrage over plagiarism and identity concealment in the real world," a situation that "brings up an interesting paradox related to authorship, and that is the simultaneous emphasis on a commitment to authorial authenticity seems untroubled by an equally prevalent dependence on intertextual links, citations, and embedded media" (Singh 32). Through their polyphonic roles, these choral members moved against the original message and speaker, while using the initial message to argue that they had been injured by MacMaster's actions.

Of all the communities Amina tried to advocate for, the LGBT community was the one who spoke out strongly when they realized that the experiences on which Amina and her rhetorical chorus had built her ethos were actually false. A blogger for *Gay in Middle East*, Daniel Nassar, angrily wrote a post entitled, "From Damascus with Love: Blogging in a Totalitarian State."

> Because of you, Mr. MacMaster, a lot of the real activists in the LGBT community became under the spotlight of the authorities in Syria … this attention you brought forced me back to the closet on all the social media websites I use; caused my family to go into a frenzy trying to force me back into the closet and my friends to ask me for phone numbers of loved ones and family members so they can call in case I disappeared myself … you feed the foreign media an undeniable dish of sex, religion and politics and you now are now leaving us with this holier-than-thou-semi-apologize with lame and shallow excuses of how you wanted to bring attention to the right people on the ground.

For Nassar and other LGBT community members and activists, MacMaster's hoax did not shed light on their situation, because he had no real experience with what their lives were like. To make things worse, MacMaster's actions brought unneeded attention to the community by Syrian security forces and potentially placed them in serious danger.

Nassar wrote multiple responses to MacMaster's deception in an effort to point out that MacMaster's ventriloquism of a lesbian woman was problematic rather than helpful. In his article for *The Guardian*, "The Real World of Gay Girls in Damascus," Nassar comments on what life is actually like for gay women in Damascus, a direct assault on both Amina's trustworthiness and her argument's credibility. Specifically, Nassar asserts that a lesbian woman is not likely to be accepted by her family as so many members of the rhetorical chorus wanted to support, and the police who came to arrest her would not have been driven off by her strangely supportive father. In response to the argument from some members of the rhetorical chorus that Amina's message could still help lesbian women in Syria, Nassar repeatedly warns that it also draws dangerous attention to them. "They don't need more attention from authorities who might target them to make sure a real Amina does not exist" ("The Real World"). For Nassar, Amina's credibility came from her self-disclosure and personal experience, but she didn't exist and the experiences she described did not occur. In addition, the argument Amina makes about the positive possibilities for the LGBT community in the Middle East loses its credibility because of the events surrounding MacMaster's hoax. Instead, MacMaster placed the LGBT community at greater risk and did the exact opposite of what he set out to do. While he claimed he was fighting against pinkwashing—the use of LGBT persecution as a reason for the West to intervene in the Middle East—MacMaster acted as a Westerner who felt he could speak for the LGBT community better than they could.

In addition to the Middle Eastern LGBT community, Western LGBT activists and bloggers found themselves having to shift their own constructions of ethos. Instead of relying on self-disclosure and self-validation online to speak, some LGBT bloggers felt they had to demonstrate to their readers that their sexual identities and gender remained the same offline as on. In a June 13, 2011, blog posting, "LezGetReal and Gay Girl in Damascus: Straight Men in Drag," a lesbian woman who identified herself as The Lesbian Conservative wrote "And as for *The Lesbian Conservative*, well, I've actually presented myself in-person to a couple of the good folks who read my blog." This statement illuminates the problem faced by the LGBT community: the authenticity of their own voices is now called into question. The Lesbian Conservative and others have to now demonstrate they are who they claim to be, that people can vouch for their existence not just online, and that they must find ways to establish that both their ethos as speaker and the message should be considered credible. This backlash potentially means that LGBT writers no longer had anonymity online to protect themselves from homophobic and dangerous responses to their work, because they must "out" themselves both online and offline to show credibility. The LGBT chorus viewed MacMaster's actions as damaging not only to their personal safety but also to their own ethos online. Because of him, LGBT in Syria and other parts of the Middle East were in danger of being scrutinized, outed, tortured, and possibly killed. To their view, MacMaster's work online created a problematic example of authorship. He lied, and therefore everything he did and said was a lie regardless of how and why he felt he could speak.

Protecting the Rhetoric

Conversely, some members of the rhetorical chorus sought to rescue the credibility of Amina's arguments from the taint of MacMaster's hoax. On June 10, 2011, Linda S. Carbonell of *Lez Get Real* added a post entitled "An Apology to our Readers about Amina Abdallah." In this article, Carbonell explains that the persona Amina contacted her claiming to be a lesbian woman from Syria. This persona fulfilled a need that the blog had; "I wanted someone in the region who could do a much better job of explaining the Arab Spring to Americans than I could from 5,000 miles away." Carbonell admits that she bought into Amina's ethos, because Amina's arguments matched those that Carbonell firmly believed ("An Apology" June 10, 2011). Carbonell felt Amina was trustworthy because Amina shared her experiences as a Syrian and as a lesbian. Further, Carbonell could rely on Amina's authenticity because they developed a working relationship with common rhetorical agendas, and Amina appeared to be acting in good faith for the benefit of the *Lez Get Real* community.

Surprisingly, despite all the evidence that MacMaster had fictionalized Amina and lied, Carbonell and *Lez Get Real* still wanted to believe Amina was a woman and a lesbian. As the news came out that Amina was not a lesbian in Syria, *Lez Get Real* in its letter of apology still bought into the fiction of gender and sexuality even when it became obvious that the person writing the work was not in Syria: "Beyond the truth about 'Amina,' who apparently is a 35 year-old lesbian living in Edinburgh, Scotland." The important aspect of the argument for *Lez Get Real* and Carbonell was that the story was being told, and they didn't particularly care who told it as long as it helped people to listen. Carbonell writes, "I want something understood, though, 'Amina' didn't say anything that wasn't the truth. The situation in Syria is no less horrific just because she wasn't actually there. People are dying, people are being mowed down in the streets, people are disappearing into the jails and secret police dungeons. IT DOESN'T BLOODY MATTER WHO TELLS US THIS AS LONG AS WE LISTEN TO THE CRIES OF PEOPLE WHO WANT TO BE FREE." For Carbonell, *Lez Get Real*, and a number of other activists online, the important and trustworthy part of the rhetorical situation was less about Amina and more about the message being presented. So in response to the destruction of Amina's ethos, the rhetorical chorus moved to make counterarguments and find merit in the message Amina once argued. At this point, the rhetorical chorus was willing to leave aside the ethos of the speaker and focus on the authority and authenticity of the message that the rhetorical chorus alone could build, maintain, or destroy depending on individuals' rhetorical agendas.

Speaker of Good Will?

The last group, while acknowledging that MacMaster had fooled people, argued that this situation was not an example of problematic authorship, but rather an example of appropriate authorship online. In her post, "Gay Girl in Damascus Blogger Hoax: Chasing Amina," Liz Henry acts as part of the rhetorical chorus who wants to protect part of MacMaster's rhetorical agency and preserve some of his rhetorical ethos. She puts inflection on one aspect of MacMaster's rhetorical stance regarding the importance of anonymity online. She argues that,

> Many people have good reason to conceal their identity and to develop relationships online under a screen name. They might like to express an aspect of their personality that would not mix well with their professional life. They might have gender identity issues they are working through. They might be in a family situation that makes it unsafe for them to come out as gay. They might write fiction using characters whose stories are under copyright. None of those, however, are excuses for deception and manipulative behavior.

While MacMaster did not present any direct argument about anonymity through his persona Amina, he used this mythos of Internet authorship as his vehicle for presenting his arguments. In an interview with *The Guardian*, MacMaster specifically articulates this premise by stating that "I started writing posts on Syria and Islam," but he found that no news organization in the U.S. would provide "a fair hearing to the Palestinian-Israeli issue." He often got responses such as "Why do you hate America?" To combat what MacMaster calls "that stupid argument," he argued, "if I sign myself with an Arab girl's name first there will be some deference from obnoxious men, just because people will be more polite to a girl than to a guy and second people won't get hung up on why do you hate?" (Addley). People who would argue against him online as a white man in Georgia would allow an Arab woman to make her case, because she would be speaking from her own position and experiences within the world. In other words, MacMaster's authorship models the utopian online world that Henry and others[7] want to protect; specifically, they sought to protect the idea that online "aspects of identity which currently form the basis for discrimination and hierarchical relationships will cease to matter" (Kendall 129–30). Despite the precedent that MacMaster sets of misusing anonymity, some people still see anonymity as a way for others to speak. They seek to reclaim this aspect of his argument and his construction of identity by dividing the activity from his failing ethos. In this move, they are agreeing with him, defending him, and yet separating their argument from him.

As the events unfolded, the rhetorical chorus revealed the extent to which problematic forms of authorship from their inception to their revelation are affected by both the choices made by the author and the interventions of other people. When Tom MacMaster created Amina, he believed (if we believe his explanation) that he was legitimately using the persona he created to help the LGBT community in the Middle East to voice its concerns for a Western audience. In his interview with *The Guardian*, he stated, "I only hope that people pay as much attention to the people of the Middle East and their struggles in this year of revolutions. The events there are being shaped by the people living them on a daily basis. I have only tried to illuminate them for a Western audience" (Addley). He advocated that it did not matter who actually made the arguments as long as the message was presented. Because of the rhetorical chorus, this example of contested authorship revealed that authority, ethos, and authenticity affect broader arguments than those offered by MacMaster. The rhetorical chorus' own rhetorical agenda often affected perceptions on the credibility of the speaker and the authority of the message. Their actions further demonstrate just how complex the situation was. While later angry for being duped, members of LGBT communities were among the first ones to lend MacMaster credibility and to vouch for his existence as Amina. They responded to the hoax by placing inflection on the aspects of his argument that mattered to them and used the opportunity to denounce MacMaster, his construction and ventriloquism of a lesbian woman, and his rhetorical agendas. Other portions of the chorus fought to maintain parts of his rhetorical message even as they eroded the ethos of his persona. And some members of the chorus were concerned that the anger of others would undermine the parts of the argument that should have value despite being articulated by a fraudulent persona. As this example shows, situations of contested authorship are just as socially constituted as any other type of authorship, because the chorus participates in the construction and demonstration of ethos as it moves through the digital space of the Internet.

NOTES

1. According to Michel Foucault in his essay "What Is an Author?," the author should be regarded as separate from the historical person who wrote the work. Instead, the individual author becomes a persona associated with a text used for purposes of classification, ownership, and censorship. Other scholars of authorship have demonstrated that the individual author mythos is a relatively recent phenomenon in the history of writing, which occurred because of changes to the economic, legal, and social status of the historical author (Woodmansee and Jaszi; Rose). In an effort to move away from this focus on the individual author in literary studies, Jack Stillinger in his seminal work, *Multiple Authorship and the Myth of Solitary Genius*, demonstrates that writers do not produce their works alone. They rely instead on a network of editors, publishers, and immediate audience members who sometimes actively participate in shaping the text. These criticisms of individual authorship as well as additional research into digital writing practices have led the field of writing studies to the conclusion that "all discourse is socially constructed" (Inge 623). In fact, studies of authorship

have shifted away from a model that privileges a single speaker as the authority to models that explore writing as a collection of social, collective, and collaborative practices (Warnick; Turkle). This decentering of the author means that the authority over the work and its credibility falls to the reader and the reader's agenda (Warnick). However, the move to decenter the author as the authority over the work raises questions regarding how to attribute authority particularly in examples of problematic authorship practices, such as cases of plagiarism, financial fraud, and hoaxes.

2. In "Online Ethos: Source Credibility in an 'Authorless' Environment," Barbara Warnick argues that website design is one of the main ways audiences determine credibility regarding a site (260–62).
3. For more information, see Andy Carver quoted in Mark Memmott and Eyder Peralta. "'Gay Girl in Damascus': Missing or Mythical?" NPR. 8 June 2011. Blog. 8 Aug. 2012; Robert Mackey. "Shifting Syrian Fact from Syrian Fiction." The lede: blogging the new with Robert Mackey. *The New York Times*. 8 June 2011. Blog 8 Sept 2012; and Joseph W. "'Amina Arraf,' Britta Froelicher & the University of St. Andrews." Harry's Place, 12 June 2011; Blog. 4 July 2012.
4. Shortly after Amina was unmasked as Tom MacMaster, Paula Brooks was discovered to be a straight man, Bill Graber. See Elizabeth Flock and Melissa Bell. "'Paula Brooks,' Editor of *Lez Get Real*, also a Man." *The Washington Post*. 13 June 2011. Blog. 5 Sept 2012.
5. In response to the article's position, Amina wrote a blog response entitled "Pink-Washing Assad?" on May 28, 2011, where she accused Davies of pinkwashing the Arab Spring, encouraging a Western audience to want to intervene in the Middle East in order to "rescue" the gay community.
6. For more details, see: Liz Henry. "Painful Doubts About Amina." *Composite*. 7 June 2011. Blog. 4 July 2012;. Mark Memmott and Eyder Peralta. "'Gay Girl in Damascus': Missing or Mythical?" NPR. 8 June 2011. Blog. 8 Aug 2012; Ali Abunimah and Benjamin Doherty. "New Evidence about Amina, the 'Gay Girl in Damascus'Hoax." 12 June 2012. Blog. 2 Sept. 2012; and all articles by Melissa Bell and Elizabeth Flock of *The Washington Post* listed in the Works Cited.
7. Melissa Bell and Elizabeth Flock. "Gay Girl in Damascus Hoax Shouldn't Spoil Online Anonymity." *The Washington Post*. 17 June 2011. Blog. 4 July 2012.

WORKS CITED

Abdallah Arraf al Omaril, Amina [Tom MacMaster]. *A Gay Girl in Damascus: An out Syrian lesbian's thoughts on life, the universe and so on*. February- June 2011. Blog. June 2012.

Abunimah, Ali, and Benjamin Doherty. "New Evidence about Amina, the 'Gay Girl in Damascus' Hoax." 12 June 2012. Blog. 2 Sept 2012.

Addley, Esther. "*Gay Girl in Damascus* Hoaxer Acted out of 'Vanity': Tom MacMaster Heterosexual American Contrite over Fictional Lesbian Blogger 'Amina Abdallah Arla al Omari.'" *The Guardian* 13 June 2011.

Arraf, Amina [Tom MacMaster]. Facebook. 3 Sept 2012.

Aristotle. *On Rhetoric: A Theory of Civic Discourse*. Trans. George A. Kennedy. 2nd Ed. Oxford: Oxford UP: 2007.

Basgier, Christopher. "The Author-Function, the Genre Function, and the Rhetoric of Scholarly Webtexts." *Computers and Composition* 28 (2011): 145–59.

Bell, Melissa, and Elizabeth Flock. "*Gay Girl in Damascus* Hoax Shouldn't Spoil Online Anonymity." *The Washington Post.* 17 June 2011. Blog. 4 July 2012.

Carbonell, Linda S. "An Apology to our Readers about Amina Abdallah." *Lez Get Real* 10 June 2011. Blog. September 2012.

———. "Syria Protests Story Apology" *Lez Get Real* February 7, 2011.

Clisby, Heather. "*A Gay Girl in Damascus*: My Brave Father." *HerBlog's Spotlight Blogger* 29 April 2011. Blog. 26 June 2012.

Davies, Catriona. "Will Gays Be 'Sacrificial Lambs' in Arab Spring?" CNN 27 May 2011. Web. 26 June 2012.

Fleckenstein, Kristie. "Cybernetics, Ethos, and Ethics: The Plight of the Bread-and-Butter-fly." *Plugged In: Technology, Rhetoric and Culture in a Posthuman Age.* eds. Lynn Worsham and Gary A. Olson. New Dimensions in Computers and Composition. Cresskill, NJ: Hampton Press, 2008.

Flock, Elizabeth "Syrian Blogger Says She Faced Arrest but Remains Defiant," *Washington Post* 27 April 2011. Web. 4 August 2012.

———. and Melissa Bell. "'Paula Brooks,' Editor of *Lez Get Real*, Also a Man." *Washington Post* 13 June 2011. Blog. 5 Sept 2012.

Foucault, Michel. "What Is an Author?" *Book History Reader.* eds. David Finkelstein and Alistair McCleery. New York: Routledge, 2002.

[*Gay Girl in Damascus*, A]. "'So You Come To Take Amina' – A Loving Syrian Father Saves His Gay Blogger Daughter from the Security Services." *Mondoweiss* 29 April 2011. Blog. 26 June 2012.

Henry, Liz. "Painful Doubts about Amina." *Composite.* 7 June 2011. Blog. 4 July 2012.

Hyer, Brian. "Homophony." *Grove Music Online. Oxford Music Online.* Oxford University Press. Web. 3 Jan 2014.

Inge, M. Thomas. "Collaboration and Concepts of Authorship." *PMLA* 116. 3 (May 2001): 623–30.

Kendall, Lori. "Meaning and Identity in 'Cyberspace': The Performance of Gender, Class, and Race Online." *Symbolic Interaction* 21. 2 (1998): 129–53.

Kennedy, Helen. "Technobiography: Researching Lives, Online and Off." *Biography* 26. 1 (2003): 120–39.

Landis, Joshua. "News Round Up (28 April 2011)." *Syria Comment: Syrian Politics, History, and Religion* 28 April 2011. Blog. 2 Sept 2012.

LaVictoire, Bridgette P. "Happy Pride Month." *Lez Get Real* 1 June 2011. Blog. 4 Sept 2012.

Lesbian Conservative, The. "*Lez Get Real* and *Gay Girl in Damascus*: Straight Men in Drag." 13 June 2011. Blog. 29 June 2012.

Mackey, Robert. "Shifting Syrian Fact from Syrian Fiction." The Lede: blogging the new with Robert Mackey. *The New York Times.* 8 June 2011. Blog 8 Sept 2012.

Marsh, Katherine. "*A Gay Girl in Damascus* Becomes Heroine of the Syrian Revolt: Blog By Half-American 'Ultimate Outsider.'" *The Guardian* 6 May 2011.

Memmott, Mark, and Eyder Peralta. "'*Gay Girl in Damascus*': Missing or Mythical?" NPR 8 June 2011. Blog. 8 Aug 2012.

Miller, Carolyn, and Dawn Shepherd. "Blogging As Social Action: A Genre Analysis of The Weblog." *Into the Blogosphere.* Ed. Laura Gurak et al. 2004. Web. 9 Sept. 2012.

Miller, Susan. *Trust in Texts: A Different History of Rhetoric.* Carbondale, IL: Southern Illinois UP, 2007.

Nassar, Daniel. "The Real World of Gay Girls in Damascus." *The Guardian* 15 June 2011. Web. 26 June 2012.

———. and Sami Hamwi. "From Damascus with Love: Blogging in a Totalitarian State." *Gay Middle East* 6 June 2011. Blog. 26 June 2012.

Rak, Julie. "The digital Queer: Weblogs and Internet Identity." *Biography* 28.1 (2005): 166–82.

Rose, Mark. *Authors and Owners: The Invention of Copyright.* Cambridge, MA: Harvard UP, 1993.

"Rising Internet Star: *A Gay Girl in Damascus.*" *WhenSallymetSally* 10 May 2011. Blog. 26 June 2012.

Singh, Amardeep. "Anonymity, Authorship, and Blogger Ethics." *Symploke* 16: 1–2 (2008): 21–35.

Sly, Liz. "'*Gay Girl in Damascus*' May Not Be Real." *The Washington Post* 8 June 2011.

Stillinger, Jack. *Multiple Authorship and the Myth of Solitary Genius.* New York: Oxford UP, 1991.

Turkle, Sherry. *Life on the Screen: Identity in the Age of the Internet.* London: Weidenfeld & Nicolson, 1996.

W., Joseph. "'Amina Arraf,' Britta Froelicher & the University of St. Andrews." *Harry's Place.* 12 June 2011. Blog. 4 July 2012.

Warnick, Barbara. "Online Ethos: Source Credibility in an 'Authorless' Environment." *American Behavioral Scientist* 48 (2004): 256–65.

Winfrey, Oprah. Interview with James Frey. *The Oprah Winfrey Show.* Jan. 26, 2006.

Woodmansee, Martha. *Author, Art, and the Market: Rereading the History of Aesthetics.* New York: Columbia UP, 1994.

Woodmansee, Martha, and Peter Jaszi. *The Construction of Authorship: Textual Appropriation in Law and Literature.* Durham: Duke UP, 1994.

2 Writing in the Dead Zone
Authorship in the Age of Intelligent Machines

Kyle Jensen

> Instead, we must locate the space left empty by the author's disappearance, follow the distribution of gaps and breaches, and watch for the openings that this disappearance uncovers.
> —Michel Foucault, "What Is an Author?"

SCENE

On September 10, 2011, *The New York Times* published a profile of start-up software company Narrative Science. The profile centered on a groundbreaking computer algorithm that transforms raw data into newspaper articles. According to the column's author, Steve Lohr, Narrative Science's algorithm exhibits sufficient stylistic dexterity to render determining human authorship difficult. In addition to mirroring the quality of human writing, the algorithm culls information from sources that humans have difficulty accessing, at a speed humans cannot replicate. For example, the algorithm can analyze real-time data entered during sporting events and write a summary before the game is complete. With a palpable sense of anxiety, Lohr assures his audience that a "real human wrote this column." Such distinctions may in time become obsolete.

On March 29, 2013, Gini Graham Scott responded to Lohr's anxious projections in a *Huffington Post* editorial. Characterizing automated writing software as an "assault on writers," Scott claimed that emerging writing technologies would erode human authorship. Suggesting that such erosion would be sponsored by industry-leading publishers such as Amazon.com and ICON International, Scott projected that the resulting economic momentum would prove difficult, if not impossible, to reverse. Before closing with a summary of the prevailing reports on automated writing software, Scott assured her audience that she authored the column.

The anxiety over automated writing software expressed in these and other popular reports is puzzling, given what media historians have discovered about machine-based writing. For example, Friedrich Kittler argued that "Once the technological differentiation of optics, acoustics, and writing exploded Gutenberg's writing monopoly around 1880, the fabrication of so-called Man became possible. His essence escapes into apparatuses. Machines take over functions of the central nervous system, and no longer, as in of times past, merely those of muscles" (16). The anxiety over automated writing is thereby puzzling because the mechanization of the "human" author is old news. Machine-based inscriptions "have regulated modern experience, making life more legible in complicated, public ways, signaling changes to the context and thereby the complexion of writing and reading" (Gitelman 11). The ostensible loss of the human author is not a loss at all. It would be more accurate (though, perhaps less comforting) to describe the contemporary author as a result of printing technologies that have gone digital.

Given these findings, it is understandable that scholars have explored "writing and reading as culturally and historically contingent" activities that blur the distinction between human and machine (Gitelman 11). My chapter adopts a somewhat different tact by asking the following questions:

> Why do we continue to witness an investment in the distinction between human and machine in the context of authorship?
> Why does the blurring of human and machine in reports on automated writing software make so many people anxious?
> What role the does the concept of *authorship* play in ameliorating such anxieties?
> Why do human writers feel compelled to announce that they are human when commenting on the emergence of automated writing software?
> Why do we witness the clustering of authenticating phrases such as "real human" (Lohr) and "I assure you" (Scott) in such reports?

I raise these questions in order to examine the ways in which popular reports on automated writing software unwittingly expose a primary feature of writing that I am calling *writing in the dead zone*. Following Brian Rotman, I define this as a virtualized time and space unique to written symbol systems that signal the bare insecurity of human finitude. I refer to writing's virtualized time and space as a dead zone. I do so because writing's virtualized time and space haunt human subjects who presume it is possible to secure themselves within written symbol systems.

Signals of *writing in the dead zone* are easiest to spot when human subjects enlist written systems to materialize their existence. Often anticipatory in nature, these enlistments attempt to unify the writers so that written text may securely represent them and their investments. Popular reports on automated writing software prove particularly useful for analyzing such enlistments because their affective tenor calls attention to the insecure nature of the process. Saturated with anxious projections about the loss of human authorship, they suggest that writing is more unruly than we typically assume. In response to writing's unruliness, reporters construe the automated appropriation of human authorship as the loss of a primary means by which humans materialize their existence. Of course, these reports are designed to insure against such loss by arguing that a human author is a securable entity. The sense of security is born from a belief that the time and space of human writers can be unified with the time and space of writing. In supporting this belief, the concept of *authorship* functions as a *bridging device*, or "[a] symbolic structure whereby one 'transcends' a conflict in one way or another" (Burke 224).

In popular reports on automated writing software, the invocation of the authorial name stages a conflict between human and machine writers. This staged conflict materializes the belief that human existence may be meaningfully secured in written symbol systems by classifying the human author as artful, conscious, locatable, and reflexive. By contrast, the writing machine is classified as mimetic, non-conscious, unlocatable, and indiscriminate. This classificatory function is arguably most apparent when the reporter announces that a human has authored the column. Such an argumentative gesture presumes that algorithms cannot refer to themselves in writing because they lack the aforementioned features that distinguish human authors.

This staged conflict effaces the criteria upon which our culture determines what constitutes an author. The effacement is not total; popular reports routinely invoke the loss of human authorship as coextensive with the loss of employment for human writers, the acceleration of capitalist enterprise, and the danger of losing track of our news sources. But it does conceal how the conceptual parameters of authorship are inevitably structured by the writing mechanisms we employ at any given moment. By concealing the structural coupling between authorship and writing mechanisms, we fail to examine that the conflict staged in these reports is not a conflict at all. Indeed, the staged conflict is better understood as an argumentative rendering of the differential time and space of writing. By resisting the impulse to invoke the concept of authorship in these debates, we may cultivate a more elaborate sense of writing's differential space and time: its dead zone.

In the pages that follow, I develop this argument with greater precision and begin by demonstrating that the prevailing popular engagements with automated writing software are anxious in nature. My overarching purpose is to examine how writing's different time and space encourages anxious projections concerning the loss of human authorship. Having this discussion demonstrates that we are dealing with a general conflict between humans and writing, not a specific conflict between humans and automated writing software. By approaching this discussion from the angle of anxiety, I may expose how reports on automated writing software gesture toward human insecurity in all writing systems. The subsequent two sections provide a more elaborate explanation of what I mean by *writing in the dead zone*. They substantiate my claim that the anxiety produced by writing's different time and space is not specific to automated writing software. Addressing the criteria upon which our culture determines what constitutes authorship is crucial to the conversation because these criteria bring into high tension the complex cultural apparatuses we use to arrest the time and space of writing. The conclusion affirms that studying the conflict between humans and writing should make us anxious and lead to projections about what the future may hold. By affirming the anxious relationship we have to writing in the dead zone, we may envision a form of writing research that is abductive in its logical orientation and thereby open to writing's complexities in ways yet to be imagined.

AGENCY

In *Ugly Feelings*, Sianne Ngai argues that anxiety is an expectant emotion. By *expectant* Ngai means that anxiety is "intimately aligned with the concept of futurity, and the temporal dynamics of deferral and anticipation in particular" (210). Because anxiety is anticipatory in nature, researchers have tended to stress its temporal dimensions. But Ngai insists that scholars assessing anxiety consider its spatial complexities as well. Specifically, she asks scholars to focus on anxiety's ability to project "onto others[,] in the sense of an outward propulsion or displacement—that is, as a quality of feeling the subject refuses to recognize in himself and attempts to locate in another person or thing (usually as a form of naïve or unconscious defense)" (210). The spatial projection of anxiety is crucial to consider because it exposes efforts to secure "a strategic sort of distance for the knowledge-seeking subject, enabling him to differentiate 'here' from 'yonder' even in the absence of the fixed positions from which nearnesses and farnesses are ordinarily established or gauged" (212). By studying the spatio-temporal interplay of anxiety, scholars may observe how it "converge[s] in the production of a distinct kind of knowledge seeking subject" who is characterized by efforts to secure or preserve interpretive agency through displacement (215).

If popular responses to automated writing software are anxious, then they should employ argumentative strategies that are consistent with Ngai's work. First, writers must create a future that projects onto people or things a feeling that they refuse to recognize. Writers must also identify a difference between the present and future, thus helping to find a location in space and time. Finally, writers must produce knowledge-seeking subjects that promise security from their projections. By applying these criteria, we may begin to identify how popular reports circumvent a direct engagement with the dead zone of writing by staging a conflict between human writers and writing machines. The projective nature of this circumvention discloses a more fundamental conflict between humans and writing, a conflict that I elaborate with greater precision in the next section.

In Steve Lohr's column, "In Case You Wondered, a Real Human Wrote This," the argumentative criteria for analyzing anxiety are on clear display. Again, Lohr's article projects a future for newspaper reporting in the wake of emerging automated writing software. As the title suggests, this future is characterized by the inability to distinguish human writers from software algorithms. In making such distinctions, Lohr anxiously locates himself in a space and time (the present) where the ability to distinguish human from algorithm is still possible. Such a distinction hinges, however, on the assumption that Narrative Science's algorithms cannot persuasively mimic self-reflexive reasoning. Audiences are thereby encouraged to trust Lohr's report without adequate evidence that the future has not already arrived. Lohr develops such trust when he describes the difference between human writers and automated writing software in terms of space and time. He writes that Narrative Science's algorithms "expand and enrich coverage" beyond the abilities of human writers and may be "posted on [a] network's Web site within a minute or two of the end of each game." When news networks use the software, they witness "a surge in referrals to the Web site from Google's search algorithm, which highly ranks new content on popular subjects." These algorithmic interfaces are important because "the combination of advances in its writing engine and data mining can open up new horizons for computer journalism, exploring 'correlations that you did not expect.'" While these assertions hail the advantages of automated writing software, rhetorically they are designed to distinguish the human from the machine.

This argumentative function is most apparent when one notes that Lohr's report is framed by the question of whether "'robot journalists' [will] replace flesh-and-blood journalists in newsrooms." In the present moment, the question seems to be settled. Narrative Science's algorithms "expand and enrich coverage" only in mundane areas of research that would bore most human writers. Moreover, the software is designed only as a remedy to editorial budget cuts. Thus, the "surge in referrals … to Google" that opens "new horizons for computer journalism" is presented as a low-cost insurance policy against a known economic threat. If Lohr's report is to be trusted, the anxiety that permeates debates over automated writing software is a faintly drawn one that can be easily resolved by attending to its present uses.

But Lohr's anxious projection is much more intense than a cursory glance would suggest. The intensity of Lohr's reasoning reaches a fever pitch in the final paragraphs of the article when he reports on Narrative Science's prediction that in five years a computer program will win the Pulitzer Prize. Lohr's prediction is noteworthy because it revises the previously held assertion that two decades would pass before software programs could exhibit artistic capacities. The imminent threat that automated writing software poses, then, is threefold. First, automated writing algorithms will usurp the highest levels of human writing and thereby trouble the concept of authorship that governs them. Second, automated writing algorithms have developed at a speed that pundits failed to adequately gauge, indicating that humans will not be prepared for the inevitable loss of their news media to such technologies. Third, automated writing algorithms are not characterized by incremental achievements but instead have larger designs to replace human writers. If, in the present moment, automated writing software is used to report on mundane data sets, its demonstrated proficiency anticipates more complex uses that render obsolete the human writer. Lohr attempts to redress the threat in the final line of his article by claiming, "should [the Pulitzer be given to a software program], the prize of course, would not be awarded to an abstract code, but to its human creators." But the responses to Lohr's article indicate that such comfort rings hollow.

All totaled, Lohr's report functions as an anxious projection that human writing will be usurped by automated writing software. Lohr's projection seems to be unaware that the blurred distinction between human and machine is old news. This point is most apparent as he reports on the mundane tasks that are currently carried out by automated writing software. Lohr contrasts such tasks with Narrative Science's prediction that within five years automated writing software will win a Pulitzer Prize. By projecting a future where human and machine writing are indistinguishable, Lohr suggests that such blurring is not operative in the present moment. His anxious projection thereby helps audiences more adequately locate themselves in the present moment where they must prepare for an inevitable future where a hard distinction between human and machine is lost. The persuasiveness of Lohr's projection is most apparent when he claims that should automated writing software be awarded a Pulitzer, it would not be given to an abstract code but to the software developers. Thus, the new knowledge-seeking subjects that secure us from this future are software authors who remain locatable in space and time despite the fact that their algorithms seem to transcend such boundaries. Or, if automated writing software does not transcend space/time boundaries, it certainly occupies a space and time that is not human.

If Lohr's column expresses an anxious concern over the displacement of human authors, Gini Graham Scott's editorial, "Assault on Writers from Automated Software" expresses the anxious projection of their outright loss. The primary purpose of Scott's editorial is to recapitulate popular reports on automated software and weigh in on the software's implications for human writers. Alongside Lohr, Scott notes that the speed and spatial reach of automated writing software will drive interest in its applications: "Sure the advantage of the software is that it can do a lot of routine writing tasks much faster and more cheaply" and, "Right now the software is primarily used to turn large amounts of data, such as sports scores, medical research, and business stats, into insightful narratives." But Scott's anxiety quickly extends beyond the software's applications, suggesting that its emergence is symptomatic of prevailing attitudes about the value of human authorship. Citing a recent prediction from Mark Coker on the state of book publishing, she notes, "If Amazon could invent a system to replace the author from the equation, they'd do that." In response to this possibility, she worries "it could be only a matter of time before the software starts taking over the work that journalists, non-fiction book writers, novelists, and other kinds do."

Although Scott's editorial adopts a decidedly economic pitch, her concerns serve as a vehicle for expressing an anxious projection about the loss of human authorship. She writes, "as this software becomes sophisticated, it can be used to create art, music, virtually any kind of art form, and perhaps it already has." Note the sense of projection that closes Scott's claim. Readers are meant to interpret "perhaps it already has" not as an admission that writers are already an effect of the technologies they employ, but that automated writing software is already so sophisticated that it may be producing art independent of human awareness. Rhetorically, Scott's claim projects a future where a distinction between human art and machinic art is obsolete. Her projection is spatially oriented insofar as it displaces her responsibility for thinking through the way existing technologies form artistic consciousness; for Scott, computers are either a tool or they assume the mantle of the artist—there is no in-between. Scott's argument thereby enables her to locate the human author in the present moment where "signals" of its inevitable extinction have yet to be fully realized.

Scott's anxious projection does not claim that software engineers will become the standard bearers of human authorship. Instead, algorithmic machines assume this mantle. Given that Scott's conclusion does not ostensibly secure a new knowledge-seeking subject, it might lead us to question whether her projection is an anxious one. But the economic underpinnings of Scott's argument indicate that the new knowledge-seeking subject will be one who can differentiate human art from machinic art. Or, if differentiation is not the goal, then the new knowledge-seeking subject will choose art despite the lack of economic incentive. This conclusion is most evident when Scott resigns herself to "taking a long vacation" and quips, "At least, a computer can't enjoy the vacation for me." Up to this point, there is nothing in Scott's claims that signal resignation. Therefore, Scott's claims read ironically, signaling to readers that they should not accept the emergence of automated writing software with resignation. Instead, readers should develop a form of counteraction that preserves a space for the human author—whatever he or she may look like as a counterpoint to machinic authorship.

The apparent function of *authorship* in these and other articles is to stage a conflict between human and machine by projecting a future where the former is usurped by the latter. Such projections position *authorship* as a bridging device that allows audiences to transcend the apparent threat that machines pose to humans. Again, this transcendence is predicated upon the assumption that a writer's time and space may be unified with the time and space of writing. However, a close reading of these articles indicates that this conflict is not inaugurated by the emergence of automated writing software but rather hinges on the conflict between the differential space and time between humans and writing. On this point, it is crucial to remember that automated writing software does not invent a different space and time for writing. Instead, it is more accurate to claim that it exploits writing's differential space and time in a manner that exposes the insecurity of writers in writing. Any reference to the space and time of writing in these articles must therefore be read as gesturing toward a more fundamental conflict between humans and writing. Thus, when reporters make reference to the speed and spatial reach of automated writing software, they are making a fundamental claim about the differential time and space of writing.

I have featured the concern over writing's differential space and time in the aforementioned articles in several ways, most notably when demonstrating how the machinic appropriation of so-called human writing motivates efforts to unify the human writer and writing in authorship. Consequently, I have characterized the anxious projections of these reports as an effort to circumvent writing's differential time and space through misdirection. Such misdirection hinges on the staged conflict between man and machine that leaves intact the authorial name.

PURPOSE

According to Foucault, the function of an authorial name is to arrest under a single heading "a certain number of texts" ... (210). The authorial heading is predicated on drawing a "relationship of homogeneity, filiation, authentication of some texts by the use of others, reciprocal explication, or concomitant utilization" (210–11). Consequently, the authorial name carves out a special place in the universe of discourse insofar as it seems "always to be present, marking off the edges of the text, revealing, or at least characterizing its mode of being" (211).

Foucault's theorization of the authorial name discloses the specific "modes of existence" that structure current debates on automated authorship (221). At stake in such debates is the possibility of securing the relationship among the various texts that writing algorithms produce. The humanist standards inaugurated by the Christian hermeneutic tradition no longer apply in the age of informatics. Or, if they are applicable, the fit is a patently incongruous one. Such incongruity is on clearest display in the aforementioned article by Steve Lohr, who reflects on Narrative Science's claim that within five years its software will win the Pulitzer Prize. Speaking directly to readers, he responds to this claim in a decidedly conciliatory tone, "Should it happen, the prize, of course, would not be awarded to abstract code, but to its human creators." Lohr's use of the phrase *of course* is telling. Specifically, it exposes how the authorial name secures stylistic attribution in order to create coherence among texts. In this instance, the software engineers would receive authorial credit for an algorithm that produced stylistic tendencies distinct from other programs. Lohr's use of *of course* indicates that the authentication process is non-negotiable. Within the context of the article, such non-negotiability amplifies Lohr's anxious projection that this software irrevocably blurs the distinction between human and machine. By invoking the continued stability of a consummately humanist project (awarding the Pulitzer Prize), Lohr asserts that humans will find a way to maintain their categorical distinction. Of course, such distinctions hinge on the award committee's recognition that stylistic innovations in writing belong to the materialized human hand, not to the processes of an "abstract code."

Within the scene of algorithmic writing, the distinction between author and writer seems tenable. As Lohr suggests, humans author the software, and algorithms write the articles. Yet the capacities of algorithmic writing software immediately trouble the hermeneutic arrangement. As Foucault explains, the most important feature of the prevailing authenticating process is its ability to split the author from the writer, producing a "plurality of the self" (215). Such splitting hinges on reconfiguring "the spatio-temporal coordinates" of the text. Whereas in non-authored texts, these coordinates "refer to the real speaker" in time, in the authored text "their role is more complex and variable" because "neither the first-person pronoun nor the present indicative refers exactly to the writer or to the moment in which he writes, but, rather, to an alter ego whose distance from the author varies, often changing in the course of the work" (215). But algorithmic writing software does not write in real time. As Lohr explains earlier in his article, the crisis posed by automated writing software is its capacity to produce prose at a rate that vastly exceeds the human writer. Moreover, the spatial transcendence promised by the prevailing criteria is complicated by the software's ability to crawl informational spaces that exceed human comprehension. In this arrangement, the software engineer works in real time while the algorithm reconfigures spatio-temporal coordinates.

We might be tempted to attribute such a hermeneutic snag to the emergence of sophisticated software technologies. But Foucault's analysis of the author function indicates that such snags are not unique to automated writing software. Instead, they are a fundamental feature of writing that is operative irrespective of the writing technology. I am calling this feature *writing in the dead zone*. To demonstrate my argument, I want to hone in on Foucault's claim regarding the distance between the real writer and the author. Notice how the distance between writer and author is constituted by the discursive construction of the authorial name, which is a written criterion designed to authenticate certain types of textual works. Such distance is inaugurated by the spatio-temporal capacities of writing (note that these are criteria borrowed from the Christian hermeneutic tradition). Writing may constitute a space and time that ostensibly secures against the finitude of human existence (the author). It may also constitute a space and time that seems to reference the time and space of human existence (the real writer). Either way, writing's differential time and space signal its unique exteriority. By *exterior* I mean that it constitutes a virtual time and space that is fundamentally different from the time and space of the human. Even when writing seems to reference the real time and space of writers, such time and space have already passed away; the writing is thereby always already dead.

Because writing precedes and exceeds us, it is best to view our bodies as a "screen through which the words of others flow and on which they are displayed" (Taylor 196). We do not and cannot control this flow, nor can we be fully conscious of the factors that call such flows into being. Foucault discusses the lack of control over writing when he argues that the author function is not consistent across historical epochs: "There was a time when the text we today call 'literary' (narrative stories, epics, tragedies, comedies) were accepted, put into circulation, and valorized without any question about the identity of the author; their [sic] anonymity caused no difficulties since their ancientness, whether real or imagined, was regarded as sufficient guarantee of their status" (212). If the author is a historically contingent figure, the concept of *authorship* does not expose an interior expression of artistic truth. Instead, the author is the effect of writing's ability to refer to itself in different times and spaces. I am claiming that writing's self-referentiality is the catalyst for the anxious projections in reports on automated writing technologies.

An example will help fill out these claims. In an interview with Claude Bonnefoy entitled "Speech Begins after Death," Foucault discusses his relationship to writing, focusing specifically on his writing process. When asked about whether the writer leads or is led by the phenomenon of writing, Foucault responds, "for me the obligation of writing isn't what one would ordinarily call the vocation of the writer. I strongly believe in the distinction, quite well known, that Roland Barthes made between authors and writers. I'm not an author. ... I place myself routinely on the side of the writers, those for whom writing is transitive. By that I mean those for whom writing is intended to designate, to show, to manifest outside itself something that, without it, would have remained if not hidden at least invisible" (69–70). Earlier in the interview, Foucault explains that an authorial view of writing treats writing as "sacred ... a kind of activity in itself, intransitive" (28). For Foucault, the distinction between an author and a writer hinges upon the difference between a transitive and an intransitive view of writing.

As Foucault explains, transitive writing designates something outside of itself, a concrete object. By contrast, intransitive writing remains in the sacred abstract, designating only itself. The crucial point is that writing is *both* transitive and intransitive. For Foucault, a transitive view of writing exposes its different time and space to a greater degree. In response to a question about his writing process, Foucault paves the way toward a clearer sense of such exposure:

> For me, writing means having to deal with the death of others, but it basically means having to deal with others to the extent that they're already dead. In one sense, I'm speaking over the corpse of others. I have to admit that I'm postulating their death to some extent. In speaking about them, I'm in the situation of the anatomist who performs an autopsy. With my writing, I survey the body of others, I incise

it, I lift the integuments and skin, I try to find the organs, reveal the site of the lesion, the seat of pain, that something that has characterized their life, their thought, and which, in its negativity, has finally organized everything they've been.

We can safely assume that Foucault is not identifying with surgeons who secure knowledge through an objective gaze, nor is he claiming that his exegesis brings the text back to life. The metaphor of surgical inspection thereby signals a need to affix writing so that it may be analyzed. The implication, of course, is that writing is otherwise unfixed. Such a claim will no doubt seem odd in light of Foucault's assertion that "writing means having to deal with the death of others to the extent that they are already dead." If, as an archivist, Foucault deals with "the death of others to the extent that they are already dead," it would seem that the writing he is analyzing should already be inanimate; there would be no need to affix it to the surgical table. But drawing this conclusion risks the assumption that writing's death is like our death (which, again, assumes the time and space of humans and writing can be co-extensive). We expect that because writing is dead, it will lie inanimate on the surgical table because the human body, when dead, lies inanimate on the surgical table.

Foucault claims, on the contrary, that although dead and affixed to the surgical table, writing cries out. He explains:

> I also understand why people experience my writing as a form of aggression. They feel there is something in it that condemns them to death. In fact, I'm much more naïve than that. I don't condemn them to death. I simply assume they're already dead. That's why I'm so surprised when I hear them cry out. I'm as astonished as the anatomist who becomes suddenly aware that the man on whom he was intending to demonstrate has woken up beneath his scalpel. Suddenly, his eyes open, his mouth starts to scream, his body twists, and the anatomist expresses his shock: "Hey, he wasn't dead!" I think that's what happens when people criticize me or complain about my writing. It's always hard for me to respond to them, except that by using an excuse, an excuse they might see as a mark of irony but which is really the expression of my astonishment: "Hey, they weren't dead!"

The "crying out" is a consequence of subjects identifying themselves in Foucault's analysis. For example, one might identify with the confessional subject described by Foucault in *The History of Sexuality Vol. 1* insofar as they too expose abnormal sexual desires to those in authority. But if we remain at this level, we miss an important clue to *writing in the dead zone* that Foucault offers when he claims, "I don't condemn them to death. I simply assume they are already dead." How is it that the living person who cries out in response to Foucault's analysis is already dead? Dead in what sense?

To understand Foucault's argument, we must assume a "naïve" orientation to writing and recognize in his claim a critique of its intransitive forms. Because intransitive writing "has a sacred dimension that has a kind of activity itself" it becomes "built on itself, not so much to say something, to show something, or to teach something, but to be there" (29). In this way, intransitive writing becomes a monument of language: stationary, controlled, and inhabitable. But Foucault is interested in a transitive form of writing that exposes "the unhealthy secret that explains [a subject's] transition from life to death" (43). As he puts it in "What Is an Author?" this involves "study[ing] discourses not only in terms of their expressive value or formal transformations but according to their modes of existence. The modes of circulation, valorization, attribution, and appropriation of discourses vary with each culture and are modified within each" (220).

A transitive orientation toward writing thus entertains the possibility that when dead, writing circulates, valorizes, attributes, appropriates, and cries out. Foucault's claim thereby asserts that human subjects are a "screen through which the words of others flow and on which they are displayed" (196). As Lynne Huffer has argued, if writing seems to express an interiority, it is because the exteriority of writing has folded into itself (29–31). Accordingly, "the inside of the subject doesn't exist as such; the subject is coincident—in space, time, and scope—with an outside that is both a function of thinking and the condition of possibility for the thinking self" (30). Because human subjects are constituted in part through the circulation of writing, they are already dead in the letter even as they meet the criteria of what we typically assign to the category of living. The crying out thereby punctuates Foucault's view that human subjects are always already dead in the letter.

When Foucault claims that writing cries out, he is making a finer point about the constitution of the human subject in writing and the difficulty of attending to writing's transitive forms. To be surprised by writing's cry is tantamount to realizing that writing is animate despite its death. Human subjects cannot raise writing from the dead because there exists no space from which such life can be granted; they cannot stand in a space separate from death because they have already made the transition from life to death in writing. As I noted in my previous analysis of the author function, writing can give us the virtualized sense of life, leading us to believe (when we write *I*) that our constitution in writing passes over death by death. But again, this act of writing always misses the mark, exposing writing's different time and space and, consequently, our finitude.

ACT

As I demonstrated earlier in this essay, reports on automated writing software are not interested in how new forms of authorship disclose writing's spatio-temporal complexities. Using the authorial name as a bridging device designed to pit the machine against the human, "[t]he author [becomes] the principle of thrift in the proliferation of meaning" (Foucault, "What Is an Author?" 221). It accomplishes this task by binding the edges of a text in a manner that seems to arrest its temporal movement (it seems always present). The presence of the human author thereby negates the possibility that authorship may be other than human.

What I have proposed in response to these reports is an abduction of the author. The purpose of such an abduction is to expand our sense of *writing in the dead zone*. Here, *abduction* refers to the logical form advanced by Charles Sanders Pierce that inferentially presumes a general rule in a "curious circumstance" characterized by incomplete information. In this case, the general rule is that writing's differential time and space will continue to expose human finitude in a manner that fosters anxious projections. This approach to *writing in the dead zone* is abductive because, as I have suggested, the nature of writing ensures that our inferences will always be based on incomplete information. This incomplete information is a consequence of writing's ability to virtualize time and space *ad infinitum*. Our constituted death in the letter ensures that we will never gain the level of separation from writing that would foster a complete analysis.

Instead of serving as a hermeneutic apparatus that secures the "expressive value or formal transformations" of a human corpus, the concept of *authorship* may be treated as a bridging device that stages a spatio-temporal conflict between humans and writing. Thus construed, the authorial name becomes a snag in the dialectical universe—to use Lynne Huffer's provocative phrase—that exposes us to the spatio-temporal features of writing. Writing might then be envisioned as a security system that continually trips its own alarms. The new task of authorship studies would be to follow the sound of sirens, with the hope that such sounds would lead to an even more elaborate sense of how writing operates.

One of the key implications of my analysis above is that a confrontation with *writing in the dead zone* will make us anxious because the awareness of our finitude means our existence is unstable. As effects of writing's circulation, we are bound to implement bridging devices that help us cope with such instability. When confronted with writing technologies that expose such instability, the question is not whether to abandon anxiety and the use of bridging devices; the question is how to comport ourselves in the study in a manner that is sensitive to the complexities of writing's operations. To raise this question already employs bridging devices and thereby punctuates the anxiety attending any act of writing. I am presuming that I am a stable entity who exerts a level of control over how I interpret written texts. This *I* is thereby a bridging device that elides a conflict with writing's time and space long enough to offer a sentence that will reach you, whoever you are. When I get there with you, who knows where we will be. I may be here, or not. If what I have said in the preceding pages is accurate, I (along with the author) have already been abducted, which points us toward nothing, nothing at all.

ENVOI

> Referring only to itself, but without being restricted to the confines of its interiority, writing is identified with its own unfolded exteriority.
> —Michel Foucault, "What Is an Author?"

Every written work can be regarded as the prologue (or rather, the broken cast) of a work never penned, and destined to remain so, because later works, which in turn will be the prologues or the moulds for other absent works, represent only sketches or death masks.
—Giorgio Agamben, *Infancy and History*

13. The work is the death mask of its completion.
—Walter Benjamin, "One Way Street"

I, Mark C. Taylor, am not writing this book. Yet the book is being written. It is as if I were the screen through which the words of others flow and on which they are displayed. Words, thoughts, ideas, are never precisely my own; they are always borrowed rather than possessed. I am, as it were, their vehicle. Though seeming to use language, symbols, and images, they use me to promote their circulation and extend their lives. The flux of information rushing through my mind as well as my body (I am not sure where one ends and the other begins) existed before me and will continue to flow long after I am gone. "My" thought—indeed "my" self—appears to be a transient eddy in a river whose banks are difficult to discern.
—Mark C. Taylor, *The Moment of Complexity*

WORKS CITED

Burke, Kenneth. *The Philosophy of Literary Form*. 3rd Ed. Berkeley: U of California P, 1973.

Foucault, Michel. *Speech Begins After Death: In Conversation with Claude Bonnefoy*. Ed. Philippe Artières. Trans. Robert Bononno. Minneapolis: U of Minnesota P, 2013.

———. "What Is an Author?" *Michel Foucault: Aesthetics, Method, and Epistemology*. Ed. James D. Faubion. New York: The New Press, 1998: 205–22.

Gitelman, Lisa. *Scripts, Grooves, and Writing Machines: Representing Technology in the Edison Era*. Stanford: Stanford UP, 2000.

Huffer, Lynne. *Mad For Foucault: Rethinking the Foundations of Queer Theory*. New York: Columbia UP, 2010.

Kittler, Friedrich. *Gramophone, Film, Typewriter*. Trans. Geoffrey Winthrop-Young and Michael Wutz. Stanford: Stanford UP, 1999.

Lohr, Steve. "In Case You Wondered, a Real Human Wrote This Column." *The New York Times* 10 Sept. 2011: n. pag. Web. 10 June 2013.

Ngai, Sianne. *Ugly Feelings*. Cambridge: Harvard UP, 2007.

Rotman, Brian. *Becoming Beside Ourselves: The Alphabet, Ghosts, and Distributed Human Being*. Durham: Duke UP, 2008.

Scott, Gini Graham. "Assault on Writers from Automated Software." *The Huffington Post* 29 March 2013: n. pag. Web. 10 June 2013.

Taylor, Mark C. *The Moment of Complexity: Emerging Network Culture*. Chicago: U of Chicago P, 2003.

3 Writers Who Forge
Forgery as a Response to Contested Authorship

Ron Fortune

In her reflections on her life as a forger, Lee Israel proclaims that after leading a writing life that accounted for several best-selling biographies, she considers her forgeries—letters purportedly written by some of the most notable writers and celebrities of the mid-twentieth century—to be her best work as a writer (126). Forgers have had such a negative reputation over the years that it is difficult to think of their forgeries as writing, as efforts that fulfill their best abilities and expectations as writers. In fact, forgery has always been seen as so offensive that we too readily group all forgers in the same criminal class without looking more closely at the variations that exist among the individuals who resort to this form of writing. Certainly many forgers, perhaps most, compose documents with nothing but criminal intentions. Yet, over the centuries, forgery has also been a resource for serious writers who find in forgery a haven that enables them to respond to the exigencies they face as writers, including the resistance to the writing they attempt to publish under their own names, their so-called "acknowledged" compositions. Ironically, while their forgeries become a means of responding to those who would deny them the success they pursue, the forged documents they produce create a basis for further contestation when the forgeries have been exposed for what they are. Without considering the nature and even the possible merits of the fabrications as pieces of writing, critics condemn them for their inherent deceptions. Looking at how writers have used documentary forgery to respond to some perceived resistance to or limitation imposed on the other writing they do not only productively complicates our view of forgery but also offers to enlarge our understanding of what we include in the concept of writing and how an expanded framework might enhance our perception of what the work of writing entails. Studying forgery as a response to contested authorship draws our attention to the frustration writers experience when they are told that their writing doesn't measure up, especially alerting us to the textual forms that expressing this frustration can take.

The forgers to be considered here are first and foremost writers; their forgeries are expressions of their efforts as writers and are a part of the stemma of their written work. How their forgeries relate to their acknowledged writing varies according to the writers and their professional views of themselves. Significantly, they don't differentiate their forgeries as writing from their other writing, and in some cases their forgeries blend their own writing with that from the pen of another writer. As writers, they retain their commitment to making the writing good *as writing*, which is consistent with Jeffrey Kahan's characterization of them as writers "who [create] a work in an acknowledged style and then [lie] about its legitimate authorship. A literary forger is not a copyist. He creates anew but within preexisting stylistic parameters" (20). Writers who forge, as opposed to forgers who write, have a keen sense of history and of the place in history they want their writing to have. How writers who forge go about situating their work historically varies according to how they see themselves as writers and how important it is for them to be identified with the writing they produce.

Writers who resort to forgery fall into two broad groups. One group consists of writers who turn to forgery as a way to achieve obliquely what they didn't or couldn't accomplish directly through the writing presented under their own names. For them, forgery is less a means to an end and more a genuine expression of what they value as writers. They are drawn to forgery because what they write as forgers suits their ethos as writers. This may be why their forgeries often combine fragments of texts they admire with stretches of their own writing. By reproducing historical documents and blending fragments with their own work, they create hybrid documents that make it easier to pass the documents off as purely historical while realizing their highest aims as writers. While responding to critical resistance is certainly a factor in the motives that drive these writers to forge, their attraction to the composing possibilities that forgery affords has a leavening effect on the intensity of their desire to prove their critics wrong. A second group of writers who forge includes writers who see forgery as a way of responding aggressively to the resistance their writing has encountered from critics and the reading public. They are more calculating and seek to use forgery as a way of drawing attention to themselves as writers and making the case that they should receive the critical respect and adulation they have been denied as writers in their own right. Significantly, these forgers who use their spurious texts to argue for their talents as writers are as invested in the quality of the forgeries as they are in their acknowledged compositions, though they want the forgeries to do the extra work of making a case for their talents as writers. This second variation will be examined in greater detail in the ensuing discussion because it exemplifies so explicitly the role forgery can play as writers respond directly to the rejection that would deny them their identity as authors. In the process of responding these forgeries become critiques of critique.

Perhaps the two most famous examples of the first variation of writers who forge are James Macpherson and Thomas Chatterton. When a growing interest in Scottish Highland poetry developed in Great Britain in the middle of the eighteenth century, Macpherson backed into a career as a forger by responding to several contemporaries, most notably John Home.

Macpherson had shown Home a sample of what he said was a larger store of such verse to which he had access; Home then pressed him for more samples. Initially, Macpherson produced wholly original writing under his own name, primarily in the *Scots Magazine*. However, as Peter Murphy has argued, he was an ambitious man, and the publishing avenues available to him, avenues limited by his background and the lack of critical enthusiasm that greeted his best efforts, could not accommodate his ambitions: "As far as escaping the Highlands goes, such publications [as the *Scots Magazine*] could do very little for him; what Macpherson needed above all was what the time called 'notice,' distinction rather than absorption in the crowd" (11). In pursuit of literary distinction, then, his writing career became dedicated first to producing what he represented as English translations of medieval Gaelic verse by the poet, Ossian, and later to defending these "translations" against charges of fraud. His authorial identity became absorbed by this work; his sense of accomplishment as an author became a function of the extent to which his forgeries succeeded.

Mostly, his forgeries are hybrids that combine authentic historical fragments with his own writing, a mixture that itself might signify a blurring in his mind of the difference between the writing of others and his own writing. In his study of the Ossianic poems in the Romantic tradition, Joep Leerson characterizes the textual mix in these terms: "Over the decades, however, it has become obvious that the question of *Ossian's* authenticity is intractable. There is no clear-cut Boolean alternative between 'true' or 'false.' There is, instead, a blurred grey zone between the authentic and the counterfeit, the sliding scale from literal translation to free translation to adaptation to reconstitution to recreation to manipulation to imitation to falsification" (1). Elsewhere, Joseph Rosenblum suggests that Macpherson may have come by this disposition to composition honestly: "Among Macpherson's tutors at Aberdeen had been Thomas Blackwell, whose *Enquiry into the Writings of Homer* (1735) suggested that Homer may have created his epic by combining and adapting various extant fragments, just as Macpherson was doing" (32). What can get lost too easily in the mix of writing practices described here is Macpherson's serious investment in the work of writing he undertook. This fact may explain why there has been in the last twenty years "a remarkable turnaround in the critical fortunes of Macpherson" as his *Ossian* poems have gone "from being literary curiosity to significant point of reference for students of the eighteenth century" (Moore 1). The overwhelmingly positive response his "translations" received initially suggested to Macpherson that he had identified the form of writing that could satisfy his aspirations as a writer.

As noted above, writers who forge typically experience two levels of authorial contestation: the resistance to the writing completed under their own names and the rejection they encounter when their forgeries are exposed. Macpherson is no exception. The indifference to his original efforts was a relatively mild form of contestation when compared to the outrage he faced when his forgeries were exposed. Samuel Johnson was the most vocal and influential critic of the forgeries, so vocal that Macpherson wrote him demanding a retraction of Johnson's attacks on the authenticity of the forgeries. Johnson responded by rejecting Macpherson's request and reiterating his criticisms: "You want me to retract. What shall I retract? I thought your book an imposture from the beginning, I think it yet upon surer reasons an imposture still. For this opinion I give the publick my reasons which I dare you to refute" (*Letters* 169). In light of the praise that has emerged from the revaluation of Macpherson's work in the last twenty years, Johnson's assessment and the larger public contestation of Macpherson's forgeries encountered in the eighteenth century is somewhat ironic. Through current ongoing revaluation, Macpherson has been "credited with reanimating Celtic poetry and, in the case of Scottish Gaelic, saving it from likely death" (Rayfield xxx). At some level, the writing talents that Macpherson brought to his forgeries were sufficient to allow him to realize his ambitions in the short term, because he achieved a level of prominence in his lifetime, and in the long term, as some contemporary critics regard the forgeries as historically significant productions.

In 1770, Thomas Chatterton committed suicide at the age of seventeen, possibly in response, at least in part, to a growing conviction that his aspirations to succeed as a poet would not come to fruition. While he wrote poetry under his own name, it is generally agreed that his forgeries were his best writing. Not only did his own writing fail to garner the recognition he sought, but from an early age he also displayed an interest in medieval history and in fabricating documents from the fifteenth century. As writing under his own name fell short of drawing the attention he deemed necessary to establish himself as a poet, he turned to writing ancient poems attributed to a fifteenth-century priest named Thomas Rowley. One impressive aspect of the forgeries is their variety and quick accumulation, as Groom has described: "The Rowley corpus was enormous, including poems, prose, drawings, and maps, and appeared to be a major literary find. Chatterton had produced more and more examples while living and working in Bristol before moving London a few months before his death in 1770" (Groom 278).

The poor response to his own writing and a predisposition to write documents imitating medieval texts might have played a role in Chatterton's ready turn to forgery. However, critics have noted that Chatterton's attraction to forgery might also be explained by his writing in an age incompatible with his dispositions as a writer. He was writing texts that anticipated the critical and textual values that would define the writing of the late eighteenth and early nineteenth centuries, a period defined by its resistance to the values operative in the middle of the eighteenth century when Chatterton was trying to make his mark. In *Lives of the Poets*, Michael Schmidt states that "[Chatterton] remained popular until the middle of the nineteenth century as a Romantic legend, a lesson in resisting to the death literary and social convention. From his setting forth he was marginal" (337). Schmidt also sees forgery as an outlet for a writer at odds with his times, insisting that "'Forgery' was a device for escaping the conventions that checked the genius of Gray and disoriented the work of Smart and Cowper" (338). He suggests that Chatterton's circumstances paralleled those of Gray, Smart, and Cowper, and that through forgery he escaped into writing that found its best audience in the writers of a later generation who celebrated him as a "boy genius."

As was the case with Macpherson, Chatterton realized his identity as a writer through his forgeries, a fact again reflected in the way in which his forgeries mix actual historical fragments with his own writing. Kaplan sees this mixture as the distinguishing feature of the forgeries: "The most remarkable feature in Chatterton's romance of Sir William Canynge [Rowley's patron] is the uncertainty throughout of the borders between creation and fabrication" (98). In their subject matter and style, the forgeries gave Chatterton an opportunity to invest himself in writing that was particularly meaningful for him in realizing who he was as a writer. Maryhelen Harmon sees the authorial empathy between Chatterton as a writer and the fictional writer he created as foundational to his life and work: "Branded as a forger and imposter for his insistence on the authenticity of the Rowley chronicle, Chatterton appears to have cherished his fabricated persona as an ideal reality to the very last. This persona, which no doubt began as an innocent, childish dream based in feelings of a purely subjective nature, resulted from a remarkable affiliation of his mind with the circumstances of a past age as he had pictured and dreamed it" (137). In a sense, his forgeries became a means of realizing his own identity as a writer, and questioning their authenticity amounted to questioning his existence as a writer.

The Macpherson and Chatterton forgeries suggest a need to re-think the line separating writing and forgery because they exemplify writers who find in forgery an outlet for who they are as writers. Writers in the second group, however, have already found an outlet for who they are as writers in their own acknowledged compositions. What they haven't found is an audience that shares their enthusiasm for these compositions, and their forgeries, which they invest with the same care evident in the writing they are defending, offer a way of demonstrating the critical inadequacies of those who would deny them the recognition they seek. Unlike Macpherson and Chatterton, the figures to whom they attach their forgeries are not fictional or semi-fictional: their arguments typically require that the authors under whose names they present their forgeries enjoy some degree of cultural recognition. They reason that if their forgeries are accepted as the compositions of these culturally sanctioned writers, the talent the reading public associates with the work of these admired writers must transfer to anyone who can produce a piece of writing that can be mistaken for theirs. We can only wonder how many other writers who believe in the value of their work but have had it rejected might contemplate, if only for a moment, something like forging a text to demonstrate the critical shortcomings of those who would contest their authorship.

One of the best-documented examples of a writer using forgery as a direct challenge to a rejection of his own work involves James Whitcomb Riley's forgery of a manuscript allegedly written by Edgar Allen Poe, a poem entitled, "Leonainie." Riley had no interest in gaining financially from the forgery. He was intensely committed to demonstrating that the rejection his writing had suffered at the hands of editors at culturally prominent magazines and journals was due to editorial bias and not the quality of his writing. He believed that regional bias and a bias against unrecognized writers were behind the repeated rejections by editors at Eastern establishment magazines and journals. One of his associates made the situation worse by goading Riley with suggestions that the rejections indicated he should give up writing and return to commercial sign painting, a job he held before becoming a professional journalist with the *Anderson (Ind.) Democrat* in 1877. Already sensitive to criticism from the succession of rejection letters he received, Riley responded to the suggestion with a determination to prove that his writing merited publication in the best magazines and journals and that others were at fault for failing to recognize this.

The issue for Riley was not the rejection of individual works but rather the denial of authorship implied in the repeated refusals to publish any of his work in the leading literary publications of the time. When he was first trying to make a name for himself as a writer, he contacted several renowned writers asking for an endorsement of him as a writer, which seems an unusual approach to embarking on a writing career. After he had become a celebrated writer himself, he questioned the tactic when, responding to the number of requests for endorsements from beginning writers that he was now receiving, he said, "A great many persons ... seem to think indorsement far more important than either hard work or special aptitude" (qtd. in Van Allen 88). At the same time, he recognized that he had once done the same, and for him the endorsement was the touchstone he used to gauge whether or not he had any business trying to be an author. When Henry Wadsworth Longfellow took the time to provide a modest endorsement, Riley's response suggests just how critical it was to his identity as an author: "I took a lot of my poems and sent them to Longfellow, asking him if he thought from them I could ever amount to anything. I made up my mind that if he said no, I would quit all that kind of thing forever" (qtd. in Van Allen 89). Even with the endorsement and his notable success in regional publications, however, his associate's suggestion that he go back to painting signs triggered a defensive reaction based on his continuing to doubt that he was an author. His subsequent decision to forge "Leonainie" became another way to prove to others and more importantly to himself, that he was an author who had the right to claim an identity as such. Being told that he should return to his previous work making signs constituted one more refusal to accept him as an author. The refusal must have hit a particularly sensitive nerve; resorting to forgery as a response would seem to be out of proportion to the insult, until we recognize what, at least in his own eyes, was at stake for Riley.

Riley exemplified a curious combination of self-doubt and self-confidence in his view of himself as an author. Certainly, his need to garner some reaffirming support from established writers such as Longfellow and his reliance on these endorsements as a basis for determining whether or not he should pursue a writing career suggests a degree of self-doubt. At the same time, he believed that he would not have encountered the bias that editors showed him if he had had an already established reputation as an accomplished writer. He saw no difference between his writing and the writing of recognized and widely admired authors. The only condition separating his work from theirs was that they were acknowledged authors and he wasn't, at least not on the scale that they were. The solution seemed obvious: He would pretend to be one of them, and once accepted as such, he could expose the inadequacies of the vetting process that denied him the authorial identity they enjoyed. Curiously, he immediately involved others in setting it up and executing his plan. For most forgers, the fewer people who know about the deception the better, since each additional participant increases the chance of a leak that could quickly lead to exposure. However, in Riley's case, the forgery had to be exposed or it wouldn't have had the desired effect, which was twofold: 1) "to demonstrate the theory I held and hold, that all that is necessary to make a poem successful and popular is to prove its author a genius known to fame" (*Letters* 16) and 2) to create an opportunity for his own writing to be accepted and recognized on its merits. Riley's survival as a writer was at stake, and the energy he invested in what became an unwieldy scheme reflected as much.

Riley's deception began with a letter he wrote to the editor of the *Kokomo* (Ind.) *Dispatch* on July 23, 1877, a letter written soon after, in his own words, he was "being rallied to desperation over the weekly appearances of [his] namby-pamby verses, by the editor of a rival [newspaper]" (*Letters* 64). In the letter, he invites the editor of the *Democrat*, J.O. Henderson, to join him in a hoax that would demonstrate the editorial bias that kept him from getting published in what he considered the most desirable journals and magazines. It is somewhat surprising that Henderson so readily agreed to join Riley in the deception, though Van Allen suggests he did so because he shared Riley's concern about editorial bias and believed that the eventual publicity would bring a welcome national attention to his newspaper and to Kokomo (101). From the beginning, Riley authored the narrative on which the hoax was based as if it were a composition. In his initial letter to Henderson, he laid out the general outline of the narrative in which the forgery would be encased and instructed Henderson to present the fabricated poem in his newspaper and in the process to "be sure to clinch the story so she'll stick." He predicted that the story would succeed from "sheer audacity and tact" and anticipated the revenge to be enjoyed when they decide to reveal that the whole thing was a hoax: "after fooling the folks a little, and smiling o'er the encomiums of the press, you understand, we will 'rise up William Riley' and bu'st our literary bladder before a bewildered and enlightened world!!!" (*Letters* 15). The contemplated irony here is unmistakable as Riley, who has been rejected as an author, will use his skills as an author to force those who have denied him to face their inadequacies as judges of literary merit.

The language of this initial letter betrays some of the animus driving Riley throughout this process. Perhaps most striking is his representation of the planned exposure of the forgery as a matter of "bu'st[ing] our literary bladder" before those who have told him that he is not an author of merit. The image of bursting their bladder communicates graphically the disdain for editors that had built up in Riley as he was faced again and again with their judgment that he was not an author. Pairing this image with that of Riley being raised up, as if from the dead, in the full glory of being the acknowledged equivalent of some great writer suggests the almost apocryphal life-giving experience Riley expected to result from the plan he was putting forward. Finally, the letters suggest with a paternalistic forbearance, the role that the public has played in keeping him from being the author he knew he was. The public would be freed from the blindness that their deference to the high priests of literary culture had forced on them to the detriment of aspiring authors. Again, irony abounds as Riley planned to deceive them through his forgery in order to enlighten them and teach them to be open to recognizing exceptional writing even when critics tell them a text is undeserving. While Riley's response may seem extreme, the sentiments are not unfamiliar to what writers generally feel when their efforts have met with a refusal to recognize them as authors, especially when these writers have absolutely no doubt that their rejected writing has merit.

As noted above, Riley did not share with Poe the kind of relationship that Macpherson cultivated with Ossian and Chatterton with Thomas Rowley; however, his ability to make the forgery work for a while required some compatibility between his work as a writer and the work of the writer targeted for the forgery. In a 1912 catalogue of Poe's work, Killis Campbell noted that "Poe had not preserved any very full collection of his writings; neither had he ... taken the trouble to make up any very exhaustive list of his publications" (327). The unsettled state of Poe's corpus could have contributed to Riley's attraction to him as a target since it would have been easy to create a place for the forgery in the unstable corpus without fear of contradiction. Even with such an accommodating material environment, however, Riley wouldn't make much headway without some connection with Poe as a writer. Marcus Dickey has noted that one "reason for choosing Poe for the ruse was Riley's fellow-feeling for the author and his style" (368). When the hoax went sour, however, Riley's disposition toward Poe changed somewhat in that he came to believe that "choosing Poe as the author to imitate for the scheme brought him bad luck and continued to do so until the end of his days" (Van Allen 110). Still, he never completely lost his sense of being connected to Poe, continuing to feel that "he was tied mystically to Poe, as he had been born on the day Poe died; and he convinced himself that

'Leonainie' only served to cement the supernatural connections between them" (Van Allen 110). Although Riley seemed to go back and forth in his sense of connection to Poe, some connection was always there and seems to have been essential to his forgery.

As a writer, Riley seemed to need a target whose writing he respected, and his ability to make the forgery work depended on this. The forgery's success required that the forged text be credible, and unlike the forgers who seek financial gain and invest their greatest efforts in constructing documents that are forensically accurate and aesthetically credible, Riley spent his greatest efforts in creating the narrative around the forgery, and in the entire affair the composition of the forged poem seems to have been something of an afterthought. If Riley felt he needed to put a different effort into composing the poem than he would put into writing his own work, his entire argument for undertaking the forgery would have been moot. The forgery needed to succeed without detailed forensic contrivances or he wouldn't have been able to say that his own poetry was as accomplished as the writers the literary establishment had exalted to the level he sought and felt he had been unfairly denied. In a letter dated June 3, 1892, Riley's description of the forgery suggests that "Leoainie" was "my invention—name, theme, everything save the certain twirl of rhyme and cadence, introduced designedly, of course, to further conspire in decoying and deceiving that ever-present class of critical assailants (who praise established poets only), eternally insisting that anything with a young poet's name to it is not a poem" (*Letters* 163–164). That the poem has been judged to be his own writing and not his writing substantially modified to look like someone else's is suggested by the facts that it is included in the definitive edition of his poetry and that Donald Manlove included the poem in his *The Best of James Whitcomb Riley*.

Many forgers who get caught express their sincere regret for having committed the crime and offer explanations seeking forgiveness. Riley did not feel that he had done anything wrong. As an author who was denied publication because of his youth, his lack of fame, and his geographical location, he felt that he was the wronged party in this whole affair. It is true that, in 1891, he characterized the poem as "the very brazen work of my profane hand and scheming brain" and stated that he "was a boy then, and deserve[d] some little charity" (*Letters* 144). However, before the letter was finished, he worked his way back to those he perceived to be the true criminals in the case—those who denied him the status of author: "The fraud was not maliciously designed, but simply to prove that a school of critics innumerable did not know nearly so much as either themselves or the public has been complacently and most persistently persuaded to believe. In other words, my poetry wouldn't go, Poe's would" (*Letters* 144–45). In a letter written in the following year, he is explicit in insisting on the rightness of what he had done: "Therefore my endeavor was to produce something that they [the critics] would pronounce a poem, thereby demonstrating the fact that they were wholly self-constituted and unfit judges of the merits of any poet, dead or living. The ruse succeeded—not only then, but is still fitfully at work on its righteous mission" (*Letters* 163–64). In her analysis of a letter Riley wrote anonymously to the *Indianapolis Sentinel* five days after the fraud was first exposed, a letter in which he was still trying to "cast doubt on the idea that he had written the poem," Van Allen suggests that he was responding as much to the inadequacies of the vetting process as he was to having his own writing rejected time and again: "This letter demonstrates how unwilling Riley was to give up his desire to prove that his poetry was just as worthy of admiration as that written by authors whom the literary establishment recognized as being great. He was so obsessed by the idea that he thought nothing about ruining his own personal reputation for integrity in the process" (107–108). She suggests, in effect, that his resentment over the power of these critics to deny authorship was expressed even on behalf of other authors who suffered as he had at the hands of these critics.

Riley understood intuitively that an elaborate narrative framework that would give his forgery the appearance of authenticity was essential to his success. A major aspect of this effort involved composing a narrative to establish a provenance that would deflect suspicions regarding the forgery's authenticity. As Fortune and Robillard have noted, forgers' "narratives are never complete; their details are sufficiently drawn to make them believable but not so finished that they become incapable of addressing the range of unanticipated challenges that invariably arise as time passes and the threat of discovery increases" (281). Riley controlled the narrative surrounding "Leonainie" from the start. As convoluted as the narrative became, through it Riley consistently pursued two themes: 1) that the forgery was credible, at least initially and 2) that a small cadre of ill-equipped critics and a reading public that slavishly followed their lead determined literary culture to the detriment of aspiring and deserving authors. While involving three co-conspirators in the project may have worked against Riley because it increased the chances of exposure, it may have worked in his favor in managing the narrative. For one, it allowed him to position himself in the story to deflect attention from him as a likely suspect when people began to inquire about the legitimacy of the document. Van Allen argues that this consideration was behind his decision to have Henderson present the forgery to the public in the pages of his newspaper: "Riley gave Henderson some suggestions for the story; but he feared that, if he wrote the introduction to the [newspaper] item himself, he might betray his own authorship through 'some peculiarity of composition'" (101–102). While Henderson was handling the presentation of the forgery to the public, Riley took the position as a critic and published an editorial in the *Democrat* questioning the authenticity of the document while praising it as an accomplished piece of writing. As Van Allen indicates, "Riley used his own reaction to the forgery as a way to stimulate a positive enthusiasm in the press" (104). More importantly as far as contested authorship is concerned, Riley's rhetorical maneuver essentially put him in the shoes of the very people who created the need for the forgery in the first place – the critics who denied him an identity as a noteworthy author. By appearing to be a neutral editorial party, he would be able to attempt to direct the kind of response he hoped the critics would render. Once he had this response, he would be in the perfect position to bring his plan to a successful conclusion by demonstrating that the critics had praised a poem that turned out to be written not by Poe, but by Riley himself. Once in this position, he could insist on the conclusion that he had hoped the forgery would force—that the literary establishment and reading public were biased in their judgments and were wrong to have denied his claim to being an author on a par with the best writers of the day.

In his editorial, Riley concluded his assessment of the poem by saying that it "certainly contains rare attributes of grace and beauty" (qtd. in Van Allen 104). However, he avoids the forgery question: "[W]e have not the temerity to accuse the gifted Poe of its authorship, for equal strength of reason we cannot deny it is his production" (qtd. in Van Allen 104). The editorial leaves the situation right where Riley needed it to be. On one hand, he established that the poem is an exceptional text worthy of Poe. On the other hand, he reached no conclusion regarding its authenticity, knowing that he would reach the point where the forgery would be exposed. This position almost made the question of authenticity immaterial. In effect, he was guiding critics and his audience to conclude that the poem was extraordinary regardless of its author. If Riley could get them to agree to this, they would have effectively conceded that, as a poet, he was on a par with Poe and deserved the high regard they assigned to the now dead writer. Further, to the extent that Riley had prepared the way for the public to apply the conclusions reached in this situation to other authors whose works have been contested due to editorial bias, his editorial potentially could have paved the way for other contested authors to be accepted as the writers they considered themselves to be.

As effectively as Riley maneuvered to bring the critical establishment to agree not only that the poem was a literary accomplishment but also that the bias he faced as an author needed to be addressed, he was less successful at maintaining control of the narrative. In the short term, he managed well even when unanticipated problems arose, but as time passed, he lost control of a not-very-complicated story. Early in the scheme, when William Gill, a Poe collector who said he had a manuscript copy of another Poe poem and could compare its handwriting with the handwriting of the forgery to determine the poem's authenticity, Riley arranged for an artist friend, Samuel Richards, to create a manuscript version of the forgery that would persuade Gill of its authenticity. Years later, Riley described his admiration for the work Richards performed in response to his request: "[Richards] did his part well, and was thus the author of the best part of the poem. He worked then as he works now—straight from the heart. He had only a line or two of Poe-facsimile to 'inspire' from, but some way the fellow caught the spirit of the whole vocabulary from it, furnishing a result that many notable and most exact critics were bewildered by, as I myself saw tested many times"

(*Letters* 63). In this instance, he exhibited the dexterity necessary to direct the narrative that encased the forgery. Soon after he worked things out with Richards, however, the hoax began to unravel, and ironically Riley played a central role in the process. Van Allen reports that he was the source for a leaked story that an employee of the *Anderson Herald* sent to the *Kokomo Tribune* exposing the forgery: "Without Henderson's knowledge, Riley had allowed the *Tribune* to discover the Poe hoax. He apologized for not conferring with Henderson on his 'ruse for throwing the exposé in the *Tribune's* hands'" (106). Then, not long after this, Riley openly admitted he committed the fraud in a letter to the editor of the *Indianapolis Journal* and explained his motive for undertaking it. When the letter appeared in the *Indianapolis Journal*, Riley wrote an anonymous letter to the newspaper suggesting that he wasn't the poem's author. Even though he had planned from the beginning to expose the scheme, he had difficulty following through when the time came, not because he had changed his mind but rather because he felt that the exposé had to be timed perfectly to have the greatest effect but he didn't have a clear idea of what the right time was.

A critical part of the right timing involved recognizing the point at which enough of the critics who had denied him authorship had bought into the hoax and allowed that "Leonainie" was indeed a long-lost Poe manuscript. The poem initially garnered considerable favor from many critics. In a letter dated October 21, 1891, John Patterson sent Riley a copy of an article from *The American Catholic Review* providing an assessment of the poem when it first appeared: "This beautiful poem is not to be found in any of the editions of Poe's works; and our opinion is that no edition should claim completeness without it. His poems are too few to allow the loss even of the most inconsiderable or least valuable; and certainly the above poem does not enter into that category; it has all the characteristics of Poe at his very best and we do not believe any other American poet could have written it!" (*Letters* 331). Even the critics who responded less enthusiastically would not go so far as to deny that the text was a poem written by Poe, which Riley took to be a positive sign: "*Everybody would like to believe*- they *want to* in the worst way" (qtd. in Van Allen 105). In this, Riley took advantage of a common pattern in the cultivation of most successful forgeries—the public's willingness and even eagerness to believe that the text was authentic even to the point of actively participating in their own deception. Forgers are schemers who recognize and take advantage of the victims' eagerness to play a supporting role in the deception. Still, with the confessions from both Henderson and Riley the hoax collapsed, and Riley was forced to deal with the aftermath.

Riley's sense of the righteousness of his cause is evident in his expectations of how the hoax would be regarded after it had been exposed, expectations that clearly drew from his confidence of his own ability as a writer. Van Allen describes Riley as thinking "that his audience would easily forgive his deceit and reward him for his cleverness and talent. He had not allowed himself to think about all the ways that his plan could backfire" (109). As an author with confidence in his ability as a writer in spite of being told repeatedly that he was not an author worth being published, Riley anticipated that the public would react to the hoax as the literary establishment that rejected him would react to "Leonainie"—both would put the past behind them and welcome Riley with open arms. Riley's letter of November 22, 1886, to a book collector who had found the dictionary on whose inside leaf Richards had inscribed the forgery, describes the aftermath of the forgery's exposure: "Papers everywhere lit into me—friends read all this, and stood aside—went around the other way. The paper upon which I had gained the meager living that was mine excused me—no other paper wanted such a man—wouldn't even let me print a card of explanation" (*Letters* 64). In part, the resentment reflected the public's anger at Riley for attempting to fool them. Significantly, while Riley recalled the period after the exposure as one of the worst phases of his life, he seems to have eked some satisfaction from the experience. He noted that, with all of the abuse that had been heaped on him after his scheme was revealed, it was a response to his attempt to fool the literary establishment and not to the quality of the writing in the forgery itself that upset everyone. When he received a letter referring to an article critical of him, he replied: "it is but a segment of the abuse that has been heaped upon ["Leonainie"] by an irate press throughout the country, and only condemned in that it was the means of duping that owl-wise institution from A to izzard" (*Letters* 16). That is, it was never condemned for falling short of the Poe standard. History would bear out Riley's lingering confidence in his abilities as a writer and in his sense that his writing should have met with a more receptive response earlier in his career. In time, the forgery brought him notoriety, which, in turn, brought him attention as a writer. Once he had his critics' attention, his work was recognized for its quality, and publication of the kind he sought followed.

Forging texts may not be the most common response to contested authorship. For some, the deception it involves may be offensive enough to cause them to pursue other options. Others may resist the idea of surrendering, at least superficially and temporarily, their own writing identities to adopt the identity of other writers. And it may not occur to many as an option. The sort of contestation authors face may also invite responses other than forgery. The extent to which writers feel that they are being resisted personally, as opposed to being denied as members of a group or class, might affect whether or not they see forgery as an appropriate response. However, the writers who do turn to forgery as a way of resisting being denied authorship share several fundamental characteristics. First and foremost, there is an existential drive, a constitutional need to be a writer and to be recognized and celebrated as such. Second, they tend to be very conscious of the textual culture that surrounds them, particularly of the writers who are not contested and who enjoy the celebrity for their writing that forgers believe should be theirs as well. Finally, their sense of themselves as writers leads them to see their writing as the best resource they have to contest being contested. Certainly they could use their abilities as writers to respond more straightforwardly to rejection, but if they are aware of the work that is being published and see their own writing as comparable, forgery affords a unique medium for pointing out a disparity that those who reject them should find unacceptable. In some ways, regardless of how the forgery plays out, there is some satisfaction in expressing one's sense of being unfairly denied authorship by tricking the critics into facing their own inadequacies as only forgery can do.

WORKS CITED

Campbell, Killis. "The Poe Canon." *PMLA*, 27:3 (1912): 325–53.

Dickey, Marcus. *The Youth of James Whitcomb Riley.* Indianapolis: Bobbs-Merrill, 1919.

Fortune, Ron, and Amy E. Robillard. "Life Writing at Cross Purposes: Documentary Forgery and the Reconstruction of Dentity." *Life Writing.* 10.3(2013): 277–93.

Groom, Nick. "Thomas Chatterton Was a Forger." *The Yearbook of English Studies.* 28(1998): 276–91.

Harmon, Maryhelen C. "Thomas Chatterton's 'Moaning Pilgrim': Fatal Pursuit of Real and Fictional Dreams." *The Kingdom of Dreams in Literature and Film: Selected Papers from the 10th Florida State University Conference on Literature and Film.* Ed. Douglas Fowler. Gainesville: UP of Florida, 1986: 136–39.

Israel, Lee. *Can You Ever Forgive Me: Memoirs of a Literary Forger.* New York: Simon & Schuster, 2008.

Johnson, Samuel. *The Letters of Samuel Johnson, 1773–1776.* The Hyde Edition. Vol. II. Ed. Bruce Redford. Princeton: Princeton UP, 1992.

Kahan, Jeffrey. *Reforging Shakespeare: The Story of a Theatrical Scandal.* Bethlehem: Lehigh UP, 1998.

Kaplan, Louise. *The Family Romance of the Imposter-Poet Thomas Chatterton.* Berkeley: U California P, 1988.

Leerson, Joep. "*Ossianic* Liminality: Between Native Tradition and Preromantic Taste." In *From Gaelic to Romantic:* Ossianic *Translations.* Ed. Fiona Stafford and Howard Gaskill. Amsterdam: Rodopi P, 1998: 1–16.

Moore, Dafydd. *Enlightenment and Romance in James Macpherson's* The Poems of Ossian. Burlington: Ashgate, 2003.

Murphy, Peter. *Poetry as an Occupation and an Art in Britain, 1760–1830.* Cambridge: Cambridge UP, 1993.

Rayfield, Donald. "Forging Forgery." *The Modern Language Review.* 107:4 (October 2012): xxv–xli.

Rendell, Kenneth W. *Forging History: The Detection of Fake Letters and Documents.* Norman: U of Oklahoma P, 1994.

Riley, James Whitcomb. *The Best of James Whitcomb Riley.* Ed. Donald C. Manlove. Bloomington: Indiana UP, 1982.

———. *The Complete Poetical Works of James Whitcomb Riley.* Bloomington: Indiana UP, 1993.

———. *The Letters of James Whitcomb Riley.* Ed. William Lyon Phelps. Indianapolis: Bobbs-Merrill, 1930.

Rosenblum, Joseph. *Practice to Deceive: The Amazing Stories of Literary Forgery's Most Notorious Practitioners.* Newcastle: Oak Knoll P, 1999.

van Allen, Elizabeth J. *James Whitcomb Riley: A Life.* Bloomington: Indiana UP, 1999.

Part II
Distributed Authorship

4 Authorial Ethos as Location
How Technical Manuals Embody Authorial Ethos without Authors

Erin A. Frost and Kellie Sharp-Hoskins

In their 2007 article, "Toward a New Content for Writing Courses: Literary Forgery, Plagiarism, and the Production of Belief," Amy E. Robillard and Ron Fortune lay the groundwork for this collection by investigating how two sites of contested authorship—forgery and plagiarism—reveal complexities of writing unavailable when "the predominant versions of process in composition studies ... emphasiz[e] *how to write* at the near exclusion of factors outside the text that contribute to belief in the value of the text" (186). In response, they show that "examining forgery and plagiarism as instances of writing yields insights into the interplay between the ways a writer tries to accumulate value to his or her work and how and why a culture accedes to or resists this effort" (208). That work, like this collection, shifts disciplinary attention from unilateral "emphasis on a codifiable writing process that can be observed, studied, and taught" to "questions of legitimacy," so that the field considers not only how to write but "who writes, who gets published, who gets to read, who you have to know in order to be published, and, perhaps most significantly, the relative arbitrariness of it all" (185). For Robillard and Fortune, as for the other contributors to this collection, then, composition scholarship must include accounts of the processes of legitimation—how authors and texts come to be marked, recognized, and understood as valuable—alongside processes of textual production.

Responding to this call to include more "factors outside the text that contribute to belief in the value of the text," in this chapter we examine processes of legitimation by discussing a specific site of seemingly *un*contested authorship: the technical manual. That is, whereas much writing in Western cultures must account for its origin(ality) through authorial attribution lest it risk the censure of inauthenticity or illegal use, technical manuals not only flout this cultural mandate but capitalize on erasing authorship as we traditionally recognize it. Indeed, a successful technical manual suppresses what we equate with marks of authorship—originality, individuality, subjectivity, embodied knowledge—in order to elicit the trust of users. A technical manual is deemed appropriately rhetorical when it appears to be neutral and objective. As we demonstrate in this chapter, the erasure of an author or authors complicates equations of authorship with individual, human bodies; in the case of technical manuals, it is the textual body *sans* author body that signifies legitimacy, usability, and expertise. This function of the author*less* text, we argue, complicates and *contests* representations of authorship in composition studies by extending processes of legitimation to include the purposeful erasure of (human) bodies in addition to the assumed presence of those bodies we more often associate with authorship. To that end, in this chapter we propose that applying scholarship on ethos that posits it as habitus, location, or "dwelling place" to a focused examination on technical manuals can provide authorship studies (as well as composition studies more broadly) a conceptual lens through which to create more robust accounts of processes of legitimation.

We begin this work by discussing authorship within Western culture as the telos of processes of legitimation structured by emotion. Thereafter, we suggest contemporary conceptualizations of ethos as a way to account for authorship *sans* traditional "authors," and we apply this conceptualization to examining one such genre of texts, technical manuals. Technical manuals, we show, draw attention to limitations of theories of authorship that ignore the so-called "authorless" text and, in so doing, provide insight into processes of textual legitimation that signify as authorship.

AUTHORSHIP, EMOTION, AND LEGITIMACY

The very fact that a case of plagiarism can become notorious on a national level is evidence of a deep cultural investment in authorship. Moreover, the angry responses to conflicts over authorship—consider the backlash against 9/11 "imposter" Tania Head (see Robillard, "Vulnerability"); Jayson Blair, the *New York Times* columnist accused of plagiarism; Maureen Dowd (who herself doggedly pursued plagiarism charges against Joe Biden); memoirist *cum* novelist James Frey (author of *A Million Little Pieces*); and author Binjamin Wilkomirski, whose account of his experience in a children's concentration camp (in *Fragments: Memories of a Wartime Childhood*) was discredited as fraudulent—demonstrate the intensity of this attachment in Western cultures.[1] We are not merely interested in but indignant over cases of questionable authorship, which affront our cultural insistence on individuality, originality, and authenticity. To understand this we can turn to what Michel Foucault terms "the author function," how an author's name lends meaning to a body of work by "perform[ing] a certain role with regard to narrative discourse, assuring a classificatory function" (107). Importantly—to understanding both our emotioned responses to authorship in question and our cultural investment in authorship itself—we must note that we come to rely on this classificatory system not only to group books on our bookshelves but to adjudicate legitimacy. We interpret a text as valuable (or not) and important (or not) using authorship as a rubric. Moreover, it, like other classificatory systems that Foucault explores in his work (knowledge production, sexuality, mental health), disciplines our judgments and practices, our understandings of normalcy, our imagination of legitimacy itself.

Helping us understand the connection to emotion—our feelings of insult, outrage, or anger that accompany instances of dubious authorship—Lynn Worsham explains the relationship between legitimacy and emotion:

> legitimate and illegitimate (or appropriate and inappropriate) objects of affective attachment ... are structurally and systemically related and, in prohibiting particular objects or persons as legitimate attachments, a society automatically invests them with great value and interest—if only for their disciplinary value in reproducing or policing authorized distinctions. ("Going" 223)

From Worsham we learn that the function of classificatory systems disciplines us affectively. Thus when authorship comes under contest, when the classificatory system through which we *should* be able to judge legitimacy of authorship fails, our affective responses discipline us to reinscribe that very system of legitimacy. Our anger at being "duped," our anxiety over plagiarism (see Howard), or our pride of recognition in an "original" secures the boundaries of legitimate authorship. We feel the legitimacy of authorship, and we feel threats to authorship: authorship contested.

Importantly, the author function is not only reified through affective encounters that shore up the boundaries of legitimate authorship, but it also draws on centuries of use as well as legal enforcement to cement its cultural validity. Manfred P. Fleischer uses the term *oeuvre* to describe the bodies of work of authors of sixteenth-century agricultural manuals, demonstrating that the attachment of particular names to those manuals affected the credibility of those manuals in the eyes of readers. In 1741, *Pope v. Curll* established that copyright of letters belongs to the author (Rose). And Deborah Brandt points out that modern "copyright law classifies writing according to its perceived social worth. It reserves for copyright protection only literary writing strongly associated with the personality of the writer or other writing that has some sort of instructive or lasting social value" (177–78). In other words, legal protection is dependent upon recognition of originality and cultural usefulness. In order to receive credit for a work, one must have written something deemed (by readers) to be both original and significant. The effect of this history on our contemporary value of authorship cannot be understated; narrated under the banner of individual rights, authorship becomes coincident with a Western epistemology of individuality, freedom, and ownership. Threats to authorship are thus threats to those values that secure and underwrite a host of cultural and national identities.

AUTHORIAL ETHOS AND BODIES

This investment in authorship as represented in the previous section is clearly predicated on the presence of an embodied author or authors. Our feelings in cases of contested authorship are directed at the person(s) we deem responsible for deception: We locate our grievance over legitimacy *on* the author. Despite the necessity of this body (or bodies), however, the body is quickly overwritten by an author's name. The shorthand allows the particulars of history and embodied experience that inflect authorship to be represented by a name; the name is both dependent on and overwrites the body of the author. Barthes, of course, explains the latter portion of this phenomenon, arguing that "Writing is that neutral, composite, oblique space where our subject slips away, the negative where all identity is lost, starting with the very identity of the body writing" (125). But with respect to Foucault, we must also acknowledge that the author function as a classificatory system remains intact. The body of the author, we might then say, leaves its trace in the name of the author, and its absence (or "death," in Barthes' terms) demands that we acknowledge a one-time embodied presence. Further, we must acknowledge the ongoing presence of such a body when authorship comes under contest. Our anger or disgust in cases of contested authorship is not directed at the author function but at the (embodied) author.

This process of emotioned structuration of the legitimacy of authorship, we argue, indicates a serious cultural investment in the sanctity of authorial ethos—the character, credibility, and originality attributed to the names of embodied individual(s) who create works of mutually agreed-upon cultural significance. As we turn to the case of technical manuals, however, especially as representative of a larger class of texts where authorship is not only absent but erased to ensure the successful function of the genre, attributing authorship to a person is no longer possible. This at once guarantees legal protection for particular bodies (who might otherwise be held personally responsible or liable for the use of technical manuals) while simultaneously denying the specific work and contributions of those bodies; authors who create technical manuals are often denied both credit and copyright, and the ethos of the text is disarticulated from the ethos of those who write it.

Initially, this phenomenon again seems best explained by Barthes' claim to the death of the author, an argument that locates meaning in effect rather than intention, in text rather that in author. That is, with respect to Barthes we might conclude that positing the erasure or suppression of markers of authorship in technical manuals merely corroborates a wider phenomenon. But in making his argument, Barthes suggests that "to give a text an Author is to impose a limit on that text, to furnish it with a final signified, to close the writing" and by contrast that by removing the specter of the author, interpretation remains open to the reader (129). Technical manuals are deemed successful, however, when they signify as closed to interpretation, such that any (that is to say, all) users interpret the text in the same (predicted) way. It is crucial to the function of technical manuals that they impose this limit for reasons that range from concerns of safety to liability to cost effectiveness. And this function of technical manuals differentiates technical manuals not only from other technical documents but from a broad range of genres where authors are neither named nor credited. The technical manual functions successfully—that is, as a technical *manual*—when it can be used as intended. And yet intentions are not traceable to embodied authors but to the text itself. While Barthes' theory is thus important to critical interpretation of texts, it does not explain how ethos becomes attached to the text of technical manuals rather than to the bodies of their authors, especially when the author body seems so important to the process of legitimation that surround authorship

To understand how authorial ethos can function *sans* traditional authors, then, we turn from authorship studies proper to the rhetorical concept of ethos and in particular to contemporary scholarship that complicates a simple conflation of ethos with individual character or credibility. Tita French Baumlin, for example, claims that "in any age, ethos necessarily shapes itself in accordance with the dominant ideologies of the culture" (230); R. Allen Harris claims that ethos describes communities; and Nedra Reynolds explains how ethos is constructed and sanctioned within groups (327). In short, ethos does not have a static definition or effects; its reputation as or conflation with individual character is a commonplace that circulates within (discursive) communities. Most helpful in understanding how authorial ethos can remain within a text in the context of erased authorship, then, is scholarship that posits ethos as a "dwelling place" or "habitual gathering place" for character rather than a description of character. Craig R. Smith provides the historical precedent of his interpretation in a hermeneutic reading of Aristotle to suggest that "Aristotle presuppose[d] the pre-Socratic notion of ethos as *dwelling place*" (2, emphasis ours); Judy Holiday claims "'that which pertains to ethos'—emerges ... as a study of the relationships among competing 'habitual gathering places' or 'dwelling places'" (389); Michael J. Hyde, Susan Jarratt and Nedra Reynolds each define ethos as a "haunt" or "dwelling place." Rather than radically disarticulating ethos from human bodies, these conceptualizations of ethos help explain how it becomes attached to bodies in the first place and thus how we might consider it separate or separable *from* bodies.

An individual described as *having* good ethos possesses such because patterns of descriptions—she is trustworthy, she is knowledgeable, she is smart—are repeatedly placed on her; they dwell at the site of her name and body or where her name and body dwell (in a particular publication, in front of a classroom or boardroom). In other words, she does not produce or author her ethos; ethos is attached to her name as a result of repetition. We might also say, following Judith Butler, that she performs ethos "by being called a name ... [wherein she] is also, paradoxically, given a certain possibility for social existence, initiated into a temporal life of language that exceeds the prior purposes that animate that call" (2). Following Butler, it is naming that animates ethos, giving it life and recognition. And thus we can begin to imagine how authorial ethos might become attached to technical manuals. If the precondition of ethos is not a body but rather a name, and if ethos gathers through repetition rather than embodiment, then ethos might justifiably attach to texts voided of authorial attributions. In short, when we consider ethos as a gathering place, a location where credibility and character accumulate rather than the possession or attribute of an individual human body, we can begin to understand the authorial ethos of technical manuals as indifferent to attributions of a traditionally understood author. It is the textual body of the technical manual that accumulates and displays credibility.

AUTHORS AND TECHNICAL MANUALS

In order to better understand the ways that a textual body can serve as a gathering place for authorial credibility without threatening our understanding of authorship in such a way that incites anger, we examine the genre of the technical manual. For the purposes of this chapter, we establish a working definition of modern technical manuals as a too-often-unexamined genre that most often exhibits a particular set of characteristics: Technical manuals 1) are written by subject matter experts, technical communicators, and other contributors in partnership, though they rarely include explicit attribution to individual authors; 2) use language that signifies as objective, neutral, and unoriginal; and 3) communicate specialized knowledge to users[2] who need to employ that information in applied contexts. Importantly, it is the interaction of these characteristics that give technical manuals their genre boundaries: While other texts (technical and otherwise) might be written collaboratively, signify as neutral, or be designed for users, the combination of these three elements adjudicates specific functions for technical manuals that, we argue, allow them to display authorial ethos without embodied authors.

These (defining) characteristics of technical manuals are attached not to the body or name of an author, but to the textual body of the manual itself. The modern technical manual typically does not include attribution to an individual author or authors. Rather, it derives its worth from an implicit claim to objective, neutral, factual communication that should be used to accomplish specific goals. This has not always been the case; Fleischer demonstrates that technical manuals were, in fact, attributed in the sixteenth century. Not only did authors take credit for these manuals, but they also used them as tools to explicitly enact social change. These authors "did not want only to raise the self-esteem of the tillers of the soil, but also to change the public image of them" (7). Over the years, however, technical communication genres, and perhaps especially technical manuals, were part of the shift Foucault describes as moving away from explicit individual authorship in scientific texts so that today, it is rare (though not unheard of) for technical manuals to explicitly display author bylines.

The writers of technical manuals—whether they are recognized as authors or not—occupy a complex position. These technical communicators often function as writing experts who work in partnership with subject matter experts to produce their work. Dorothy Winsor, examining authorship practices at a manufacturing firm, found that press releases contained content created by both writers and engineers, but those same press releases usually did not include authors' names at all. If an individual was named as author, it was always an engineer—the choice of byline obviously being intended to locate authorial ethos on the body of the expert/engineer. More often, no author is listed and the textual body of the technical manual serves as the repository for whatever ethos is necessary to make the manual function as intended. Joseph Jeyaraj notes that subject matter experts—like engineers—may culturally devalue technical writers' authorship because their own experiences with writing often come from working for organizations that value this corporate authorship model; experts "may not always be able to validate notions of autonomous authorship by being able to put their names on written documents at all times" (20). Therefore, this erased authorship is enforced as a genre convention.[3] Jeyaraj notes that even in cases where an individual is credited with authorship of a technical document, "the rhetorical authority the document possesses comes from the organization that produces the document rather than from the people or person who wrote it" (20). In other words, even when an author is specifically named in a technical manual, the authorial ethos of the manual is derived from the manual's textual body rather than from the name of the author, and any characteristics it displays are thus understood to contribute to the character (read: ethos) of the text rather that to its author(s). This can be contextualized and understood vis-à-vis the relationship of technical manuals to their audience of users, who rely on the objectivity and neutrality of the technical manual to be not only successful but also safe. Authorial ethos derived from a textual—rather than human—body retains no hint or haunt of human fallibility; it merits the trust of users by eliminating human error. Even in rare cases when technical manuals display author names, then, users continue to imagine the texts as distinct from bodies writing.

Disembodied rhetorical authority has been in large part sponsored by intellectual property legislation, which made possible the concept of corporate authorship. The Copyright Act of 1909 and the Copyright Act of 1976 each removes the legal ownership of paid employees over texts they write (Brandt 169). In other words, "work made for hire" becomes the property of the employer; writing as paid labor is now commonplace. Brandt argues that "workaday writers" are "willingly coerced corporate voices" whose claim to authorship has been completely severed (166). The corporation then owns the work, while the author—whose authorship has been erased—acquires economic capital. Brandt, like Foucault, turns to history for context. She suggests that this work-for-hire scenario is a throwback to feudal law. However, even though feudal law would have subjects relinquish authorship completely in exchange for sustenance, Brandt found that this exchange is not so clear-cut. She interviewed 50 workaday writers, finding that "neither credit nor responsibility seems able to be completely lent nor relinquished" (177). Brandt concludes that "Workaday writing is most accepted as a form of labor and thereby conducive to commodification and contract. But what kind of labor it is remains poorly understood" (182). Indeed, writing done for hire often includes the byline of the individual writer, as in most newspaper stories. Thus, even in the context of corporate authorship, technical manuals are notable in their apparent authorlessness. Helping to contextualize this phenomenon for the genres of technical writing, Jennifer Slack, David Miller, and Jeffrey Doak argue that "the politics of organizations and organizational politics often have as their goals limiting, obscuring, or hiding information"—sometimes including the author—and purposefully perpetuating the myth of technical communication as a "neutral activity" (33). Occluding authorial attributions obscures the complex practices whereby technical manuals are produced by removing evidence of collaboration, communication, and workaday writing that often sponsors these texts. The effect is a nullification of threats to the text's authorship; it cannot be as easily doubted when author bodies are absent for (read: erased from) blame.

We can further understand this displacement and erasure of authorial bodies by paying attention to gendered representations of writing that converge in technical manuals in complex ways. As Howard argues, authorship is gendered based on both content and genre, and this gendering manifests in "the equation of masculinity, abstraction, strength, and originality. It also involves a less straightforward equation of women, specificity, and plagiarism" (477). In the case of the technical manual, however, these equations are even less straightforward. The manuals are gendered masculine—based on unqualified prose (a strength), their levels of abstraction and objectivity, and a lack of personal details—but they are also highly specific and unoriginal: stereotypically feminine attributes.[4] With the important goals of signifying as not only objective and instructive but *usable*, these feminine markers threaten to undermine authorial ethos. First, if users assume that the specificity or details of the text emerge from the person of the author (or a combination of experts, technical writers, and workaday professionals) the manual loses its objectivity and ability to instruct dispassionately. Importantly, and returning to the language Robillard and Fortune offer, the "production of belief" necessary for a technical manual must extend to its usability—the audience of a technical manual must be able to use the information within the manual. And because the level of specificity required in technical manuals is one of the characteristics necessary to convince readers of the value of the manual, it cannot dwell within an individual author.

Examining the history and qualities of technical manuals as we did above, we see that the genre requires authorship devoid of authors. That is, in order to function successfully and without the censorious repercussions, technical manuals must limit interpretation as much as possible, such that users imagine the characteristics of the text representing a coherent, credible author, but that authorship cannot be located at the site of a human body or bodies, lest it risk the criticism of partiality or subjectivity. The user of a human resources manual, for example, must not assume that the details of the text emerge based on the writerly style, perspective, or proclivities of a work-for-hire writer; the user of a safety manual does not assume that the prose of the text was debated by a team of engineers and technical writers under deadline for production. Authorship is not absent; its traces signify in a particular expectation and arrangement of the text that allow human author bodies to be subsumed under the rubric of the ethos of the text itself.

The concept of disembodied authorship, wherein traditional author bodies have been subsumed under the ethos of a textual body, of course, invites the question, is authorship *sans* authors still, in fact, authorship? Or, to bring the question to the specific case of technical manuals: is their function an author(ship) function? To these questions we answer with an emphatic yes, and in so doing situate this project as itself a contest to the boundaries of authorship. The complex relationships among human bodies writing, the textual bodies of technical manuals, and their specific function and use make apparent authorship as irreducible to authenticity, originality, or veracity. These relationships posit authorship as a system of legitimacy that disciplines and protects our "belief in the value of the text" (Robillard and Fortune 186).

ABSENT(ED) AUTHORS AND THE OTM

The importance of the technical manual to authorship studies lies in this genre's context of use. Many genres signify as abstract, objective, neutral, specific, and usable; that is, many genres exhibit the characteristics that signify credible authorship in a technical manual. However, because technical manuals rely upon closing down interpretation in order to facilitate the communication of specialized knowledge for applied purposes, those characteristics produce effects that are specific to the genre. To explain, the interactions of these characteristics with the technical manual's context of use alter users' understandings of what constitutes ethos and authorship. Because attachment to a human authorial body would undermine the prescriptive nature of the text, technical manuals elide traditional authorship *without* raising threats to our core cultural values by attaching ethos to a different sort of body—the textual body.

To better illustrate our contention that technical manuals locate authorial ethos in their own textual bodies rather than utilizing the author function in a more traditional sense, we demonstrate how some of the aforementioned characteristics—abstraction, objectivity, neutrality, specificity, usability—generate attachments between the text and the authorial ethos necessary for the document to function. To begin this work, we turn to the Occupational Safety & Health Administration (OSHA) Technical Manual (OTM) as a primary example (though we will use other supporting examples). The OTM is useful in this way because of its widespread use, as well as its legal enforceability; it is a technical manual with significant cultural influence. Further, it serves as a digital haunt for ethos associated with a large and widely recognized organization—OSHA—that has authority over a large number of people. Further, the OTM is a publication of the U.S. Department of Labor, and it is a technical manual that—like most technical manuals—does not list individual authors.[5] The identified purpose of this publication is to serve as "a reference for technical information on occupational safety and health issues." It is distributed via OSHA's website (OSHA.gov) and went into effect on January 20, 1999.

The OTM's content includes significant information about safety, which requires thinking about bodies. However, engagement with human bodies threatens the text's ability to signify credibility in the absence of a human author. To mediate this threat, the document eclipses evidence of attachments to particular human bodies. However, the OTM includes several places where we can see by juxtaposition the difficulty of writing abstractly about bodies. For example, the OTM acknowledges that different bodies have different capabilities: "Age, weight, degree of physical fitness, degree of acclimatization, metabolism, use of alcohol or drugs, and a variety of medical conditions such as hypertension all affect a person's sensitivity to heat" (Section III, Chapter 4, Part I, A, 1). In addition, several sections of the OTM discuss regulations and recommendations specific to women of child-bearing age (Section VI, Chapter 1, Part IV, B, 2, b) and pregnant women (Section VI, Chapter 2, Part III, F). The OTM further discusses how bodily practices ("mouth pipetting" in Section VI, Chapter 1, Part IV, C, 5; "housekeeping" and "personal hygiene" in Section V, Chapter 3, Part II, B) affect safety and health. The OTM steadfastly uses third-person language throughout these sections, thereby creating a rhetorical barrier between thinking about human bodies and actual recognition of personhood. This barrier suggests that any discussion of bodies within the OTM is produced by OSHA as a governing organization rather than embodied authors (who, themselves, would be subject to the technical guidance being narrated).

In thinking about rhetorical spaces where bodies are discussed, we find that embodied ethos is vital to communication about bodies (which most often centers on health and medicine). The ethos of the doctor in Western culture, for example, is well established and often anchors medical texts and advertisements. In the same way that the doctor's embodied presence as author or sponsor serves as a gathering place for credibility, the technical manual constitutes a unique site in which the body of the text stands in as a marker of abstraction significant enough to validate the text's claims about bodies.

In contrast, passages in the OTM less directly concerned with bodies involve less risk of moving the text far enough from abstract ideas to introduce a challenge to ethos, and the OTM includes second-person language in several places, including sections on "Shipping Instructions" (Section II, Chapter 4, Part II), "Chemical Protective Clothing" (Section VIII, Chapter 1), "Ventilation Investigation" (Section III, Chapter 3), and "Legionnaires' Disease" (Section III, Chapter 7). In these sections, the use of second person does not threaten authorial ethos by invoking bodies produced through abstraction: it is the bodies of the users themselves who are hailed and carry the burden of correct (read: closed) interpretation. But their own embodied reading practices continue to rely on the authorless text, the text *sans* human authorial bodies, entrusted to provide objective, neutral, instructions to guide such interpretation. The OTM also signifies as credible by pointing to other textual bodies as affirming resources. This rhetorical positioning once again erases authorial markers while, we argue, reaffirming authorial ethos. The content is framed in terms of existing regulations about sampling and measurement methods, health hazards, safety hazards, construction operations, health care facilities, ergonomics, personal protective equipment, safety and health management, and miscellaneous issues. Further, the document consistently demonstrates that all recommendations are based not only on existing laws, but also on existing facts—established via empirical studies—regarding health and safety; most chapters include detailed bibliographies or reference sections. The text also continually and insistently references other sources—from laws to research studies—as the origins of the material it presents. In one place in the OTM, for example, this rhetorical move strongly points to mitigating liability and responsibility:

> NOTE: This technical manual is based upon the outdated API Specification 4E, which has been superseded by API Specification 4F, June 1995. The API RP 4G provides a "Recommended Guyline Anchor Spacing and Load Chart." AESC has published "Guidelines on the Stability of Well Servicing Derricks." There has been considerable progress within the industry to design procedures to assure the integrity of the stability system without the necessity of conducting individual pull tests on each of the anchors. (Section IV, Chapter 1)

The OTM presents itself as a secondary source—a reporter of previously established fact—but never a primary source of culturally significant content. It signifies as a vessel, a communicative vehicle, rather than a site of knowledge production, which serves to affirm its credibility/ethos without creating susceptibility to threats of contested authorship.

Specificity is a characteristic used so ubiquitously to demonstrate credibility throughout the OTM that it becomes difficult to isolate particular examples; this very impenetrability signals that authorial ethos has successfully been integrated into the body of the text. At the same time, the OTM utilizes specificity in ways that both shore up authorial ethos (when needed) and avoid specificity in cases that might undermine it. One example of specificity implemented very early in the manual occurs when the text explicitly states its own value and purpose: "The information herein is valuable in establishing sound safety and health programs" (Section I, Chapter 1, Part B). The text also uses specificity by demonstrating, as mentioned above, its understanding of the potential differences between users: "Employers should develop training programs based upon the employees' educational level and language background" (Section VIII, Chapter 2, Part XI). This language is fairly representative of this section; like the "neutral" language examined above, it assigns ethos to the text itself, indicating "its" own acknowledgment that employees are individual people with specific needs that may be different from each other. At the same time that the text seems to recognize this and allows space for different kinds of bodies, it also takes up this specificity in ways that separate humanity from bodies; that is, the text discusses humans in a specific function, as employees (and, in some places, as teachers and users) rather than as people. Only specific functions of people are relevant, so as to retain authorial ethos by limiting the scope of what the text professes to lay claim to.

We can see similar patterns in other authorless texts that function as manuals on a micro-level (insofar that they are designed for use), such as an un-bylined newspaper announcement; such texts, which invariably deal with subjects that signify as objective, like community event announcements, include a secondary byline (in the absence of a primary byline that would attach to a particular author) that locates the authorship of the piece with the newspaper itself or its editorial board. In other words, and returning to the argument of this chapter, the absence of traditional authors in texts that function as technical manuals is critical to the ethos of a text. To be clear, we do not claim that all authorless texts accrue ethos in the same way as technical manuals. However, texts that are valuable because of the claims they make to conveying technical information for audiences interested in application do rely upon their positioning as authorless to signify credible authorship through the textual body. Without traditional authors from which to extrapolate or assign motive or blame, the text of a technical manual like the OTM or an exhortation to attend a community event nevertheless signifies strong, consistent, and, at times, unassailable authorship.

These patterns of language use, like the others, assign to the text what we might elsewhere consider exclusively human capacities: command, instruction, recognition, acknowledgment. These rhetorical patterns suggest how we can begin to conceptualize authorship when authorial ethos accumulates within a text without pointing to human, embodied authors. Attaching authors' names to a document such as the OTM would ultimately undermine the ethos of the document by threatening its claims to the aforementioned characteristics. Ethos can only be sanctioned as legitimate, in the case of this technical manual, when the names of those fallible human beings who authored it remain absent. The erasure of author names—but not authorship practices—is part of the system of authorship that creates conditions in which this text's ethos legitimates its function.

IMPLICATIONS OF AUTHORSHIP SYSTEMS

Recognizing that systems of authorship are at work in ostensibly authorless texts allows us to see how those systems are changing—how, in the terms introduced earlier, a wide array of processes of legitimation contribute to our cultural recognition and understanding of authorship. Paralleling changing perspectives on what counts as technical communication (see, for example, E. Flynn; J. Flynn), common conceptions of what a technical manual is and what authorship of a technical manual might look like may be changing. Joan Livingston-Webber argues that strict interpretations of modern copyright law run contrary to postmodern notions of public domain and fair use held by young authors. Douglas Noble, in his article on software architecting, explores the failures of current technical manuals and suggests a move to computer-based models. Adobe Systems Inc. is perhaps representative of this move. For its popular Creative Suite software, Adobe provides an online technical manual. Not surprisingly, no authors' names are mentioned. However, this is not the site that users are directed to when they click "Help" while using their software. Rather, they are sent to a site where users can interact, a site that Adobe calls "part of the Adobe Community Help environment," where Adobe specialists, users, and expert moderators all create content. Adobe conceptualizes this space not as a product that the company owns, but rather as a community or environment that is collectively shaped. The authorial ethos that makes this space valuable, then, dwells in the space itself rather than in any physical or corporate body or any name attached to it. And while named individuals participate in the production and distribution of knowledge in this space, it is the location of the text(s) that invests those names with authority. If we do find value in such manuals—as seems to be the case, given the success of this example—then a shift to a community-based model for the production of technical manuals may be underway. This collaborative—and perhaps feminist—model represents a new path for shifting and exploring both the authorship of technical manuals and authorship writ large. Recognizing location as a sponsor of authorial ethos extends the parameters of authorship studies, of authorship itself.

The case study of authorship in technical manuals also impels us to resist any simple call for the return of authorship. While feminist scholar Diane D. Brunner, for example, suggests that feminism is about reclaiming the author and advocates teaching technical writing students to use the personal, the specific, as a means for both reaching one's audience and accumulating authority, and Jim Henry suggests that technical communication teachers need to discuss authorship to get at issues of power, reinstating a traditional conceptualization of author (with the responsibility and agency that implies) in our study of technical manuals introduces problems. Technical manuals are invested with responsibility in a way that produces potential liability (Paradis). Reinstating an author would make those authors economically vulnerable, when they are already marginalized workers. Further, the attempt to reinstate authors of technical manuals would likely result in a problematic reduction of a complex system of distributed agency. As Clay Spinuzzi argues, agency not only should not, but cannot, be traced to an individual human actor who is always already enmeshed in complex systems of communicative practices. Positing the contributors to technical manuals as authors with the cultural expectations that implies—and the affective disciplining it relies on—could undermine the protection that corporate or organizational authorship offers those contributors. Here we do not suggest that contributors be absolved of responsibility for participation in writing activities with the potential for harmful or unethical effects. We continue to follow Robillard and Fortune, however, in pursuing lines of inquiry that acknowledge "factors outside the text that contribute to belief in the value of the text" (186).

In addition to taking into account large concepts like liability and distributed agency, this work with technical manuals also calls attention to our need to explicitly discuss authorship in relation to technical communication and the practices of professional writers. Doing so promises a twofold benefit: It opens up our understandings of writing practices, and it expands authorship to include sites where we don't imagine authors. While we don't advocate merely reinstating explicitly named authors for technical manuals, we do suggest that studying erased or hidden authorship can be a fruitful endeavor for both authorship studies and technical communication. We seek to shift authorship studies to include unapparent authors at a number of levels.

In thinking about making writing practices—and thus, different kinds of authorship—more apparent and opening up our understandings of writing practices, we look to the model offered by the technical manual *Our Bodies, Ourselves*. This manual was first conceived by a group of 12 women in a 1969 workshop on knowledge about women's bodies. Those women formed the Doctor's Group and published a booklet entitled *Women and Their Bodies*. Members of the group wrote this booklet collaboratively, and they used it to communicate specialized knowledge to women users. Since then, the Doctor's Group has developed into the Boston Women's Health Book Collective. The BWHBC has authored, re-authored, revised, published, and re-published the original manual, re-titled *Our Bodies, Ourselves*, in many editions and many forms, including the modern website at www.ourbodiesourselves.org. In all forms, this manual and the process by which it came into existence provide a model for thinking about collective, distributed authorship and its products. Further, the BWHBC shows one way in which non-traditional authorship practices—rendered unapparent in the resulting technical manual—can help us to think differently about who an author is, what an author does, what an author values, and how we come to understand authorships itself.

Authorship scholars also might think about expanding the definition of authorship to include sites where authors do not initially seem to be present.

For example, the *Sustainable Building Technical Manual: Green Building Design, Construction, and Operations* manual includes many attendant entities: It is produced by Public Technology Inc. and the U. S. Green Building Council, sponsored by the U. S. Department of Energy and the U. S. Environmental Protection Agency, managed by four individual officers of Public Technology Inc. and Gottfried Technology Inc., edited by a number of consultants—and authored by no one. Or, we might contend, its authorship emerges within a complex relationship among all of the aforementioned entities. Each of this manual's producers, sponsors, managers, and editors certainly lends meaning to the work itself; even if they do not actively participate in what we might recognize as writing, their presence alters the final form of the text and our ability to believe in its value. Authorship scholars might gain significant insight into authorship practices by considering the complexities of what each of these entities contributed to the text, how those contributions were managed, what effects they had on other authors, and what effects they have on users.

CONCLUSION

In writing this chapter, we noticed that technical manuals usually point to intentions to keep people safe, and, yet, they most often resist acknowledging the presence of people at all. Technical manuals close down meaning because there is apparently no one with intention behind them; the text points back to itself or to other authorless texts, refusing to acknowledge authorship at all. However, our point is not that authors still exist, unacknowledged, in technical manuals; something more complex is happening here. Instead, we argue that when we dismiss the authorless text as a domain outside the purview of authorship studies, we risk missing the ways that authorship can potentially be constructed. The authorless text extends our understandings of authorship in composition studies by extending processes of legitimation to include the purposeful erasure of authors. We don't need authors to have authorship.

NOTES

1. See Robillard, "We Won't Get Fooled," for a discussion of the relationship between anger and authorship at length in the context of plagiarism.
2. We utilize the term *user*, as differentiated from the term *audience*, following a tradition of technical communication and technology scholars who emphasize the importance of user agency (Hallenbeck, Oudshoorn and Pinch, Sun, Wajcman).
3. Technical writers often straddle disciplines that value authorship differently. This sometimes leaves technical writers in a liminal space where they are not considered experts and have little power to exert authority. Jeyaraj uses postcolonial

theory to show how constructions of authorship—or lack thereof—in technical communication circles reify the marginalization of the profession.
4. In addition to contributing to authorship studies, this chapter also follows and adds to an existing body of technical communication scholarship that pays attention to feminist and authorship issues. Katherine Durack, for example, argues that women have been left out as authors of technical communication literature not because of a lack of production on their part, but because key terms for technical communication—*technology*, *work*, and *workplace*—are gendered in ways that prevent female authors from being taken seriously. Further, the journal *IEEE Transactions on Professional Communication* devoted a 1992 issue to the effects of gendered assumptions on understandings of rationality and the *Journal of Business and Technical Communication* and *Technical Communication Quarterly* both have produced issues on gender and technical communication.
5. The OTM's abstract does mention that it is published under the authority of the assistant secretary of the Department of Labor. However, this information is conveyed in a note at the bottom of the abstract page rather than as a traditional author credit.

WORKS CITED

Barthes, Roland. "The Death of the Author." *Authorship: From Plato to the Postmodern*. Ed. Sean Burke. Edinburgh: Edinbugh UP, 1995: 125–30.

Baumlin, Tita French. "'A Good (Wo)man Skilled in Speaking': Ethos, Self-Fashioning, and Gender in Renaissance England." *Ethos: New Essays in Rhetorical and Critical Theory*. Ed. James S. Baumlin and Tita French Baumlin. Dallas, TX: Southern Methodist UP, 1994: 229–55.

Boston Women's Health Book Collective, Inc. "Information on Women's Health & Sexuality—Our Bodies Ourselves." *Information on Women's Health & Sexuality—Our Bodies Ourselves*. N.p., n.d. Web. 02 June 2013.

Brandt, Deborah. "When People Write for Pay." *JAC* 29.1–2 (2009): 167–97. Web.

Brunner, Diane D. "Who Owns This Work? The Question of Authorship in Professional/Academic Writing." *Journal of Business and Technical Communication* 5.4 (1991): 393–411.

Butler, Judith. *Excitable Speech: A Politics of the Performative*. New York: Routledge, 1997.

"Creative Suite Help and Support." *Adobe*. 2010. Web. 25 Nov. 2010.

Durack, Katherine. "Gender, Technology, and the History of Technical Communication." *Technical Communication Quarterly* 6.3 (1997): 249–60.

Fleischer, Manfred P. "The first German Agricultural Manuals." *Agricultural History* 55.1 (1981): 1–15.

Flynn, Elizabeth. "Emergent Feminist Technical Communication." *Technical Communication Quarterly* 6.3 (1997): 313–20.

Flynn, John. "Toward a Feminist Historiography of Technical Communication." *Technical Communication Quarterly* 6.3 (1997): 321–29.

Foucault, Michel. "What Is an Author?" *The Foucault Reader*. Ed. Paul Rabinow. New York: Pantheon, 1984: 101–20.

Frey, James. *A Million Little Pieces*. New York: N.A. Talese/Doubleday, 2003.
Hallenbeck, Sarah. "User Agency, Technical Communication, and the 19th-Century Woman Bicyclist." *Technical Communication Quarterly* 21.4 (2012): 290–306.
Harris, R. Allen. "Generative Semantics: Secret Handshakes, Anarchy Notes, and the Implosion of Ethos." *Rhetoric Review* 12.1 (1993): 125–59.
Henry, Jim. "Teaching Technical Authorship." *Technical Communication Quarterly* 4.3 (1995): 261–82.
Holiday, Judy. "In[ter]vention: Locating Rhetoric's Ethos." *Rhetoric Review* 28.4 (2009): 388–405.
Howard, Rebecca Moore. "Sexuality, Textuality: The Cultural Work of Plagiarism." *College English* 62.4 (2000): 473–91.
Hyde, Michael J. "Introduction: Rhetorically We Dwell." *The Ethos of Rhetoric*. Ed. Michael J. Hyde. Columbia: U of South Carolina P, 2004: xiii–xxviii.
Jarratt, Susan C., and Nedra Reynolds. "The Splitting Image: Contemporary Feminisms and the Ethics of Êthos." *Ethos: New Essays in Rhetorical and Critical Theory*. Ed. James S. Baumlin and Tita French Baumlin. Dallas, TX: Southern Methodist UP, 1994: 37–64.
Jeyaraj, Joseph. "Liminality and Othering: The Issue of Rhetorical Authority in Technical Discourse." *Journal of Business and Technical Communication* 18.1 (2004): 9–38.
Noble, Douglas. "Pitfalls in Software 'Architecting': Some Issues in Transforming Paradigms from Manual to Computer-Supported Methods." *Journal of Architectural Education* 51.3 (1998): 166–76.
"Osha Technical Manual (OTM)." *Occupational Safety and Health Administration - Home*. 20 Jan. 1999. Web. 25 Nov. 2010.
Oudshoorn, Nelly, and T. J. Pinch. *How Users Matter: The Co-construction of Users and Technologies*. Cambridge: MIT Press, 2003.
Paradis, James. "Text and Action: The Operator's Manual in Context and in Court." *Textual Dynamics of the Professions: Historical and Contemporary Studies of Writing in Professional Communities*. eds. Charles Bazerman and James Paradis. Madison: U of Wisconsin P, 1991: 256–78.
Reynolds, Nedra. "Ethos as Location: New Sites for Understanding Discursive Authority." *Rhetoric Review* 11.2 (1993): 325–38.
Robillard, Amy E. "Vulnerability, Precariousness, and the Paradox of the 9/11 Imposter" *JAC* 33.1–2 (2013): 41–64.
———. "We Won't Get Fooled Again: On the Absence of Angry Responses to Plagiarism in Composition Studies." *College English* 70.1 (2007): 10–31.
Robillard, Amy E., and Ron Fortune. "Toward a New Content for Writing Courses: Literary Forgery, Plagiarism, and the Production of Belief." *JAC* 27.1–2 (2007): 185–210.
Rose, Mark. *Authors and Owners: The Invention of Copyright*. Cambridge, MA: Harvard UP, 1993.
Slack, Jennifer Daryl, David James Miller, and Jeffrey Doak. "The Technical Communicator as Author: Meaning, Power, Authority." *Journal of Business and Technical Communication* 7.1 (1993): 12–36.
Smith, Craig R. "Ethos Dwells Pervasively: A Hermeneutic Reading of Aristotle on Credibility." *The Ethos of Rhetoric*. Ed. Michael J. Hyde. Columbia: U of South Carolina P, 2004: 1–19.

Spinuzzi, Clay. "Who Killed Rex? Tracing a Message through Three Kinds of Networks." *Communicative Practices in Workplaces and the Professions: Cultural Perspectives on the Regulation of Discourse and Organizations.* eds. Mark Zachry and Charlotte Thralls. Amityville, NY: Baywood, 2007: 45–66.

Sun, Huatong. "The Triumph of Users: Achieving Cultural Usability Goals with User Localization." *Technical Communication Quarterly* 15.4 (2006): 457–81.

Sustainable Building Technical Manual: Green Building Design, Construction, and Operations. Tech. Public Technology / U.S. Green Building Council / U.S. Department of Energy / U.S. Environmental Protection Agency, 1996. Wajcman, Judy. *TechnoFeminism.* Cambridge: Polity, 2004.

Wells, Susan. *Our Bodies, Ourselves and the Work of Writing.* Stanford, CA: Stanford UP, 2010.

Wilkomirski, Benjamin. *Fragments: Memories of a Wartime Childhood.* New York: Schocken, 1996.

Winsor, D. A. "Owning Corporate Texts." *Journal of Business and Technical Communication* 7.2 (1993): 179–95.

Worsham, Lynn. "Going Postal: Pedagogic Violence and the Schooling of Emotion." *JAC* 18.2 (1998): 213–45.

5 The *Kairos* of Authorship in Activist Rhetoric

Seth Kahn and Kevin Mahoney

For people who study activism and activist rhetorics, 2011 was a banner year. Two major activist movements—One Wisconsin and Occupy Wall Street—emerged onto the national scene. Each has its own distinct rhetorical stances and purposes, framed by movement leaders and needs. Each has spawned primary texts, aimed at both internal audiences (organizing strategies and tactics documents) and external (manifestos, policy statements, blogs, websites, and so on). Both share a deep commitment to radical democratic politics and to using persuasive tactics and strategies to fight systemic class inequity.

These movements and their offspring fruitfully contest conventional definitions of *authorship*, as treated in the editors' introduction. Instead of warranting or critiquing judgments about the value(s) and status of writers and their texts, authorship is a tactical issue; democratic activists deploy or reject the concept *kairotically*, a term we invoke in two distinct but overlapping ways: 1) *a la* Gideon Burton's definition of *kairos*: "the opportune occasion for speech," *kairos* is a way of understanding not just the context (time and place) for persuasion, but also the way context advances persuasion; and 2) perhaps more pointedly, as John Poulakos argues, *kairos* can be "creating and managing self-consciously opportunities within rhetorical compositions" (90). That is, we contest the privileged status of *authored* texts via case studies of two leftist activist campaigns, contending that in activist settings authorship has significant tactical value—so much so that its rejection can speak as loudly as its proclamation.

The two activist campaigns we discuss deploy authorship claims both *in response to contextual demands* and *in order to advance their political agendas*, in service of democratic movement building: Occupy Wall Street, and Raging Chicken Press—a regional independent media project spawned following the Wisconsin Uprising in February 2011. They deploy authorship, by which we refer primarily to authorial credit, in opposite ways even though the two campaigns are in many ways sympatico. Furthermore, each has been explicit in its purposes for doing so, in ways that amplify those purposes.

THE AUTHOR MAY OR MAY NOT BE DEAD, BUT *SOMEBODY* WROTE THIS

Although Occupy Wall Street and Raging Chicken Press have made very different decisions about author attribution, the political/rhetorical impulse behind the decisions is similar if not identical. Both campaigns build from a theory of rhetoric-as-democracy very different from the traditional Aristotelian (or more recently Habermasian) notion of *deliberation*. At heart, traditional deliberative rhetoric and traditional authorship are problematic in very similar ways, particularly in their assumptions of enlightenment rationality and individualism. Both OWS and RCP recognize that the halcyon days (would that they were so) of the *agora*, or the *public sphere*, are gone. However, both also realize that *collective responses to power* must happen. The decisions to name (RCP) or not to name (OWS) authors represent two different ways of expressing that collectivity. Put simply, to be complicated as we go: OWS directly invokes Hardt and Negri's notion of "the network," a decentralized, anti-hierarchical structure that makes squelching a movement by removing its "leadership" impossible because there's no leadership to remove. Raging Chicken Press has roots in Hardt and Negri's argument regarding the need to both struggle within and construct against Empire—accepting that there is no "outside" to authorship, only *kairotic* institutional and tactical configurations of authorial power.

OCCUPY WALL STREET

Occupy Wall Street doesn't only *contest* authorship; OWS *refuses* it and in that refusal is kairotically constructing its own persuasive context. From its inception, understanding who speaks for the campaign, who authors its positions and statements, has been all but impossible. Nobody officially claims to speak for the movement, and as a result, the movement (as voiced on the website that's generally considered the closest thing to an "official" voice) rejects any such claim by anyone and sharply contests anybody's right to speak for it.

The rejection of authorship is visible from the inception of the campaign. Most of us who followed OWS in its early days know that the idea originated with the Canadian anti-corporate activist organization, Adbusters. A July 13, 2011, blog post, unsigned, presents an explicit call to action and uses the phrase on graphics in the Twitter hashtag #occupywallstreet. (See Figures 5.1 and 5.2.)

The post explains the rationale for targeting Wall Street as the object of a "worldwide shift in revolutionary tactics" (Adbusters) and argues for the radical participatory democracy that would become both the core of Occupy's project and its biggest problem.

The Kairos of Authorship in Activist Rhetoric   91

Figure 5.1

Figure 5.2

Fast-forward to September 17, 2011. Adbusters' call for 20,000 people to "flood into lower Manhattan, set up tents, kitchens, peaceful barricades, and occupy Wall Street for a few months" didn't turn out those numbers (estimates of the first week range from "a couple of hundred" to 2,000—protest crowd estimates are notoriously unreliable), but a significant and growing crowd landed at Zuccotti Park, across the street from the entrance to the New York Stock Exchange, and set up not only "tents, kitchens, [and] peaceful barricades," but also restroom and bathing facilities, libraries, first aid stations, and duty rosters according to which people cooked, cleaned, and made sure the encampment was orderly. These procedures, along with the organizing of demonstrations and public statements, emerged from daily, sometimes more frequent, General Assemblies.

Since the beginning, OWS has deployed a consensus model of self-governance, making all decisions in the General Assemblies. On the website (www.occupywallst.org), the page "How to Occupy" provides extensive information and advice on operating by consensus including links to documents on "dialogue management," "consensus building," and the like. There are blog posts that translate and elaborate various forms of political philosophy and explain the mechanics of running meetings. Other sections explain legal requirements for obtaining protest permits in various cities where Occupy sites might spring up, provide directions for keeping camps healthy and practicing Civil Disobedience, and advise activists on working with the press and developing social media presences. Here many of us first learned the concept of the "mic check," a method for simultaneously amplifying speakers' voices and regulating them—without using any mechanical amplification—as a speaker talks, the crowd repeats what the speaker has said; if the crowd refuses to send the message onward, it dies unheard. At the same time, the message becomes property of the crowd rather than the originator, who is often unknown to the larger audience—again, a *kairotic* moment in the sense that "voice" is inescapably collective, and it's from that collectivity that its persuasiveness emerges.

Likewise, no OWS webpage, link, document, or site is attributed to any individual writer(s). One page ("General Assembly") offers links to the minutes of every single General Assembly from September 17, 2011, to March 27, 2012; to audio recordings of many of those meetings; and to pages of live tweets from those meetings, as well as smaller group meetings occurring in the camp. Not one of those pages mentions anybody's name as an authority or spokesperson. Phone numbers and e-mail addresses to contact people appear, but even then names don't appear—except, one has the name "Drew" in an e-mail address that's been struck through but not erased from the page. Since there is no last name and no other indication of who he is, all we know is that somebody referred to him by name, and somebody else wanted to document the fact that the minutes shouldn't include it.

There are two tactical, and interrelated, reasons for the decision not to attribute any of these texts. First and more practical, to the extent that any or all Occupation activities risk running afoul of the law, writers are protecting themselves by hiding their identities. Or, as Hardt and Negri argue in *Empire*, postmodern democratic resistance to empire requires *networks* that decentralize lines of authority and thus make defeating movements by removing "leadership" much more difficult. The *context of persuasion* is very much double-edged. For movement insiders, it doesn't matter who wrote or said anything; to movement outsiders, it shouldn't matter because the collective voice has spoken it (and because it's none of your business anyway!).

Second, and more about principle than practical concern, the commitment to collective decision-making requires the movement's participants to resist credit for texts and ideas, in the same way OWS refuses to identify spokespeople or media contacts. The OccupyWallSt.org website insists repeatedly that the movement is leaderless, as in this statement on the front page:

> **Occupy Wall Street** is a leaderless resistance movement with people of many colors, genders and political persuasions. The one thing we all have in common is that We Are The 99% that will no longer tolerate the greed and corruption of the 1%. We are using the revolutionary Arab Spring tactic to achieve our ends and encourage the use of non-violence to maximize the safety of all participants. (Home page)

Furthermore, the administrators for the website go beyond simply asserting leaderlessness, to disaffiliating from (among other organizations) Adbusters—which clearly coined the concept of Occupy:

> OccupyWallSt.org is the unofficial *de facto* online resource for the growing occupation movement happening on Wall Street and around the world. We're an affinity group committed to doing technical support work for resistance movements. We're not a subcommittee of the NYCGA nor affiliated with Adbusters, Anonymous or any other organization. (About)

The effort to make sure that the *voice* of the movement doesn't belong to anybody in particular is explicit. Nobody/everybody speaks on behalf of anybody/everybody else. Nobody/everybody owns the language. Nobody/everybody earns praise (or blame) for acts of singular genius (or buffoonery).

In that light, it's ironic that the first text to receive national media attention was a "Proposed List of Demands," attributed to a Lloyd Hart, whose name is nowhere else to be found. Posted to OccupyWallSt.org on September 28, 2011, the document drew no response except a comment disowning it because it hadn't come out of a General Assembly, until Keith Olbermann shared the document on his October 3 *Current TV* show. Olbermann's *ethos* as a liberal pundit, along with the fact that he didn't say OWS had disowned the statement, answered for some what was one of the most significant challenges the movement faced in the mainstream media. Finally, a text made specific, concrete points and *voiced* the Occupy agenda in a *clear* and *compelling* way (and had somebody's name on it). Finally there was a text that had been *authored*.

OWS's unwillingness to name anybody drew sharp criticisms from reporters and even ostensible allies. On September 23, 2011, *New York Times* opinion-writer Gina Bellafonte acknowledged that the project was "a diffuse and leaderless convocation of activists against greed, corporate influence, gross social inequality and other nasty byproducts of wayward capitalism not easily extinguishable by street theater," while at the same time declaring one participant—seemingly plucked at random from the crowd and chosen because she was wearing only cotton underwear and didn't mind having her picture taken—"a default ambassador" (Bellafonte). *Times* media reporter Brian Stelter notes, on November 20, 2011 (two months after the occupation began, and weeks after OWS had issued declarations), "Lacking a list of demands or recognized leaders, the Occupy movement has at times perplexed the nation's media outlets" (Stelter). If Occupy's collective voice was clear and consistent to its participants, if the context for persuasion was constructed convincingly for insiders, it's clear from these accounts that such *kairotic* elements weren't broadly effective.

That's true even from ostensible supporters and sympathizers. From sympathizers, the argument struck a different tone, generally "We'd love to support you, but ..." or "We support you in spirit, but. ..." One very detailed letter among dozens of its kind, by an ostensible ally named William Stodden, was posted on Google+; the original post no longer exists, so we're citing from one of the 300+ reposts (Patterson). Stodden argues at some length, excerpted here:

> [I]f you are going to disrupt our society ... at least for me, a person who wants to actively support your efforts, ... PLEASE do two simple things. ...
>
> 1) Tell the people of this country PRECISELY what you are protesting. We have seen vague statements, we have heard very esoteric grievances on the radio. We want to know WHAT you are protesting against, or WHO you are protesting against, and WHY. ... [I]f you want to get ... people out into the street to join you, you have to be a bit more specific. ...
>
> 2) Tell the people of this country PRECISELY what it would take to get you out of the streets and back to your homes. Will you quit protesting if we get a 5% unemployment rate like we had before our economy corrected for our country's rampant speculation? ... Give us an end point to the protests, so we have something to work TOWARD. ...
>
> (Patterson)

That Stodden's letter was reposted more than 300 times on Google+ is part of what's noteworthy about it, as are the very contentious debates it set off. Dan Patterson's post drew 56 comments in just a few days—at the time, given that Google+ was still in beta, a remarkably large number.

Stodden doesn't use the term *authorship*, and to a large degree his criticisms are more applicable to what he sees as bad writing than they are to authorial absence: lack of clarity, precision, incisiveness, and specificity. In many of the comment threads, participants praised Stodden's writing as superior to that of any of the Occupy documents. He strikes a strong tone and is clear and consistent. He elaborates points. OWS activists tried to explain in response that the inherently messy messaging emerging from a collective isn't a flaw but a feature of the movement; in authorial terms, that is, emphasizing originality and ownership of ideas is flatly contrary to the project.

Late in the conversation, Seth—without doing this consciously—began reacting to Stodden's author-persona (his style, his demeanor), and this in turn helped Seth see more clearly what Stodden thought was missing: clear, forceful declarations, rather than multi-vocal, confusing masses of words more important for the process they embodied, for the persuasive context they created for themselves, than for anything they said. Although Seth wouldn't have used the terms *authorship* or *kairos* at the time, the following comment questions Stodden's ability to author a movement he isn't participating in:

> You seem very confident that you understand the movement better than its participants do. I see that as a rather aggressive form of intellectual appropriation; we don't think what you think, so we must be wrong about ourselves. ... [W]here I come from, people who proclaim themselves sympathetic find ways to work together, rather than insulting people who they say they sympathize with.
>
> (Kahn)

At the risk of conflating authorship with authority—or as we prefer to see it, by pointing out the overlap between the terms—Stodden's willingness to speak for a movement he doesn't participate in demonstrates the intellectual colonizing that traditional authorship so often results in. By making a very public statement that he understands the movement better than its participants do, he signals very clearly that he doesn't really understand the movement at all. At the same time, in much the same way as the early news coverage points to, his letter and the ensuing discussions indicate that the rejection of traditional authorship in the movement had only so much persuasive effect, or more precisely, that the persuasive context OWS worked to establish was limited.

Since late 2011, the major shift in the Occupy movement has been its expansion to other sites (nearly every major U.S. city and many smaller ones have had encampments) but a shrinking public presence as a driving force in our political discourse. It's arguable, that is, that the movement's unwillingness to claim authors has cost it the chance to fulfill its ostensible purpose. We disagree, taking the long view that a massively polyvocal network has in fact shifted political discourse substantially and productively (that you recognize the phrase "We are the 99%" but have no idea who coined it is an example). Income inequality has become a commonplace in the discourse, and as we'll elaborate in the conclusion, without the gigantic majority of participants worldwide knowing the names of anybody but our own friends and comrades.

RAGING CHICKEN PRESS

Whereas Occupy Wall Street began with a call to use a "Tahir Square" tactic to initiate a process of collective deliberation and action in the front yard of the very institutions that brought the U.S. economy to its knees in 2008, Raging Chicken Press was responding to a call initiated by more than 100,000 people who occupied the Wisconsin Capitol building for more than two weeks beginning February 15, 2011. The Madison protests erupted after Wisconsin Governor Scott Walker introduced Assembly Bill 11, or the "Budget Repair Bill." Walker claimed that the purpose of the bill was to help plug a $3.6 billion budget hole. However, as Ezra Klein explained on his *Washington Post* blog on February 11 of that year, "The best way to understand Walker's proposal is as a multi-part attack on the state's labor unions" (Klein).

As protests grew so did a network of progressive media activists. Blogs and websites such as Dane101 [http://www.dane101.com/], bluecheddar [http://www.bluecheddar.net/], and Uppity Wisconsin [http://www.uppitywis.org/] combined with emerging social-media savvy journalists and long-time progressive institutions like UW-Madison's Center for Media and Democracy to provide up-to-the-minute reports on the protests. Progressive media activists also investigated the genealogy of Walker's "Budget Repair Bill" and the money behind it. In July 2011, the Center for Media and Democracy launched a new web page, *ALEC Exposed*, which brought an otherwise obscure and secretive organization, the American Legislative Exchange Council (ALEC), into public view. The *ALEC Exposed* "About" page explains the launch of their site and the ALEC agenda as follows:

> On July 13, 2011, the Center for Media and Democracy (CMD) unveiled this trove of over 800 "model" bills and resolutions secretly voted on by corporations and politicians through the American Legislative Exchange Council (ALEC). These bills reveal the corporate collaboration reshaping our democracy, state by state. ...
>
> ... Before our publication of this trove of bills, it has been difficult to trace the numerous controversial and extreme provisions popping up in legislatures across the country directly to ALEC and its corporate underwriters.

ALEC Exposed laid bare a national strategy for a generational power shift that was expertly coordinated but played out largely outside of the national spotlight in state legislation and elections.

ALEC Exposed contested conventional notions about how bills are authored. It would be naïve to say that most Americans believe that the 1975 *Schoolhouse Rock* cartoon, "I'm Just a Bill," represents anything close to the actual legislative process. Americans know that money, lobbyists, and "special interests" speak loudly on Capitol Hill, influencing politicians to legislate in their favor. For the first time, however, *ALEC Exposed* showed Americans that some legislation making its way through their state legislatures was not even authored by elected state legislators. Many right-wing state legislators were simply slapping their names on ALEC authored "model bills" (their term) and ushering them through the legislative process. In one 2012 case, Florida Representative Rachel Burgin (R) forgot to remove ALEC's mission statement from the model bill before she introduced it in the Florida legislature (Seitz-Wald). *ALEC Exposed* was successful in carrying out a *kairotic* act in John Poulakos' sense of "opening a seemingly settled account and by introducing new ways of reasoning ... leading to the formation of new beliefs" (95). But, it wasn't the mainstream media that assured that *ALEC Exposed*'s revelations became widely circulated—especially among activists and progressive legislators. It was an emergent network of progressive blogs and non-profit organizations using social media.

While Pennsylvania Governor Tom Corbett did not seek the national spotlight as vigorously as other newly elected right-wing governors in Wisconsin, Ohio, Indiana, Michigan, and Florida, his first budget address in March, 2011, signaled that he intended to compete for the "cut, gut, and punish" Blue Ribbon. According to the Pennsylvania Budget and Policy Center's (PBPC) analysis of Corbett's budget proposal, his administration called for austerity-level cuts, including a 50% cut for the 14 universities of the Pennsylvania State System of Higher Education (PASSHE); a nearly 50% cut in state support for the four "state-related" universities (Penn State, University of Pittsburgh, Temple, and Lincoln); a $1 billion cut to public schools—including basic and special education; deep cuts in the Department of Environmental Protection (while unleashing Big Gas and Oil companies to "frack" Pennsylvania's Marcellus Shale in search of natural gas); and a 29% cut in the Department of Conservation and Natural Resources. Both Kevin and Seth work at PASSHE universities and are active in their faculty union, the Association of Pennsylvania State College and University Faculties (APSCUF). APSCUF's contract would expire on June 30, 2011, and the union was in negotiations when Corbett's budget proposal hit the newswires.

Kevin's vantage point at Kutztown University, which had already undergone several rounds of austerity resulting in the retrenchment (dismissal without cause) of faculty and staff and the elimination of several academic programs and departments, pushed him to launch an experiment in activist media rooted in Pennsylvania that mirrored the efforts of Wisconsin's progressive blogosphere. *ALEC Exposed*'s work coupled with the emergent media activism in Wisconsin provided two important touchstones for the project. First, ALEC-type legislation on the right had found a way to circumvent, even break, the relationship between a legislative author and audience and, by extension, accountability. Second, few mainstream journalists seemed able or willing to do the investigative work necessary to understand what was happening. Nonetheless, progressive media activists found ways of constituting a different kind of journalist-subjectivity that contested both what it meant to "be a journalist" and to "do journalism" that was inseparable from new institutional configurations. Progressive media activists were echoing, in practice, Aaron Barlow's argument in *The Rise of the Blogosphere*, that bloggers and new media activists were calling up the specters of the early American Republic in which "[t]he press ... was not seen as distinct from the political debates that raged in taverns and coffee houses, in political meetings both formal and informal. The pamphlet, the magazine, and the newspapers were seen as tools in the debate, not as some entity outside or beyond" (xvii).

Having done significant work integrating blogs into composition classes, developing new courses in "Rhetoric, Democracy, Advocacy" and "Activists Writing Media," and running his local faculty union blog (APSCUF-KU XChange) for several years, Kevin decided it was time to expand his work beyond the walls of the classroom and university. Raging Chicken Press was born.

Figure 5.3

On April 8, 2011, Kevin published Raging Chicken Press's first post and call for participation, "Spawn of Raging Chicken." Explaining his reasons for starting Raging Chicken Press (Raging Chicken, hereafter), he wrote:

> I've come to appreciate the critical importance of alternative media networks in helping sustain social movements. During the first couple of weeks of the Wisconsin protests, I stumbled upon a great progressive blogger from Wisconsin, bluecheddar ... [S]he was frustrated with mainstream media's coverage of the protests. Yet, in defiance of the despair that can seep in when you watch your experience being erased on the nightly news, bluecheddar was defiant, noting that she became convinced that the alternative media, that network of bloggers, twitterati, vloggers, and more established alternative publications, did a much better job of critically reporting local issues. She reminded me of similar conversations I've had with friends over the years that ended up with us producing a 'zine or alternative newspaper. ...
>
> ... So, I figured, what the hell ... let's give it a shot.
>
> (Mahoney, "Spawn")

Raging Chicken sought to aggregate stories from activist bloggers across the state and report on local and regional struggles that had a direct impact on the lives of Pennsylvanians. In addition, and just as important, Raging Chicken would be a venue for activists to *practice doing activist media*. Practicing "doing activist media" meant contesting the entrenched notion of what it means to "be" a journalist—to engage in a protracted, daily struggle over who gets to tell our public stories and the material networks necessary to sustain such an author.

Raging Chicken was to be an activist media site devoted to building a progressive media infrastructure and movement; the writing and reporting it published would not be what students learn in most of their journalism classes. As Barlow documents in *The Rise of the Blogosphere*, following the Civil War, American newspapers turned away from a century of partisan writing.

> Instead of being *participants* in politics, however, the papers now saw themselves as *reporters* of politics, leaving advocacy to the magazines and to editorials deliberately set off from the news aspects of the papers. ... [A]s a profession, they had begun, for the first time, to really see themselves as somehow aside from the events they covered and no longer as part of the stories. ... Like the cameras carried by the photographers who were becoming their colleagues, they were simply recorders—in their minds at least.
>
> (Barlow 76)

The rise of this professionalized journalism and its accompanying insistence upon "objectivity," "reporting," and "balance" is still standard fare in journalism courses today. Students majoring or taking classes in journalism are disciplined, in the Foucauldian sense. New journalists are not only trained to "do" professionalized journalism, they learn how to "be" a *particular kind of journalist*. This is an important point.

The "journalist" and the writing she or he does is embedded in an institutional structure that expects and reinforces professionalized journalism. The best way for a journalist to succeed, of course, is to do excellent journalism within the terms set by professionalized journalism. That is, the "author" is not divorced from her or his material and discursive infrastructure. What if a journalist or journalism student wanted to do a different kind of writing? What if she or he wants to do activist media? Where does that individual find the same kind of institutional structure to support that writer identity, that kind of journalist? Sure, there are well-established progressive media sites and magazines such as *AlterNet* and *The Nation*, but those sites don't have their own schools of journalism to help cultivate the next generation of activist writers. Progressives do have periodic gatherings like the Z Media Institute and Netroots Nation that offer media activists opportunities to network and learn tactics. As important as those sorts of gatherings are, they can't offer sustained time, space, and practice for new participants/writers/*authors*. Asserting new author identities, without simultaneously asserting new material and discursive infrastructures, is an exercise in wishful thinking.

It may sound like Raging Chicken is just advocating for a different kind of journalism or a different kind of journalist. That is true, to an extent. However, to stop there is to miss a bigger point. Our public stories are not just authored by one or two individuals. They are collaboratively authored texts that are *authorized* by historically specific institutional and discursive frameworks. For generations now there has been a relatively *un*contested author of our public story: the professional journalist as "reporter" producing "objectivity" within an increasingly corporatized media environment (let's call that uncontested author "establishment journalism"). To be a different kind of journalist, then, means to not be "doing journalism" at all—that is, not to be a recognizable author of our public story.

But that aggregated "author" of our public stories—the journalists *and* the media environment *and* the rules of writing—is increasingly being contested. ALEC represents one kind of challenge to establishment journalism: Our public stories are becoming increasingly authored in the shadows, using the official media network as a mere delivery device. However, we have also seen the instability of establishment journalism from writers more associated with the kind of progressive media activism witnessed in Wisconsin.

Take for example, the June 30, 2013, edition of NBC's *Meet the Press*. Host and establishment journalist David Gregory interviewed Glenn Greenwald of *The Guardian* about his reporting on whistleblower Edward Snowden's disclosure of secret documents concerning the NSA's collection of data on millions of Americans. Even as public debate raged as to whether Snowden was a "criminal" and "traitor" (the claim of the Obama administration) or a "whistleblower" and "hero" (to civil libertarians on both the left and the right), Gregory directed his questions to Greenwald's status as a journalist:

> To the extent that you have aided and abetted Snowden—even in his current movements—why shouldn't you, Mr. Greenwald, be charged with a crime?
>
> (Greenwald)

Greenwald's response resonated with the critiques posed by progressive media activists and went to the heart of the contestation over what it means to "be" a journalist, to be an author of our public story. Greenwald pulled few punches:

> I think it's pretty extraordinary that anybody who would call themselves a journalist would publicly muse about whether or not other journalists should be charged with felonies. The assumption in your

question, David, is completely without evidence—the idea that I have aided and abetted him in any way. The scandal that arose in Washington before our stories began was about the fact that the Obama administration is trying to criminalize investigative journalism by going through the emails and phone records of AP reporters, accusing a Fox News journalist of the theory that you just embraced—being a co-conspirator with felonies, for working with sources.

If you want to embrace that theory, it means that every investigative journalist in the United States who works with their sources, who receives classified information, is a criminal. And, it is precisely those theories and precisely that climate that has become so menacing in the United States. That's why *The New Yorker's* Jane Mayer said investigative reporting has come to a "standstill," her word, as a result of the theories you just referenced.

On the one hand, this exchange is well within the framework of establishment journalism. After all, Greenwald worked for *The Guardian* at the time. However, Greenwald cut his teeth in 21st century public writing with the launch of his 2005 blog, *Unclaimed Territory*, moving on to one of the Internet's earliest new media magazines *Salon.com* until his short stint at *The Guardian*. In October 2013, Greenwald announced he was leaving *The Guardian* to team up with eBay founder Pierre Omidyar to launch a new media enterprise (Brandom). Omidyar said the new venture would embrace the "personal franchise model of journalism" most closely associated with progressive, new media:

> individual journalists who have their own reputations, deep subject matter expertise, clear points of view, an independent and outsider spirit, a dedicated online following, and their own way of working.
> (qtd. in Brandom)

If the Gregory/Greenwald exchange marks a momentary bubbling of contestations over establishment journalism's authority over our public story, Greenwald's decision to partner with Omidyar to build a different kind of collaborative author is one of the most public challenges to establishment journalism. It is a recognition that a new author needs a new house. And while establishment journalism's goal is to "report" the news, Omidyar hopes to "find ways to convert mainstream readers into engaged citizens" (qtd. in Brandom).

While the success of Greenwald and Omidyar's experiment has yet to be seen, their endeavor echoes the progressive media activists in Wisconsin and the purpose of Raging Chicken. Unlike the decision of Occupy Wall Street activists to refuse authorship for very specific and principled tactical and strategic reasons, Raging Chicken actively and aggressively cultivates "authors"—writer identities—more consistent with the raucous and vibrant

21st century progressive, political, social media world. And, for complex and at times contradictory reasons, that writer identity, that emerging collaborative author of our public story, has strongly identifiable, public personae out in front. Whether we're talking about bloggers like bluecheddar or internationally known figures like Greenwald, the author is out in front as a distinct persona.

Raging Chicken has quickly become a crucible for nurturing an activist journalistic identity. And the more practice writers and editors have doing the work of progressive, activist journalism, the more successful the site has become. The site has grown from a one-person project to a media site featuring a regular group of writers producing original reporting and a rich collection of aggregated content from progressive sites around the region. The first "issue" of Raging Chicken was published in July, 2011. In that month just over 1,100 visited the site. One year later, just short of 11,000 readers visited the site. As of July, 2013, the site averages between 10 and 15,000 visits a month with a high of over 31,000 visits in June, 2013. The Facebook page for Raging Chicken has grown from a few dozen "likes" to over 2,700 as of this writing. Several Raging Chicken contributors have had their work picked up in national progressive publications such as TruthOut.org and Counterpunch.org; and, Raging Chicken Press has been cited in *MotherJones*, *The Nation*, and the *Daily Kos*. In May, 2013, Raging Chicken was credited by the Allentown, PA, based *Morning Call* and *Philly.com* with breaking a story about a quiet move to allow concealed weapons on PASSHE university campuses. In that short time, Raging Chicken writers have also learned a lot about what it means "be" an activist writer, what it means to "do" journalism in a different key and to collaboratively author a different public story.

Figure 5.4

Raging Chicken's decision to aggressively cultivate author identities has been critical to its success. Raging Chicken is a creature of the progressive blogosphere and social media that relies upon social interaction. Alan Rosenblatt, Director of Online Advocacy at the Center for American Progress Action Fund, is one of the leaders in social media consulting for progressive organizations in the United States. He argues that

> Social media is fundamentally about engagement, which is the interaction among people. Engagement includes conversations with your audience and efforts by your audience to promote your messages to their networks.
>
> (Rosenblatt)

Progressive social media strategist Beth Becker says that over the past several years she has opened every social media presentation or training session with the following statement:

> It's called social media. You have to have the conversation. The Internet isn't just about pushing information out broadcast style, it's about growing and connecting community. If you're just going to broadcast, go build a better website.

Rosenblatt and Becker both point to one of the most important differences between establishment journalism and progressive, activist journalism: that the writer is a *participant* in the communities that she or he is writing about or to. It's a return to pre-Civil War notions of journalism that Barlow documents so well.

Being a participant-journalist requires that the writer be a person. Readers in particular communities don't build relationships with web pages; they build them with flesh-and-blood people. Raging Chicken contributors are very much engaged with their readers in the comment sections of their articles and on the ground with other activists. Wendy Lee, for example, is an anti-fracking activist who writes about the resistance to Big Oil and Gas companies' environmentally destructive natural gas extraction practices in the Marcellus Shale (think: Josh Fox's film, *Gasland*); her day job is as a philosophy professor. Wendy has engaged in extensive debate with gas industry proponents in the comment section of her articles, allowing her to develop "longer analyses of corporate collusion, issue evasion, and corruption" (Lee). When a water company working with a natural gas company sought to evict residents of the Riverdale mobile home community in Jersey Shore, PA, so it could pump millions of gallons of water out of the Susquehanna River for fracking operations, Wendy became part of the blockade and resistance. Several of her photos and blog posts for Raging Chicken were picked up or cited by national progressive publications such as *Mother Jones*. Wendy was the *only* "journalist" on the ground in Riverdale; her posts and photo essays captured the growth of a community of resistance—the residents of Riverdale, a group of young men and women from Occupy Cleveland who dropped what they were doing in Ohio to help establish a blockade at Riverdale, and a philosophy professor at a state university. It's a good bet that the story of Riverdale would never have been publicly told had it not been for Wendy.

Many of Raging Chicken's contributors do such work *because* Raging Chicken has sought to build relationships with activists and community members online and on-the-ground. Part of this relationship-building is about re-establishing trust and accountability between citizens and journalists. Each time an article is published on Raging Chicken, activists and community members who are close to the issues get to see *their* realities reflected back to them and can hold writers accountable because the writers are known. The collaborative author constructed in Raging Chicken is made up of strong author identities that gain their credibility and authority by linking their action with their words, videos, and images.

Sites like Raging Chicken can serve as training sites for the next generation of activist journalists who are actively contesting establishment journalism, the "author" of which has left behind critical citizenship and deep democracy. It is that struggle over the collaborative author of our public story with which Raging Chicken is engaged.

CONCLUSIONS, OR, THE MULTITUDE ALWAYS FINDS A WAY TO SPEAK

Occupy Wall Street and Raging Chicken Press offer two venues in which traditionally privileged notions of *the author* (originality, creative genius, ownership of ideas, and so on) must take a back seat to the interests of democratic collectives, *while at the same time* serving roles for activists when circumstances demand them. Raging Chicken, for example, has demonstrated the power that traditionally *authored* texts (or at least "authors") can have. Wendy Lee's work has served not only to make her a national anti-fracking leader, but also to bring Raging Chicken readers and the ethos that comes with featuring prominent activists. On the other hand, OWS's refusal to name authors/spokespeople is likely to have contributed to its most significant impact: injecting arguments about income inequality into U.S. political discourse by popularizing terms like "the 99%" and even "occupy" itself. By eliminating *ad hominem* attacks against ostensible spokespeople, OWS avoided problems like the collapse of the Kony 2012 campaign, catalyzed by the public meltdown of film-maker and campaign leader Jason Russell and the attacks against Edward Snowden and Glenn Greenwald deflecting attention from the government abuses of investigatory power that they were blowing the whistle on.

We don't mean to say simply that sometimes claiming authorship is smart and sometimes not, although that's one version of the point. Another version of it is to say that this *kairotic* conception of authorship problematizes the privilege generally attributed to it while highlighting its concrete rhetorical/persuasive/political values, two of which strike us as most significant: 1) the credibility some activists need in some settings to act as leaders; and 2) the validation of spaces in which to practice and sharpen the rhetorical skills necessary to advance democracy. Our experiences in activist settings also help us see that although the traditional "author" function is easy to write off in terms of class privilege (*a la* Roland Barthes, Foucault, etc.), there are places for it—or its close relative—in leftist activist rhetoric/discourse, even if we want to call it something else: "writer" or "activist" or "citizen journalist." That is, the *concept* of author may be more valuable when detached from the term itself and its history.

Finally, if Poulakos is right that *kairos* is as much about producing context as responding to it, then our key finding might be that while Raging Chicken Press and OWS are very different in how they produce texts, the differences do not signify competing goals or purposes. The tactical differences, taking place at different nodes in a radical democratic activist network, together produce a context for sustained movement building. The dialectic the practical (journalistic conventions, interviewing techniques, setting up encampments, or getting permission for marches) and the ethical (the good those practices do) offer arguably calls for *author-activists*. They appear when needed and disappear when not, they sometimes take credit for their work but only when it furthers the collective effort, and their commitment to democracy is at the same time the context to which they respond and the context they produce.

WORKS CITED

Adbusters. "#occupywallstreet." Blog, 13 July 2011. Accessed 12 April 2013.

Barlow, Aaron. *The Rise of the Blogosphere*. Westport, CT: Praeger, 2007.

Bellafante, Gina. "Gunning for Wall Street, with Faulty Aim." *New York Times*, 23 Sept 2011. 13 April 2013.

Brandom, Russell. "NSA Reporter Glenn Greenwald Partners with Billionaire eBay Founder for New Venture." *The Verge*. 16 Oct 2013. 4 Jan 2014.

Greenwald, Glenn. "Greenwald: Obama Administration Known for Targeting Whistleblowers." Interview by David Gregory. *Meet the Press*. 30 Jun 2013. 2 Jul 2013.

Hardt, Michael, and Antonio Negri. *Empire*. Cambridge: Harvard UP. 2001.

Kahn, Seth. Comment on "Interesting Idea. How Do You Feel about This?" 28 October 2011. Google+.

Klein, Ezra. "What is Actually Being Proposed in Wisconsin?" *The Washington Post*. 18 February 2011. 15 May 2013.

Kroll, Andy, with Nick Baumann and Siddhartha Mohanta. "What's Happening in Wisconsin Explained." *Mother Jones*, 17 March 2011. 15 May 2013.

Lee, Wendy. "Re: Article I Am Writing." Message to Kevin Mahoney. 26 June 2013. E-mail.

Mahoney, Kevin. "Spawn of Raging Chicken." *Raging Chicken Press*. 8 Apr 2011. 25 June 2013.

"Occupy Wall Street: The Movement Continues #*occupywallstreet*. worldwide." http://occupywallst.org. 1 May 2013.

Patterson, Dan. "Interesting Idea. How Do You Feel about This?" 28 October 2011. Google+.
Pennsylvania Budget and Policy Center, The. "Budget Analysis: Governor's Proposed 2011–2012 Budget." 8 Mar 2011. 25 Jun 2013. Web.
Poulakos, John. "*Kairos* in Gorgias' Rhetorical Compositions." *Rhetoric and Kairos: Essays in History, Theory, and Praxis*. Ed. Phillip Sipiora and James Baumlin. Albany, NY: SUNY Press, 2002: 89–96.
Rosenblatt, Alan. "Rules for Social Media Engagement." *Frogloop*. 20 Oct 2010. Accessed 02 Jul 2013. Web.
Seitz-Wald, Alex. "Oops: Florida Republican Forgets to Remove ALEC Mission Statement from Boilerplate Anti-tax Bill." *ThinkProgress*. 2 Feb 2012. 2 Accessed Jan 2013. Web.
Stelter, Brian. "Protest Puts Coverage in Spotlight." *New York Times*, 20 Nov 2011. Accessed 13 April 2013.

6 In the Author's Hands
Contesting Authorship and Ownership in Fan Fiction

Rachel Parish

> That a writer can create fictional characters who come alive so fully that readers feel they know them, can understand their motives, predict their actions, continue their stories and grieve when they "die." That, surely, is as close to God as any author can come.
> —Sheenagh Pugh, *The Democratic Genre*

For as long as there have been stories, there have been authors. Whether that author is a transcribed deity, a corporate entity comprised of numerous co-writers, or an ordinary citizen, the crafters of texts are typically assumed to possess ownership and control over their words. With the development and the expanding accessibility of the Internet and the social media frenzy of technology that followed, however, the very nature of the term "author" is on the verge of a cataclysmic shift. Fan fiction, a growing genre of composition, poses the potential to completely rewrite the "rules," so to speak, of how we define authorship, now more than ever before. And corporations are already jumping on board with fan fiction, even in spite of some authors'—and fan fiction writers'—protests. A recent Amazon press release announced that the company is preparing to launch a new publishing platform called "Kindle Worlds" on their handheld digital devices. Kindle Worlds will "enable any writer to create fan fiction based on a range of original stories and characters and earn royalties for doing so. ... Through these licenses, Kindle Worlds will allow any writer to publish authorized stories inspired by these popular Worlds and make them available for readers to purchase in the Kindle Store" (Amazon).

The questions "What is fan fiction?" and "Should it be allowed?" have been asked in previous scholarship on fan fiction, with answers being offered by scholars such as Sheenagh Pugh, Henry Jenkins, Rebecca Black, Karen Hellekson, and Kristina Busse, among others, who define and attest to fan fiction's value as a form of writing. Fan fiction has been prevalent in the writings of literature for centuries; the ability to distribute these works so easily to mass audiences and for free, though, has only helped this genre to flourish and become more noticeable by commercial readers and writers. The question we should be asking is perhaps no longer "What is fan fiction?" but instead, "Why is it contested?" and "What can we do with fan fiction?"

THE FAN'S FICTION

To understand why fan fiction is contested, we must first understand what it is. Rebecca W. Black in her text, *Adolescents and Online Fan Fiction*, defines fan fiction as "a fiction written by fans about pre-existing plots, characters, and/or settings from their favorite media" (10). Fan fiction serves as a way of extending a reader's beloved story, but there's more to this genre than extension. Renowned scholar Henry Jenkins additionally notes that fans of a particular text(s) use the writing genre to "play with the rough spots of the text—its narrative gaps, its excess details, its loose ends and contradictions—in order to find openings for [their] elaborations of its world and speculations about character" (74). One considerable draw of fan fiction is the amount of control the readers themselves gain. Unresolved plot lines are a thing of the past; the actions of a minor or deceased character may be carried on into their own stories, and a fan fiction author can even pluck from one tale and transport characters into a different setting, often described in the fan fiction community as a "crossover."

The introduction of technology such as the Internet and social media have helped to distribute, but also transform, fan fiction. In the introduction to their collection of essays, *Fan Fiction and Fan Communities in the Age of the Internet*, Kristina Busse and Karen Hellkson note fan fiction's availability to fans far prior to the Internet or even the computer. Written or typed stories were compiled into "hard-copy zines" and distributed among avid readers (13). However, as accessibility to the Internet has grown, the space online fan fiction encompasses has increased—though unless you specifically typed "fan fiction" into a search engine, it may be more difficult to immediately discover online. In retrospect, the seeming invisibility online may have helped fan fiction to flourish under the radar of those who would deem it copyright infringement or seek to have the content removed. Luckily for fan fiction aficionados, rather than "feeling lucky" on Google or attempting to search for a web page dedicated to a single story, many readers and writers are members of massive online communities where they share and peer review one another's fan fiction. The Web's largest fan fiction site is Fanfiction.net, hosting millions of pieces including works "based on the Bible, Shakespeare, TV shows ... cartoons ... and video games" (Alter). Fanfiction.net organizes its immense content by several sub-categories, including length, the story or stories the book is based upon, and even the rating of content, allowing for fairly easy search capabilities within the site.

Fanfiction.net's main draw to readers and writers is arguably that of the genre itself: it's free. Anyone with a pad of paper and a pen can theoretically write fan fiction. Proactively, though, anyone with a keyboard and Internet access can type and find a web domain to host and more importantly, share, his or her work. The lack of profitability has been one way in which fan fiction helped to keep its legality in check amidst growing alterations to copyright law. "Most experts agree that fan fiction qualifies as fair use under copyright law, provided that it differs substantially from the original and its creators don't attempt to profit from it" (Alter). Companies like Amazon have transformed fan fiction from the whimsical scribblings of fans to a form of monetary gain, resulting in further contestation, which I will elaborate on momentarily. Contestation may be the result of recent commercial successes such as E.L. James's *Fifty Shades of Grey*, which was originally a fan fiction of Stephanie Meyer's *Twilight* series published on Fanfiction.net (Alter).

Sheenagh Pugh points out a further appeal of fan fiction in *The Democratic Genre* stating, "there have been several studies of fan fiction as a sociological phenomenon," (11) in which readers use publicized works as inspiration for their own expansions, and Henry Jenkins similarly uses the notion of De Certeau's "poaching" to establish fan fiction as a "cultural bricolage through which readers fragment texts and reassemble the broken shards according to their own blueprints, salvaging bits and pieces of the found material in making sense of their own social experience" (De Certeau qtd. in Jenkins 26). However, I would argue that fan fiction readers and subsequent authors and artists define their craft beyond "poaching" others' materials; rather, participants use the "original" writings as a means of constructing their own authorship and of cultivating a sense of identity both across various social networks and for themselves privately. Instead of "salvaging" parts, these authors and artists are utilizing the works as inspiration and a catalyst for their own ideas. The inspired writings transform readers to writers, whose works attract new readers, and thus the fan fiction "circle of life" continues. Here, however, the contesting of authorship begins, as the "birth" of fan fiction writers is equated to the "death" of the "original" authors.

CONTESTING FAN FICTION

Fan fiction exists in an interesting limbo, as a sort of "third type of creation, neither pure copies of another author's work nor authorized additions to the original" (Tushnet 67). The discussion, as I noted at the beginning of this chapter, has primarily centered around the validity of fan fiction itself. Should fan fiction writers be granted authorship of their texts? If we follow the route of Roland Barthes's well-known "The Death of the Author," one could conclude that Barthes's essay eloquently argues for the value of the fan creator: "As soon as a fact is narrated … the voice loses its origin, the author enters into his own death, writing begins" (142). By Barthes's notion, authorship is never concretely established; once you pick up a pen and write something down, the idea and ownership of that idea itself flows from your being onto the page. And if commercially distributed, that page can belong to anyone, to do theoretically anything with it. The evolution of authorship into a career path and profit stream, though, creates murky paths for Barthes's theories to tread.

With corporate commercialization of fan fiction, a more apparent separation of disapproval versus support emerges. Scholars like Abigail Derecho note that fan fiction ensures the significance of the "original" works in that "the [primary] text is never solidified, calcified, or at rest, but is in continuous play, its characters' stories, and meanings all varying through the various fics written about it" (77). Some published authors, however, find the prospect of their works in never-ending flux to be detestable, if not terrifying.

Anne Rice, author of the bestselling novel *Interview with the Vampire*, voiced her opinion of fan fiction in a *Chicagoist* interview, stating, "I don't ever want to read about my characters in someone else's writing. It's too upsetting for me, because they are mine and from my mind. I never read fan fiction. Other writers feel differently about it and are happy and encouraging of it. I don't make judgments—I prefer to ignore it" (Sudo). For her, authorship has granted her the power to "own" her characters, and in turn, she believes in her sole power to hold onto those characters and "protect" them from being exploited in undesirable ways via fan fiction. Despite her seemingly apathetic, non-judgmental stance in the interview, though, Rice's post on her website more abrasively states, "I do not allow fan fiction. The characters are copyrighted. It upsets me terribly to even think about fan fiction with my characters. I advise my readers to write your own original stories with your own characters. It is absolutely essential that you respect my wishes" (Rice). Since her post in 2010, sites such as Fanfiction.net have not allowed fan fiction of Rice's novels to be published on their site, perhaps out of fear of a potential copyright lawsuit.

Another contesting author is fantasy writer Mercedes Lackey, whose stance against fan fiction takes an intriguing twist. "At this point, it is not legal nor permissible for you to publish any fiction based on my copyrighted works on the net. Nor is it legal for you to publish a novel-length work in ANY form. My agent reluctantly permits paper publication of short fiction in fanzines; he is inclined to go ballistic over anything longer than a short story. He has not yet granted permission to anyone to publish net fan-fiction" (Lackey). The power of authorship is interestingly co-owned by Lackey and her agent, and her disdain for fan fiction seems less about attachment to characters and more about upsetting her agent with the seeming financial devastation publishing fan fiction on her stories may invoke. Or, one could argue Lackey is merely deflecting blame off herself to keep fans happy, and therefore, continually buying her novels.

Not all writers choose to keep fans from composing fan fiction, though they do express a need to control what types of fan fiction are published online. Authors such as J.K. Rowling, who has stated she is "very flattered by the fact there is such great interest in her Harry Potter series and that people take the time to write their own stories," encourage fan fiction creation, as long as it is "PG-rated and non-commercial only" (Waters). Many authors, such as Stephanie Meyers, who has taken no legal action against E.L. James's *Fifty Shades of Grey* trilogy, seem to be in agreement. George Lucas has even allowed fan fiction to be commercially published in the past, as long as there is not "any sex and minimal swearing in the fan-fiction" (Writersco).

Returning to Amazon's Kindle Worlds, the only titles initially licensed for publishing fan fiction were a few graphic novel series, *Pretty Little Liars*, *Gossip Girl*, and *The Vampire Diaries*; however, the addition of famed author Kurt Vonnegut's works into the pool has drawn sparks ranging from disapproval to bold outrage, claiming writers should not be allowed to profit by tampering with the creations of culturally established authors (Bricken). But in the cases of Rowling and Lucas, and other authors who support fan fiction, I argue they align with Derecho's theory on extending the "original" text, and do so for reasons having more to do with commercial profit than creativity or play. Even if the most beloved classics are offered up like sacrificial lambs to the key-bound hands of rabid fans, it will still be fans who read, crave, and perhaps contest these fan fiction creations. Fans who undoubtedly own, or may become owners of, the source material. Fan fiction is, in a manner of speaking, free promotion for these authors. If you read a fan fiction of *Slaughterhouse Five*, chances are you have already read or own Vonnegut's novel. If not, you may find yourself persuaded to give it a read, and see if the fan fiction you've just read makes more sense or seems like utter rubbish. Either way, encouraging a fan's extension of their work is just another way to reinforce authors' fan base, and in return the future profitability of their franchise.

INTO A NEW AUTHOR'S HANDS

Writers of fan fiction claim their craft is not stealing but instead reshaping and evolving the role of the author itself. Fan fiction and subsequent fan-created media, I argue, function in a sense as a resurrection of the author. The storyteller is revived; the tale continues beyond "The End," with creative expansion and unimaginable transformation. Social networking sites ranging from Facebook, Tumblr, Pinterest, to DeviantArt.com allow individuals to cultivate their own identities as artists and authors based on their expansion of others' works, helping to shed some light on answers to the question, "What can we do with fan fiction?"

DeviantArt.com boasts itself as "the world's largest online art community ... showing 257 million pieces of art from over 27 million registered artists and art appreciators" (Sotira), who all share their work and offer each other critiques, sell commissions and merchandise, and help network with those who share their passion personally and professionally. The sub-category of "Fan Art" has become immense on the site, with artists and authors taking the form of fan fiction to new levels, creating comics, paintings, drawings, sculptures, even plush doll creations based on the characters of valued shows, books, and movies. Similar to Fanfiction.net, DeviantArt requires the creation of a pseudonym or "username" in order to submit artwork or literature, immediately shaping the user's identity as a writer on the site. This isn't immediately surprising, as Rebecca Black points out how "computer-mediated communication" allows for the construction and enacting of "identities in online environments" (77). These identities, which can be semi-anonymous usernames, function similarly to handles constructed through the social media site Twitter and allow a degree of separation from an individual and copyright law, much like a pen name grants an author semi-anonymity and privacy from fans and life as an author.

While identities are developed among these artists and writers, the ever-present availability of these fan-created works increases tensions, as Rebecca Tushnet notes: "Visibility [of fan fiction and fan art] invites study, and sometimes legal threats, as shown by the section of chillingeffects.org that hosts copies of cease and desist letters received by various fan sites" (63). Scholars such as Julie Levin Russo would criticize that "fan fiction is always subordinate to its father text" (qtd in Stasi 118), and deem fan-created works as stealing from the "original" author for their own gain.

The contestation among fan art pieces becomes harder to pinpoint due to the nature of the medium itself. Unlike fan fiction, fan art is physically transformative, often becoming an entirely new, non-textual creation. This in turn makes legal disputes of copyright infringement trickier to articulate. With the "transformative" nature of fair use, fan artists have found innovative ways to make a career of combining their skills with the source material of others. New York-based artist Alice X. Zhang profits from selling fan art on DeviantArt, but has expanded her marketing from the site to hosted art gallery showings and web merchandising. She has even gone so far as to have her work trademarked and purchased by companies such as BBC[1], transforming what some might call an act of stealing into entrepreneurship. Zhang communicates with fellow artists about her art process and love of the source materials she bases her own artwork upon, but also respectfully seeks to educate others of her process in obtaining copyright of her work, which allows her to interestingly become a sort of co-author of the franchise.

Several professional artists use DeviantArt as a way to see various artwork from around the globe and also to share information with younger or up-and-coming artists. DeviantArt member "Techgnotic," also known as Brian Kesinger, began working for Disney at the age of 18, with the feature film *Tarzan*, Disney's adaptation of the Edgar Rice Burroughs series. From there, Brian molded the various influences around him into his own artwork that has been celebrated by fans via fan art of their own, including Cosplay, which is the act of transforming 2D work into 3D by dressing as the characters. Regarding these fans, specifically those engaging in Cosplay, there is complete support. "I can't think of a higher compliment. It truly is special to see your work embraced in such a way that a person is compelled to pull a character that you created off the page and transform his or her physical appearance in order to bring my work to life." Further, "Fan art allows you to take bigger ideas, either be it from a movie or a comic book and ... you can create concepts from there based on what you've read or watched ... you ask yourself why you are doing [fan art], and what do you like about [these characters]?" (Techgnotic). Brian describes fan art as a means to come full circle, connecting to existing stories and characters, which in turn will help to develop newer ones that will eventually be taken up by readers.

Similarly, DeviantArt member Hoai Minh, known as "NanFe" on the site, boasts a unique style of digital painting that resembles gothic impressionistic style,[2] featuring broad coarse brushstrokes and monochromatic palettes with red color-spotting. Her fan art of the Japanese graphic novel series *Bleach* gained her a large following on the site, though now she does a lot of artwork starring her own original characters. With these three artists, the question of which "text" is subordinate to the other becomes an increasingly tangled and murky discussion, and arguably this is the "nature of the beast" that is fair use. Fair use has four main principles: The purpose and character of use, nature of copyright work, amount and substantiality of portion taken, and effect on the potential market (Stim). These four principles are to many as vaguely described as they are contested and leave authors of fan fiction and fan art with a large gray area to work with, especially online.

Rebecca Black argues, though, that sites such as DeviantArt.com and Fanfiction.net are meant for more than just making a profit. These sites provide readers ways to "use new media to communicate, develop relationships, access and share information, and author socially situated identities in online spaces" (49). Pugh likewise observes how interacting within these spaces can encourage reading and peer review practices, iterating how the fan fiction community allows "a far more supportive community than most profic[3] writers get to work with;" emboldening the notion that "good readers make good writers ... [writers] cannot expect to improve at their craft without reading both their predecessors and their contemporaries" (238). Variety creates exposure, practice makes progress, experience develops understanding; fan fiction offers a fresh means of examining character and plot development, grammar, and dialogue and adhering to genre conventions, among other facets of composition. The added bonus is the "cushion" of being able to work within established threads of plot, setting, and character that can be fine-tuned and transformed in limitless ways. Fan fiction strives not to "pirate" an author's work, but to create new authors and expand existing stories without claiming them as their own. Instead of the death of the author, fan fiction aspires to reshape the role of the author and alter both how one is allowed to become an author and given distribution control via authorship.

CONCLUSION

In 2004, my friend Auzzie[4] and I were, as Sheenagh Pugh declares, "not ready for a story to end" (31), when we collaborated on our first fan fiction,

"Merry Memories," and later co-authored in 2006 a fan fiction titled, "Pirate's Gold,"[5] both based on J.R.R. Tolkien's *The Lord of the Rings* trilogy. A counter on the site indicated that "Merry Memories" only had 28 views, but "Pirate's Gold" boasted 362 views by the end of 2006. We were elated despite the fact that some fans were less than enthusiastic about our departure from Tolkien's writing style. Our overuse of exclamation points and vernacular did not, in their view, fit Tolkien's style of writing. As reviewer "Cookie Monster's Crystal Ball" stated, "I want to believe this story is a troll, since I can't imagine anyone putting 'lil princess' in a LOTR [Lord of the Rings] story and expecting to be taken seriously" (Fanfiction.net).

Yes, our story was contested, but for Auzzie and me, writing those chapters was more than simply carrying the story farther than the DVD player or theater seats. We were developing our own identities as writers; Tolkien's texts were prompts that fueled the creative fires our adolescent minds were harboring. "Pirate's Gold" became our answer to the question plaguing Pugh, "whether a fanfic writer, working with someone else's material, can ever develop her own individual voice and become more than a pastiche of someone else" (193). That our writing was a departure from Tolkien's style was a mark of our own identity, which we construed as a rite of passage, of authorship, a right that our creations could freely intermingle with Tolkien's Hobbits without reprimand. Once a character is created and released to the public, it "has [its] own reality, which [the primary author] does not necessarily understand perfectly, or even better than a reader" (Pugh 16), and readers can extend this understanding by becoming the new narrator of the story, with a new identity that is exhibited through fan fiction or fan art.

The commercialization of fan fiction, as desired by Amazon's Kindle Worlds, creates issues of contested authorship among writers of multiple genres, as *Forbes* writer Carol Pinchefsky voices her hesitation with the platform:

> I'm concerned about the quality of Kindle World's content. In traditional publishing, a manuscript has to be approved by an editorial staff with exacting standards. There's nothing in Amazon's press release—and a query to Amazon about this has currently gone unanswered—that suggests an editorial process. Fan fiction is wonderfully fun if it's free, but if I'm paying for content, I would want something worth paying for.

One can see how an author might be disturbed at the thought that fans may read poorly composed stories involving the characters and plots they've worked so tirelessly to create.

Her sentiments seem to be shared by fan fiction writers. One author with the pseudonym "Singing Flames" writes, "Overall, I find the new Kindle Worlds an intriguing concept. I like the idea of being able to publish, in an official format, our fan fictions. The legalese is a bit daunting, and should be examined closely before anyone agrees to it. I do worry about less-than-stellar stories coloring people's opinion towards all of the stories offered. Like the independent authors who publish Kindle books, I'm sure quality will vary greatly." Other fan fiction writers share in the prospect of conceptualizing their work as having monetary value, as "Archsage328" comments at the bottom of "Singing Flames'" post: "I know that in Japan, you're allowed to sell Doujinshi,[6] so if and when *anime* gets added to the [Kindle Worlds] roster, this could truly be something I could celebrate with every fiber of my being." Perhaps such a move by Amazon will reverse negative connotations surrounding fan fiction pointed out by Pugh: "The fact that fan fiction isn't written for money causes it to be held in low esteem by many who have never read any, but are convinced that writers who were any good would be getting paid" (229).

Kindle Worlds could open the realm of fan fiction reading and its appreciation to a larger audience, but skepticism remains. Pinchefsky warns, "from experience, I can tell you that fan fiction is fun, but it doesn't teach the writers how to write" and seems to fear the exposure may do more harm than good to the reputation of fan fiction. However, "Singing Flames" offers her own rebuttal to Pinchefsky's claim. "I believe any practice helps a writer's skill, regardless if it's done as a fan or original fiction. I have read a novel-length fan fiction that was better than numerous printed novels I've read. Now, I'll admit there are some aspects of fan fiction writing that are provided for the author (like world building), but to make such a blanket statement seems condescending and not a little prejudice [sic]."

Fan fiction calls for a major shift in how we view the role of the author, to see texts not as documents with one or two major owners but as stories that once told can be expanded, transformed, and continued on by the readers who enjoy them. The possibility that fan fiction may be undertaken for profit, sparked by Kindle Worlds, has no doubt left individuals contesting the right these new "authors" will have and questioning how the public will react to their favorite stories being essentially re-written. However, I argue this is not the "death of the author" but the "birth" of a new role, to reshape the power of the reader for the better. Until the role of the author is further re-evaluated, there will be contestation of fan fiction and its developing role in the literary world. But it is clear that fan fiction is changing views of authorship, perhaps faster than any could have imagined. The advent of media streaming from device to device, coupled with maximum multimodal capabilities and the ever-expanding development of the Internet's accessibility make this movement undeniably kairotic, and worth examination by scholars and writers alike.

NOTES

1. The following links to Alice X. Zhang's, "Virtuoso" which has had rights purchased by the British Broadcast Company, BBC. Clicking on the link to her username, "alicexz," will take you to her homepage on Deviant Art: http://alicexz. deviantart.com/#/art/Virtuoso-256536410?_sid=5295c5e0.

116 *Rachel Parish*

2. The following links to Minh's Deviant Art page: http://nanfe.deviantart.com/. There you can see her various artwork, an indiscriminate mingling of original characters and *Bleach* fan art.
3. "Profic" describes writers who create fictional texts for profit; often considered the opposite of fan fiction writers.
4. Auzzie is not the actual name of my friend but a nickname given to her in high school. I use the name here because it is also her name on the fan fiction we co-authored. She also was developed into a character in our fan fiction, "Merry Memories."
5. The first *Lord of the Rings* film arrived in theaters around the same time as Disney's *Pirates of the Caribbean*. Our shared love of both film franchises could explain the title more than the actual content of the story.
6. Doujinshi refer to fan fiction in the form of graphic novels that are based off Japanese comics or animated television series.

WORKS CITED

Alter, Alexandra. "The Weird World of fan Fiction." *The Wall Street Journal Online*. 14 Jun. 2012. Web. 22 Mar. 2013.
"Amazon Publishing Introduces 'Kindle Worlds,' a New Publishing Model for Authors Inspired to Write Fan Fiction—Launching with an Initial License of Popular Titles from Warner Bros. Television Group's Alloy Entertainment." Business Wire: Seattle. 22 May. 2013. Web. 29 May. 2013.
Ash. "Fan Fiction Owner Bans & Guidelines." Writersco. writersco.heddate.com. 11 Mar. 2011. Web. 06 Dec. 2013.
Barthes, Roland. "The Death of the Author." *Image-Music-Text*. Trans. Stephen Heath. New York: Noonday Press, 1977.
Black, Rebecca W. *Adolescents and Online Fan Fiction*. New York, NY: Peter Lang Publishing. 2008.
Black, Romania. "Merry Memories." Fanfiction.net. 9 Feb. 2004. Web. 14 May. 2013.
———. "Pirate Gold." Fanfiction.net 6 Oct. 2005. Web. 15 May. 2013.
Bricken, Rob. "Amazon Has Added Kurt Vonnegut to Its "Official" Fan Fiction Program." IO9. io9.com. 6 Aug. 2013. Web. 18 Dec. 2013.
Derecho, Abigail. "Archontic Literature: A Definition, a History, and Several Theories of Fan Fiction." *Fan Fiction and Fan Communities in the Age of the Internet*. Karen Hellkson and Kristina Busse (eds.) Jefferson, NC: McFarland & Company, 2006.
Hellekson, Karen and Busse, Kristina. "Introduction." *Fan Fiction and Fan Communities in the Age of the Internet*. Jefferson, NC: McFarland & Company, 2006.
Jenkins, Henry. *Textual Poachers: Television, Fans, and Participatory Culture*. New York: Routledge. 1992.
Lackey, Mercedes. "FAQ: Ask Misty Archive: Writing" *The World of Mercedes Lackey*. mercedeslackey.com. 2003. Web. 18 Dec. 2013.
Pinchefsky, Carol. "Fan Fiction is Finally Legitimized with Kindle Worlds." *Forbes*. 22 May. 2013. Web. 29 May 2013.
Pugh, Sheenagh. *The Democratic Genre: Fan Fiction in a Literary Context*. Brigend: Seren. 2005.
Rice, Anne. "Important Message from Anne on Fan Fiction." Anne's Message to Fans. annerice.com. 2010. Web. 15 Dec. 2013.

Singing Flames. "Paid Fan Fiction Opportunity." Deviant Art. Deviantart.com. 28 May 2013. Web. 28 May 2013.

Sotira, Angelo. "DeviantArt: Homepage." Deviant Art. Deviantart.com. n.d. Web. 15 May. 2013.

Stasi, Mafalda. "Toy Soldiers from Leeds: The Slash Palimpset." *Fan Fiction and Fan Communities in the Age of the Internet*. Karen Hellkson and Kristina Busse (eds.) Jefferson, North Carolina: McFarland & Company, Inc. 2006: 115–131.

Stim, Rich. "Measuring Fair Use: The Four Factors." Copyright & Fair Use: Stanford University Libraries. fairuse.stanford.edu. 2013. Web. 24 Dec. 2013.

Sudo, Chuck. "Anne Rice on Monsters, Facebook and *Fifty Shades of Grey*." *Chicagoist*. Chicagoist.com. 4 Apr. 2012. Web. 16 Dec. 2013.

Techgnotic. "Otto and Victoria: Octovictorian Etiquette" Deviant Art. Deviantart. com. 29 May. 2013. Web. 30 May. 2013.

Tushnet, Rebecca. "Copyright Law, Fan Practices, and the Rights of the Author." *Fandom: Identities and Communities in a Mediated World*. Jonathan Gray, Cornel Sandvoss, and C. Lee Harrington (eds.). New York: New York UP. 2007: 60–71.

Waters, Darren. "Rowling Backs Potter Fan Fiction." BBC News Online. news.bbc.co.uk. 27 May. 2004. Web. 20 Dec. 2013.

Part III
Excluded Authorship

7 Writing after Stonewall
The Lost Forms of Gay Authorship

James Zebroski

> Only that historian will have the gift of fanning the spark of hope in the past who is firmly convinced that *even the dead* will not be safe from the enemy if he wins.
> —Walter Benjamin (qtd in Mark Merlis, *American Studies*)

> I can't help but notice that when I finally write a book in which there are no men sucking each others' dicks, I suddenly win the Pulitzer Prize.
> —Michael Cunningham in 2000, author of *The Hours*

THE CRYSTALIZATION OF GAY AUTHORSHIP OUT OF A SHIFT IN POWER RELATIONS

My claim is that only by recognizing the deeply political nature of gay life and writing and evoking the experiments of the post-Stonewall counterculture of the 1970s can one begin to do justice to the writing called retroactively gay literature and the writing that is not canonical or even literary but no less a witness to the dead.

This chapter studies the shifts in authorship forms that emerge from Stonewall and develop to the present day. The structure of the argument is:

1. Revolution: *The Violet Hour.* Gay literature is seen through two received narratives. David Bergman has presented the first and, perhaps the most important, argument for the emergence of gay literature as a total break and revolution, in the work in the 1970s' Violet Quill group based in New York. Bergman has done an enormous amount of primary research on this and related issues. For decades he has collected the work of the Violet Quill, kept in contact with its surviving members, and dedicates this book to them.
2. Evolution: *Eminent Outlaws.* While spending a good deal of time analyzing the work of the Violet Quill, Christopher Bram offers essentially the opposite received narrative—that gay literature comes out of a long continuity and evolution going back at least to World War II, including authors like Gore Vidal, Tennessee Williams, Allen Ginsberg, Truman Capote, James Baldwin, and many others he terms eminent outlaws. Bram

is himself a creative writer who has published a long string of successful, sensitive, generous, and well-written gay novels. He admits his recent history comes at gay literature from this creative writer perspective.

3. Sam Steward and Alternatives: The recently recovered work of Sam Steward detailed in Justin Spring's amazing and extremely important biohistory, *Secret Historian: The Life and Times of Sam Steward, Professor, Tattoo Artist, and Sexual Renegade,* as well as his edited mammoth collection *An Obscene Diary: The Visual World of Sam Steward*—what can only be called a collection of anti-art artifacts and writing—raises serious questions about Bergman's and Bram's narratives. Steward's life, writing, and visual practices simply do not fit into either narrative. Sam Steward presents all kinds of problems for those two narratives and is wedged between these standard views. In the space created by this wedge, an entirely alternative view of gay and gay authorship arises.

4. Stonewall as History, Counterculture, Myth: In this section, I expand the meaning of Stonewall to go beyond being the riot that is the origin of gay literature. It is also a countercultural and political way of life (and sex) and writing.

5. Post-Stonewall Gay Writing 1969–1978: In this final section I describe the larger project out of which this essay comes. This section traces the emergence, and often the death, of alternative forms of authorship. When one theorizes authorship, one begins to see significant patterns.

REVOLUTION: *THE VIOLET HOUR*

In his book *The Violet Hour* David Bergman argues that the Violet Quill group (hereafter VQ) is crucial to understanding gay literature, and American literature, in the last quarter of the twentieth century. VQ was made up of seven male writers who started a creative writing group in New York in the early 1980s to workshop their gay writing. Bergman states that "Two of the writers—Edmund White and Andrew Holleran are simply among the best writers in the United States ..." (1). A little later he notes that "In short, one reason to read the *Violet Quill* is that their works present the most articulate and passionate expression of the ethos of a certain aspect of New York gay culture during that period. To ignore the Violet Quill is to construct a history of twentieth-century American culture with a floor missing" (21). Bergman's book—erudite, readable, insightful, persuasive—is excellent literary formalist criticism, although it is seemingly totally unaware of the last fifty years of theory in literary studies. The book is literary in a narrow sense of canonical literature. *The Violet Hour* is essentially Bergman's formalist argument to English studies for letting these writers into the canon.

Not only does Bergman construct his project to be literary in a formalist sense, but he grounds that approach in what can only be described as the anti-political aesthetic of the VQ writers: "Its aspirations were literary, not therapeutic or political" (23). Political activities were "extraliterary," and their doctrine might be said to be that "writing well is the best political activism" (23). "Literary excellence is the only commitment" (49). He defines the goal of the VQ as to explore "... the possibility of a truly gay fiction—namely, one that was written for gay men, by gay men in the language and with the assumptions of gay men ..." (41). Bergman, in a somewhat savage critique of Ethan Mordden and his comments on Holleran's writing, goes further:

> The gay writer remains in a precarious position. If gay writing is to be great writing—which is Larry Kramer's expressed desire—it cannot be held to serve some preestablished social agenda the way Nazi art or the social realism of the Stalinist Soviet Union did. (36)

Bergman argues that the writing of the VQ changed gay literature and in the process, American literature, forever. He claims that the VQ writers were not very much influenced by their post-World War II gay forebears. Despite his formalism, Bergman's narrative is a story of revolution. Despite his generous review of the work of the forties and fifties, Bergman begins in what is a kind of gay Dark Ages and ends with the Golden Age of the VQ. The chapter on gay writing of the forties and fifties is significantly entitled "Gay Writing before the Violet Quill" as if the only function that writing could possibly serve is as a precursor of the VQ. He concludes a review of the pre-VQ writing with this:

> Why didn't these novels of the late forties and early fifties, despite their limitations, start a continuous line of gay writing? Why, after so large an outpouring of works that dealt with homosexuality, did the number slow to a trickle? Why did it take a quarter of century for the development of the Violet Quill? The short answer is ... the Cold War. ...

In this progress narrative is embedded a very carefully presented argument for "great literature," which almost always means literary modernism and creative writing ideology. In the quest for greatness, it would seem most gay men's lives do not measure up, and the wide range of popular, pulp, and porn writing of this period simply doesn't count.

EVOLUTION: *EMINENT OUTLAWS*

Armistead Maupin gets it right for his non-fiction writing as well as for his novels, specifically *Exiles in America*, when he blurbs that book: "Bram is the rarest of creatures: a gifted writer who wields his wit without malice and his wisdom without pretense" (inside flyleaf). Christopher Bram, who happily accepts the label of gay writer (to this day, surprisingly few gay writers do), presents in his *Eminent Outlaws* the most comprehensive (and fun: it is full of deep dish) accounts of gay writing since World War II. In this ambitious and generous book, Bram starts with this sentence: "The gay revolution began as a literary revolution" (ix). Bram devotes a chapter to each decade of gay writing from the fifties to the nineties. He argues that it did not all begin with Stonewall—or the VQ—that gay literature starts with the boys coming back from war (and often a lot of man-to-man sex during it). Bram, then, includes Gore Vidal (he calls him a sort of fairy godfather of gay lit knowing Vidal would hate the appellation and even more the credit. Vidal always resisted labels of gay and homosexual, seeing in them the beginning of oppression) and goes on to talk of Tennessee Williams, Allen Ginsberg, James Baldwin, Truman Capote, and so on down to Kushner and Maupin in the nineties. He admits from the start his biases, including the fact that he is a novelist and sees this history as story. He adds that "The story of these men has never been told in a single narrative before, which is surprising" (x). The sort of literature Bram writes is popular, but also committed to modernist principles; the carefully modulated pacing of a good storyline with subplots and not fragmentation and experimentation are typical of his novels. Like his novels, his story of gay writing is beautifully paced and smartly populated with interesting people, writing, and events. In many ways, this essay builds on Bram's account. Yet in two ways, this essay parts ways with Bram.

First, Bram (like Bergman though less fanatic) accepts the binary of political versus literature. This binary implies that good literature is not and cannot be political. Bram says it this way when crediting these activists with preserving Stonewall:

> Gay politicals like Craig Rodwell and Frank Kameny did not like *Boys [in the Band]*, but political activists rarely like fiction of any kind. Literature is about ambiguity, mixed emotions, and guilty pleasures. Politics is about ideals and action. *Boys* was attacked not because it was behind the times, as some claimed, but because it reflected real life all too accurately. (142)

Here we can see—just as we observed in Bergman who is more virulent about it—an acceptance of the antithesis between politics and literature that is a regular part of American modernism. Here we see that once you split off the political, you make invisible the fact that all writing is always political if by political one means the exercise of power. To work from the premise that writing is not political, as the generation of activists disparaged here noted, is to accept the political status quo. It is to flee from the very idea of the Stonewall and the Women's Movement—the personal is political.

So it is an oxymoron for Bram to say that the gay revolution began as a literary revolution and that we do not have to see writing as political. This is creative writing ideology, a view attached to profit and dispensed in university programs and workshops throughout the land to any student who gets an MFA, although Bram comes to this honestly, outside of such "writing tribunals."

Bram disagrees with Bergman on the import of the VQ: "It is sometimes claimed that the Violet Quill as a group created a new gay literature. I don't see that. ... I'm not convinced their work marks a real break with what was written before Stonewall" (197). Yet, he does admit that with the publication of Ed White's *A Boy's Own Story* in 1980, "The mainstream had finally accepted a gay novel as a real work of literature. The high quality of White's prose certainly helped" (209). The narrative then progresses to the present day, now that gay and gay literature have won acceptance. He starts with Vidal coming home from World War II and Nagasaki, moves through fifty years of stories and moves, in the chapter titled "High Tide"—itself telling— to Michael Cunningham's Pulitzer Prize-winning *The Hours*. Bram finishes the book with a novelistic flourish: Gore Vidal coming home in old age to die. After recounting the sad decline of Vidal and generously crediting him with the revolutionary work that started things rolling after World War II, Bram, looking over fifty years of progress, notes:

> When you stop to think about it, the transformation is nothing short of amazing. And the process was reflected in the written word. In just over fifty years, between 1948 and 2000, a tiny literary species, a handful of books and plays appeared only now and then to disabuse or silence, grew into a lively ecology of many animals, hundreds of titles that came out every year and sometimes won national praise and prizes. The world changed, too, but the literature itself was an agent of that change, feeding it, and reporting it, serving both as cause and effect. During a half century when books and plays lost much of their importance in American culture at large, they played a major role in the growth of gay life. (303)

Bram, through the quality of research and writing of this book, as well as through his generosity and (dare I say it?) kindness, has earned the right to be celebratory and to offer an upward and onward progress narrative. But as we break out the champagne, it behooves us to ask who and what is left out by this progress narrative.

SAM STEWARD AND ALTERNATIVES

Spring's "discovery" and resurrection of the works and life story of Sam Steward is perhaps the most important contribution to the study of gay literature in the last two decades. Spring begins his study by identifying Steward:

> Samuel Steward—a poet, novelist, and university professor who left the world of higher education to become a sex researcher, a skid-row

tattoo artist and pornographer—may seem at first an odd candidate for a biography, for he is practically unknown and nearly all of his writing is out of print. (ix)

Yet Steward presents the case of the gay man who lived from 1909 until 1993 and who fits neither pre-Stonewall nor post-Stonewall labels, neither in Bergman's nor in Bram's stories. His writing is vast—he constantly wrote and published—the published writings list in Spring runs to nearly eight pages and contains over two hundred entries (442–50). Steward made his fame through the Phil Andros pornographic novels that were popularized after the Stonewall riots (though Steward had been trying through the 1960s to get them published). The Phil Andros novels were subsequently republished in the 1980s with Tom of Finland cover illustrations and have been in print ever since. Today some of the early copies are collectibles and go for over $200 each.

But Steward was hardly "just" a pornographer, and a good one. The list of his writing includes every sort of genre and publishing venue imaginable: poetry, a dissertation, novels, short stories, numerous articles in a dental journal, many essays, letters, articles and stories for a ground-breaking homophile European journal *Der Kreis*, reviews, pieces about tattooing, pieces for emerging gay magazines and newspapers in the 1970s, a book on tattooing culture, an account of his friendship with Stein and Toklas, and an autobiography. This is the *published* writing, which does not include the even more voluminous unpublished pieces and illustrations, a sample of which Spring collected in *An Obscene Diary*, or Steward's actual diaries, kept religiously for decades. How can any account of writing or even literature not include Steward? It also does not include the numerous interviews he had with gay magazines after Stonewall made such subject matter accepted. If we want to know about authorship from about 1930 till 1990, Steward's work must be studied. If we want to know anything about gay sex and gay sexual practices in the everyday life of most gay men in this period, following Kinsey, again it is to Steward we must go. Yet Steward is hardly more than a footnote in both Bergman and Bram.

Born in Ohio, a graduate of Ohio State University, receiving his Ph.D. in English from Ohio State in 1934 at 25, Steward lived mostly in Chicago. He was an academic and novelist through the first part of his life until he was fired in 1956 without explanation—his contract was simply not renewed—by the president of De Paul University where he had worked for almost a decade and was a popular teacher among students. He had just before that become very interested in tattooing, something at the time that was rarely seen as acceptable except among working class and navy men (unlike today when it has become wildly faddish among all of the young social classes). He left academe never to return and set up a tattoo shop in a seedy part of downtown Chicago. This combined his interests in illustration (his talents were considerable) and young men's bodies.

But perhaps what is most remarkable are his collections that document his sex life. He seems to have recorded every sexual contact he had in his entire life and, more, this documentation itself is vast and takes many forms. He developed an extremely detailed card catalogue filing system he terms the Stud File, but he also used one of the first instant development cameras to take hundreds of snapshots. He was a prolific illustrator, and this also contributed to his chronicle of gay sex from the 1930s through the 1980s. This evidence, which supports the claim for sexual experimentation not to mention a vast sexual appetite, was unheard of especially before the 1960s. As Spring clearly notes, keeping such documentation was itself punishable by long prison time. A man having sex with men was also a felony that sent large numbers of gay men to prison. Spring says, "Even as he was compiling his Polaroid collection, Steward was well aware that in creating so much documentary evidence of his sexual activities he was essentially courting prison time" (133).

Why risk prison to keep records of sex? Spring argues that:

> Steward's many forms of self-documentation now seem to me, in retrospect, a single lifelong body of work through which he hoped to demystify homosexuality for generations to come. As a young man Steward had hoped to establish himself as a popular novelist, but by his early forties he realized he would not be able to do so without censoring, condemning, and pathologizing his own homosexuality to suit the expectations of his publisher. And so instead, he decided to write a secret history—one that was playfully cross-referenced, illustrated, and footnoted—telling the absolute truth about his sexual life in every detail … it was, in fact, his great consolation in a life that was otherwise characterized by constant disappointment, discouragement, isolation, and rejection. (xiv)

Spring in his "Afterword" concludes that even Steward's Phil Andros novels—and I would argue many of his other writings as well if we start from a democratic notion of writing—"… can easily be seen as precursors to post-Stonewall gay literary writing, in which the worlds of homoerotic experience and everyday living are one and the same" (413). Spring's incredible and important work was not published until 2010; Bergman refers to Steward (under the name of Phil Andros) in three pages of the Dark Ages pre-VQ chapter; Bram not at all.

So, bringing this together, how does Steward fit into either Berman or Bram's narratives? Not very well.

Let me name just a few of the differences.

The VQ and Eminent Outlaw	Sam Steward
Bi-coastal, mostly New York based	Midwesterner, mostly Chicago based
Literary successes (ultimately)	Literary failure

(Continued)

Creative writing culture and values	Popular culture and values
Modernist writing	Counter-modernist writing
Upper class values privileged in writing	Working class values accepted in tattooing and his pornography, though Steward tried to commit to elitist modernist values early on
Explicitly anti-political	Not political though in practice a true sexual outlaw
Depictions of gay sex are few	Constant and complete representation of sex/life
Elitist	Democratic
Progress Narrative	?

Taking up only the last point, Bergman and Bram, in different ways to be sure, are both committed to a progress narrative of gay literature; things are getting better because of the heroic work of our forebears. The progress narrative comes out of the Enlightenment and is widely accepted today regarding the gay movement: President Obama's Second Inaugural address, putting Stonewall in the same sentence with Seneca Falls and Selma, shows that. Bergman and Bram do have differing starting points for that narrative: Bergman the Violet Quill in the late 1970s and early 1980s; Bram with Vidal and others right after World War II. But Steward's work is a monkey wrench in these progress narratives because he was a literary failure and gave up literature and academe—though significantly he did *not* give up writing (or authoring). He came long before the earliest of Bergman and Bram's canonical writers and stayed late. His writing after he abandons literary modernism takes up values that are diametrically opposed to both the Violet Quill writers and the eminent outlaws. His work is not simply important; it is crucial.

My point here is that unless we find a way of fitting Steward into our notions of authorship—he wrote and published probably hundreds more pages than the VQ put together—we are ignoring his huge corpus of writing not to mention the life of someone who, as unique as he was, may have had more in common with the typical gay man (whatever that may be) than any of the writers on which Bergman or Bram focuses. Given this, let us return to one of the key historical moments in both Bergman's and Bram's narratives: Stonewall. Let us try to imagine history that avoids the linear progress narrative.

STONEWALL AS HISTORY, COUNTERCULTURE, MYTH

It is commonplace now to recognize that Stonewall as origin of gay culture is largely arbitrary, that gay culture and gay writing existed before Stonewall, and that other protests and riots could just as legitimately be tapped as the beginning of the modern gay movement. Christopher Bram notes that:

> The Stonewall riots were an expression of change, not a cause of it—not by themselves, anyway. There had already been similar protests in Los Angeles and San Francisco that are now forgotten. Stonewall might have been forgotten, too, except that a year later in 1970, a group of activists including Craig Rodwell marked the riot with a march. ... Rodwell suggested they do it a week earlier as a protest march in New York, commemorating the street battles of last year. (146)

But Bram here is too conventional in his acceptance of the idea that history is one linear thing. He ignores the fact that history is not set of irrefutable events and hard facts—but from the start history is interpretation. His is a positivist illusion. Even if there were only Stonewall, it would always be open to multiple interpretations; it would signify in multiple ways. The idea that a video camera or cell phone would "capture" history as reality rather than interpretation ignores the fact that the camera is positioned and viewed by a person with interpretive slants.

Interpretations are political and, despite Bram, they do change the world in complex ways. In a way, Stonewall is a collection of events—and interpretations—both before and after the June 27, 1969, the first day of riots in Greenwich Village in New York City that provided a site for new interpretations and further claims for what was emerging from the counterculture as gay. Stonewall is a trace of a part of the movement that fragmented into a political and cultural separatist set of movements. As Les Brookes shows, Stonewall (and gay fiction) is deeply political—it is no coincidence that one of the loudest and first gay organizations that sprang up in Stonewall's wake took the name of the Gay Liberation Front (GLF). That name came directly from numerous third world political movements and organizations working against colonialism, specifically the National Liberation Front (NLF, the political arm of the Viet Cong), very much in the forefront of the media of that day due to the Paris peace talks to end the Vietnam War. As Brookes notes the culture of that day was clear about being ideological:

> Ideological conflict was therefore inevitable at this moment of revolutionary change; and the basis of this conflict was the fundamental opposition between assimilationism and radicalism. The subculture of the early 1970s was in fact a battlefield: on one side were those who had no quarrel with the social order, while on the other side were those who wished to see it razed to the ground. (2)

Sex was the practice both central to every human being and important in society's formation of identity, let alone social and individual reproduction. And sex and new sexual *alternatives* were viewed in this gay counterculture as the motor that would drive *liberation*. (The two most important key words of Stonewall, aside from *sex*, were *alternative* and *liberation*.) Stonewall was, literally, after all, the Stonewall Inn, a bar, where a wide range of people met to drink, dance, and to select sex partners. Like bars to this day in gay culture, even if one does not drink, the bar is the premier gay institution because it is (still) one of the few safe public places where gay men can gather and where one can be surrounded entirely by one's own kind and not have to assimilate to the dominant straight heterosexist milieu that strangles nearly every other form of social life.

As Patrick Moore argues, sexual liberation seems to have released an explosion of creativity in other fields and endeavors. The huge increase in gay organizations but also consciousness raising groups, the inundation of underground magazines and manifestoes, and the relatively immediate passing of the word about Stonewall all point to this explosion of alternative writings and creativity.[1]

Then it is not surprising that history became symbol and symbol became myth. Stonewall is already being cited by gay writing and film by 1970. The gay organizations that formed immediately after the riots in Columbus, Ohio, at Ohio State had in their newspaper in June 1971 plans to go to the very first gay pride march in New York City that month.[2] Word was out, with lightning speed.

POST-STONEWALL GAY WRITING 1969–1978

What we see from 1969 to the present day in gay writing is an oscillation in authorship that follows the events of history, a periodic alternation between moments in which power is recognized as creating new forms of authorship and moments when literature is seen in isolation and a creative writing ideology prevails. As creative writing ideology gains hegemony, many forms of gay authorship, which came out of Stonewall, are lost.

When we study this extensive sample of the diverse materials produced under the first years of Liberationist Authorship from 1969 to 1978,[3] we discover:

1 The social formation of gay authorship is not vested in one author, but is rather a collective project. It is about developing a new way of being—and being gay and lesbian—in writing. It directly and immediately is linked to the politics of sexual practices.
2 While we see in these data what seem to be the slow creeping of conventional authorial practices disseminating across time/space, this actually all happens very quickly: This sample covers nine years, and commercial authorship takes over beginning around year six. The texts track a shift from collective authorship in which individual names are never mentioned to its opposite—a creative writing authorship and its "charisma

of authorship" (McGurl) that is tied directly into profit making in the business world.
3 Gay authorship emerges not from elite culture (*Boys in the Band*, *The Great Gatsby*, or *The City and the Pillar* or later VQ) but from a) the counterculture and b) popular culture. Both are democratic and include a wide span of people left out of previous accounts of gay writing. We must accept and learn how to read pop culture especially formula fiction democratically rather than as failed elite literature.[4]
4 Pop culture is especially helpful to scholars because it demands that we get back immediately into history. Pop culture artifacts, more democratic than elite literature, disappear with time. Reading a pop culture artifact from 35 years ago is impossible if one does not return to history. To return to history means a return to the power relations of that time. To return to history means returning to the political.
5 A surprising focus on social class runs through these writings. *Rubyfruit Jungle* is as much working class lit as gay lit. Maupin depicts a range of social classes just as he does a range of sexualities but social class is still central to *Tales*.
6 Stonewall enters into the gay culture very early on and is mythologized and cited very early on.[5] Stonewall becomes a mythic commonplace within a year of the event.
7 Major book publishers and film studios were not involved in the emergence of gay lesbian literature. Small presses, counter-cultural broadsides, and magazines and newspapers, as well as mainstream newspapers, were the sites of emergence. The Unitarian Universalist Church sponsored the pioneering film, *A Very Natural Thing*, in 1973. Also bar rags (e.g., *Bay Area Reporter*) played a crucial role in reviewing straight- and gay-themed books and gay literature and in such reviewing helped collaborate in opening up a space for gay authorship. (see Zebroski)
8 Special mention seems warranted for Maupin's *Tales* newspaper columns and books. Aside from their very early production and wide reception, the number of intertexts with popular and elite culture references is amazing. His construction of 28 Barbary Lane and Anna Madrigal serves as a metaphor for the creation the "house of gay literature." Barbary Lane is a sort of temporarily open space where experiments can be tried out, alternatives can be shaped, gay is equal to straight but, in an impish way, better.
9 With the exception of *Tales*, gay lit contrary to stereotypes is not, in these texts, very open to what later is called "promiscuity." Monogamy of various sorts is represented as preferable even in gay lit that presents other alternatives. "Promiscuity" in these texts is always on the way to something more permanent—and more socially acceptable. So-called promiscuity increases only in later texts starting with John Rechy's *The Sexual Outlaw* in 1977.
10 That said, perhaps the most important mark of emerging gay writing is an openness to sex, sexual practices, and a sex-positive view. The gay

writing in this database increasingly and ever more explicitly represents sex—straight and lesbian and gay and other. It is interesting that straight sex is represented as much as it is in early gay literature. Gay sex in these texts can be a weapon against straight society, but it is also a liminal space in which a new society, new relationships, and new sorts of families, are imagined and built.

Only by acknowledging and embracing the Stonewall counterculture, which is political, and by taking a broad view of what counts as authoring that begins with popular culture, can one begin to do justice to the living and the dead.

NOTES

1. See especially *San Francisco / Bay Area Gay and Lesbian Serial Collection*, one of the most stunning databases out there. Also see my chapter "Rhetoric, Anti-Structure, and the Social Formation of Authorship" for further evidence for this claim.
2. See the Columbus, Ohio, gay counter cultural Central Ohio Gay Newsletter 1 (June 5, 1971): 1. Ohio Historical Society collection. This issue of the newsletter called for car pools of gay folks in Columbus to go to New York City to celebrate Christopher Street Liberation Day on June 27. It notes New York (and Chicago and L.A.) will celebrate and that New York is planning on 50,000 people. A phone number—464–0333—is given and interested people are asked to contact that number before June 23.
3. This analysis draws on my related scholarly project titled "Speaking with the Dead: Stonewall and the Forming of Gay Authorship." In that essay, I examine these early post-Stonewall texts in some detail: Mart Crowley, *Boys in the Band* (film) [1970] ; Phil Andros (Samuel Steward), *Roman Conquests* (pornographic novel) [1971/ 1983]; Rita Mae Brown, *Rubyfruit Jungle* [1973]; Christopher Larkin, director, *A Very Natural Thing* (film) [1973]; Patricia Nell Warren, *Frontrunner*, [1974]; Armistead Maupin, *Tales of the City* [1976 (1978)].
4. Jamie Harker draws similar conclusions in her erudite study of the 1950s reception in the U.S. of the work of Christopher Isherwood, who desired his writing to be twentieth century high modernist. He failed, not unlike Sam Steward; yet his work, also like Steward's, had immense positive effects on gay authorship when that work was taken up as popular culture (often as pulp) or what Harker calls "middlebrow" culture. See Harker's *Middlebrow Queer: Christopher Isherwood in America*.
5. The references to Stonewall begin in the periodic literature—countercultural newspapers and magazines within the year of the riot in June of 1969. Major books about gay life begin to refer to Stonewall in 1971 (see e.g., Altman and Murphy). One 1972 gay social guide refers not only to Stonewall and gay, but the emergence of gay authorship and gay literature in 1972 (Hunter). Finally, one of the first references to Stonewall in a novel is Warren's *The Frontrunner*, which was published in 1974. Warren in fact places the novel's main character Harlan at Stonewall and makes him a participant in the Stonewall Inn riots.

WORKS CITED

Altman, Dennis. *Homosexual: Oppression and Liberation*. NY: Avon, 1971.

Andros, Phil [a.k.a. Sam Steward] *Roman Conquests*. San Francisco: Perineum Press, 1983 (1971).

Bergman, David. *The Violet Hour*. New York: Columbia UP, 2004.

Bram, Christopher. *Exiles from America*. New York: Harper Collins, 2006.

———. *Eminent Outlaws: The Gay Writers Who Changed America*. New York: Hachette Book Group, 2012.

Brookes, Les. *Gay Male Fiction: Ideology, Conflict, and Aesthetics*. New York: Routledge, 2009.

Brown, Rita Mae. *Rubyfruit Jungle*. New York: Bantam, 1977 (1973).

Cardone, Tom. *The Lost Library: Gay Fiction Rediscovered*. New York: Haiduk Press, 2010.

Central Ohio Gay Newsletter 1 (June 5, 1971): 1. Ohio Historical Society Collection, Columbus.

Crew, Louie, ed. *The Gay Academic*. Palm Springs: ETC Publications, 1978.

———. with Ricktor Norton, eds. Special Issue: "The Homosexual Imagination." *College English* 36. (Nov. 1974).

Harker, Jaimie. *Middlebrow Queer: Christopjer Isherwood in America*. Minneapolis: U Minnesota P, 2013.

Holleran, Andrew. *Dancer from the Dance*. New York: Harper Perennial, 2001 (1978). *Ground Zero*. New York: William Morrow, 1988.

Hunter, John Francis. *The Gay Insider: USA*. NY: Stonehill, 1972.

Kramer, Larry. *Faggots*. New York: Warner Books, 1978.

Maupin, Armistead. *Tales of the City*. New York: Harper and Row, 1978.

———. *Michael Tolliver Lives!* New York: Harper Perennial, 2007.

Meyer, Christian, and Felix Girke (eds.) *The Rhetorical Emergence of Culture*. New York: Berghahn Books, 2011.

McGurl, Mark. *The Program Era: Postwar Fiction and the Rise of Creative Writing*. Cambridge: Harvard UP 2009.

Murphy, John. *Homosexual Liberation; A Personal View*. NY: Praeger, 1971.

Moore, Patrick. *Beyond Shame: Reclaiming the Abandoned History of Radical Gay Sexuality*. Boston:"Queer Nation Manifesto." ["I Hate Straights"], 1990. www.historyisaweapon.com/defcon1/queernation.html. January3,2013.

"Radicalesbians: The Woman-Identified Woman." "1970" In Schlager (ed.) *St. James Press Gay and Lesbian Almanac*. Detroit: St James Press, 1998: 70–72.

Rechy, John. *The Sexual Outlaw*. NewYork, Grove and Weidenfeld Press, 1977.

San Francisco/Bay Area Gay and Lesbian Serial Collection. A joint project of the San Francisco/Bay Area Gay and Lesbian Historical Society and the University of California Berkeley. Microform. 1966 to 1991. Special funding provided by the UC Shared Purchase Program, 1991.

Schlager, Neil (ed.) *St. James Press Gay and Lesbian Almanac*. Detroit: St James Press, 1998.

Spring, Justin. *Secret Historian: The Life and Times of Sam Steward, Professor, Tattoo Artist, and Sexual Renegade*. New York: Farrar, Straus, and Giroux, 2010.

———. *An Obscene Diary: The Visual World of Sam Steward*. Italy: Antinous P and Elysium P. 2010.

A Very Natural Thing. Dir. Christopher Larkin. 1973 Water Bearer 1999. Film.

Warren, Patricia Nell. *The Front Runner*. New York: Bantam, 1977 (1974).
Wittman, Carl. "Gay Manifesto 1969" [Refugees from Amerika]. In Schlager (ed.) *St. James Press Gay and Lesbian Almanac*. Detroit: St James Press, 1998: 67–70.
Zebroski, James T. "Rhetoric, Anti-Structure, and the Social Formation of Authorship." In Christian Meyer and Felix Girke (eds.) *The Rhetorical Emergence of Culture*. New York: Berghahn Books, 2011: 264–81.

8 The Sound of Silence
Defense of Marriage, Don't Ask, Don't Tell, and Post-Authorship Theory

Paul Butler

On June 26, 2013, Kristin Perry, one of the respondents in the landmark *Hollingsworth v. Perry* case, stood outside the United States Supreme Court Building and stated, "This is a great day for American families and children" (Perry). Her words captured not only the significance of the U. S. Supreme Court's ruling striking down California's Proposition 8, a state ballot initiative that defined marriage as a union exclusively between a man and a woman, but also the strategy of those who had initiated the case. On the same day, in the Windsor decision, the Supreme Court ruled part 3 of the Defense of Marriage Act (DOMA) unconstitutional. In a press conference after the ruling in her case, Edith Windsor, who had brought suit based on federal estate taxes levied due to the non-recognition of her same-sex marriage to her now-deceased partner, stated, "[The ruling] makes me feel incredibly proud and humble" (Windsor).

In an earlier but also highly significant appearance on *The Rachel Maddow Show* (TRMS), West Point graduate and Army linguist Lieutenant Dan Choi adopted a similar strategy in opposing the military's Don't Ask, Don't Tell (DADT) policy. Returning to speak about DADT after previously coming out publicly on TRMS, Choi emphasized the importance of honor for everyone in the military, including his fellow West Point graduates, and of doing the right thing in their roles: "Our group (of gay military officers) stands shoulder-to-shoulder with all of those soldiers that are serving their country selflessly" (Choi).

What is remarkable about the common response in these diverse examples is the nature of the discourse used by the individuals involved. In each instance, what seems crucial is what is *not* said, just as much as—and possibly more than—what *is* said. The successful Supreme Court decisions ruling Part 3 of the Defense of Marriage Act unconstitutional, and overturning California's Proposition 8, as well as the repeal of the U.S. government's Don't Ask, Don't Tell policy, suggest that the strategy has been a form of what composition scholar Cheryl Glenn describes as "silence, or the language of the powerless" (25). In effect, I argue that the gay community has co-opted the discourse of the dominant group (including words like "honor" and "marriage," for example) to achieve its stated objectives. In the process, as Glenn, French theorist Michel Foucault, and others have posited, there has been a subtle yet systematic way of subverting societal power, knowledge, and assimilation through discourse. As Foucault explains in *The Discourse on Language*, there are certain rules of exclusion that give some members of society a privileged right to speak on subjects like politics and sexuality. Foucault claims that these rules of exclusion can impose discursive limits in a way that denies access to some individuals: "We must conceive discourse as a violence that we do to things, or, at all events, as a practice we impose upon them" (229).

My argument, following Foucault and others, is that the outcomes attained in the Supreme Court cases and in the reversal of DADT emanate directly from a strategy used by the activists opposing them. The strategy is a result of these groups' finding a way to circumvent—and, in essence, to redirect or redeploy—the selective silencing that Glenn articulates in *Unspoken: A Rhetoric of Silence*, where she writes:

> The dominant group in a social hierarchy renders "inarticulate" subordinate or muted groups (any traditionally disenfranchised) and excludes them from the formulation, validation, and circulation of meaning. Thus, the inability to speak fluently in certain social interactions can indicate mutedness, and *silence itself becomes the language of the powerless.*
>
> (25; emphasis added)

In suggesting that subordinate groups can be effectively deprived of discourse, Glenn echoes the same disenfranchisement of the marginalized that Foucault does, and she goes on to delineate the cost of silence for them: "All language, then, is the language of the dominant order, and if they speak at all, subordinate groups must speak through ... 'double-voiced discourse,' a discourse that reflects and refracts the social, literary, and cultural heritages of both the dominant and muted groups" (28). Glenn's description postulates a kind of post-Orwellian double-speak, influenced by principles of Bakhtin's double-voiced discourse but emphasizing a subordinate group's ability to speak *only* through the refracted lens of someone else.

In light of the decisions on DOMA, California's Proposition 8, and Don't Ask, Don't Tell, then, an important question presents itself: How did these groups succeed? Given the collective silencing that took place with the enactment of DADT and DOMA statutes, how did these groups find a way to circumvent the dominant discourse they faced? I argue that the appropriation of dominant discourse renders the members of the community fighting these laws a *counterpublic*, that is, a form of oppositional public principally defined in tension with the larger public sphere. In her influential article, "Rethinking the Public Sphere," theorist Nancy Fraser defines counterpublics as "parallel discursive areas where members of subordinated social groups invent and circulate counterdiscourses, which in turn permit them to formulate oppositional interpretations of their identities, interests, and needs" (123). I contend that this Frasier-style counterpublic is precisely what groups opposing Proposition 8, DOMA, and DADT were able to enact.

An additional elaboration of Fraser's notion that subordinated groups circulate self-interested discourses in opposing a dominant public can be found in *Publics and Counterpublics*, where Michael Warner illuminates the importance of a counterpublic's knowledge of its role: "A counterpublic maintains at some level, conscious or not, an awareness of its subordinate status" (119). Hence, the groups that stood against DOMA, California's Proposition 8, and the DADT policy navigated in highly specific ways through the counterdiscourses that served their identities, interests, and needs. At the same time, however, they remained keenly aware of their subordinate status in attempting to make public arguments to effect change. In addition, as Warner suggests, counterpublics must circulate their counterdiscourses widely, mixing them with the discourses of dominant publics and interacting with audiences composed of strangers. He writes, "Fundamentally mediated by public forms, counterpublics incorporate the personal/impersonal address and expansive estrangement of public speech as conditions of their common world" (121).

In addition to these groups operating as counterpublics, I argue that the existence of their unique counterdiscourses produces a special, new type of authorship, a theory I am calling *post-authorship*. Briefly stated, post-authorship theory postulates that authorship emerges organically from a confluence of competing and often contested social factors, including the necessity of counterpublics seeking ways to navigate their own silencing. In his influential essay "The Death of the Author," Roland Barthes anticipates post-authorship theory when he writes, "A text is not a line of words releasing a single 'theological' meaning (the 'message' of the Author-God) but a multi-dimensional space in which a variety of writings, none of them original, blend and clash" (146). Barthes's understanding anticipates post-authorship theory in signaling that the potential influence of a text depends on its mixture with other texts and on how it is received and redeployed by its audiences. In the case of DOMA, DADT, and Proposition 8, dominant texts were managed by subordinated groups: reintroduced to various publics and renegotiated by them, ultimately resulting in the reversal of the laws and regulations in question.

Indeed, post-authorship theory suggests not only that discourse is ultimately not in the control of its original authors but that a discourse like DOMA or DADT, designed to control others, necessarily blends dominant discourses and counterdiscourses to arrive at its meaning, drawing from multiple writings and audiences. Barthes anticipates this idea when he says, "[The writer's] only power is to mix writings, to counter the ones with the others, in such a way as to never rest on any one of them" (146). This is effectively the lesson marginalized groups have internalized. Thus the very nature of post-authorship theory includes the idea of *silence speaking*, that is, blending, along with more dominant voices, the collective voices of the disenfranchised—all of those whose discourse has been suppressed or subordinated. Glenn states that "silence itself becomes the language of the powerless"; post-authorship theory redefines silence, giving it agency and showing how silence is not really silent at all but works underground, sometimes surreptitiously, to affect change in discourse and culture.

Post-authorship theory also complicates the thinking of Foucault, who explains that the control of discourse often consists of "determining the conditions under which it may be employed, of imposing a certain number of rules on those individuals who employ it, *thus denying access to everyone else*" (*Discourse* 224; emphasis added). While what Foucault says is true, at least on the surface, post-authorship theory implies that discourse ultimately cannot be denied or silenced. Rather, I contend that post-authorship theory can offer members of some marginalized communities access to language and, ultimately, to full participation in society. The idea of post-authorship suggests that silence ultimately finds a way to speak, which is what happened with the Defense of Marriage Act, California's Proposition 8, and the military's former Don't Ask, Don't Tell policy, in which subordinated voices ultimately won widespread acceptance in public discourse.

DON'T ASK, DON'T TELL

To give an example of this counterpublic dexterity and of the sound of silence, it is instructive to look at a few comments from the U.S. Department of Defense's "Report of the Comprehensive Review of the Issues Associated with a Repeal of 'Don't Ask, Don't Tell.'" Some comments, reported in *The Washington Post*, are from those who opposed the repeal, including a soldier who stated: "I cannot rely on someone who I don't feel comfortable with, nor can they trust me. A lack of trust turns into a lack of cohesion, which eventually leads to mission failure" (Somashekhar). On the other hand, the LGBT organization, "Knights Out," formed to offer gay service personnel support for their sexuality, was careful, and disciplined, in the way it used language to counter these sentiments and to help bring about an end to the Don't Ask, Don't Tell policy. Former Army lieutenant Brenda Fulton cites the following text published in the Knights Out newsletter: "Don't Ask compromises unit cohesion. Forcing soldiers to lie about who they are, and who their families are, tears down trust, and erodes the bonds that make military units strong" (221). The Knights language is similar to the dominant discourse of repeal opponents and includes some of the same words (e.g., "unit cohesion" and "trust") as well as associated words like "bonds," "strong," and "families," with their broad resonances. The language reflects an obvious effort to co-opt dominant discourse to serve the ends of a subordinate group.

Opponents of repeal also resisted that outcome by trying to make the issue about gay equality and identity. One opponent stated, "How far are we going to go with this whole gay thing? Am I supposed to celebrate gayness—do they get to wear a rainbow flag on their uniform? If that is the case, this uniform isn't worth wearing" (Somashekhar). By contrast, news releases from Knights Out made it clear that the discourse of equality, as used above by opponents of DADT repeal, was not controlling. Instead, the Knights Out group directly addressed DADT by using words like "honor," "duty," and "military code": "Integrity and honor are, and should be, central to our military code. The Don't Ask, Don't Tell policy forces soldiers to choose between their honor and their military duty." Indeed, by appropriating the discourse of the dominant group, the Knights Out organization "speaks" volumes; its self-silencing on issues of fairness and equality is, in effect, a defining form of its discourse.

Another noticeable strategy used by those seeking repeal of DADT is based on the discourse of national security and military readiness. The following blog post about gay linguist Dan Choi, "Obama to Fire His First Gay Arabic Linguist," by college professor, activist, and author Aaron Belkin, appears on *The Huffington Post*: "I spent a day with Dan Choi last month, and he is not someone we want to fire from the military. He loves the armed forces. He served bravely under tough combat conditions in Iraq. His Arabic is excellent, and he used his language skills to defuse many tough situations and to save lives, both Iraqi and American." In this excerpt, as in much of the discourse put forth by proponents of the repeal, there is an emphasis on issues of *national security* and *military readiness* revealed in words such as "bravely," "tough combat conditions," and "excellent Arabic." Indeed, the military establishment itself adopted discourse about the DADT policy harming "institutional integrity" and, as *Unfriendly Fire* author Nathaniel Frank, writing in *The New Republic*, emphasized with respect to military readiness, "[T]he current policy hinders gays and lesbians from accessing the support services that are critical to morale and readiness because they can't speak openly to chaplains, doctors, or psychologists without fearing reprisal." It is clear that discourses supportive of military goals are used to appeal to broad audiences, diminishing issues of sexuality, equality, identity, and diversity.

Other examples reveal similar strategies at work. For instance, the Human Rights Campaign, a leading national gay rights organization, launched the "Voices of Honor Tour" with former gay Army linguist Jarrod Chlapowski, once again appropriating dominant discourse ("honor") while hinting at a distinctly new connotation for the word. A *The New York Times* editorial, in the aftermath of President Obama's 2010 State of the Union Address in which he promised to repeal DADT, read: "Gay people serve openly and effectively in the armies of Britain, Israel, Australia and Canada," broadening the global nature of the policy and emphasizing its pragmatic aspects. Even though the explicit specter of equal rights is absent, however, issues of fairness and equality always lie just beneath the surface, pushing the argument forward in unexpected ways.

The strategy adopted by counterpublics and, in some instances, by their dominant group counterparts, proved successful. As the final compromise bill that led to the repeal of the DADT statute made its way through Congress, according to Nathaniel Frank, lawmakers "dropped the nondiscrimination language that the legislation had contained since it was first introduced in 2005" (*Unfriendly* 194). What's more, in a 2010 district court decision ruling the Don't Ask Don't Tell statute unconstitutional, the judge wrote that "The Act not only is unnecessary to further unit cohesion, but also harms the Government's interest [by] impeding the efforts to recruit and retain an all-volunteer military force" and "by causing the discharge of otherwise qualified service members with critical skills" (*Log Cabin Republicans v USA and Robert M. Gates, Secretary of Defense*). Here, it is clear that the reconstituted dominant discourse has been widely adopted by everyone involved in repealing the policy. Once the Pentagon report on repeal was issued, even President Obama, echoing the discourse of both dominant and counterpublic groups, stated, "[The report] confirms that, by every measure—from unit cohesion to recruitment and retention to family readiness—we can transition to a new policy in a responsible manner that ensures our military strength and national security."

The repeal of the U.S. military's Don't Ask, Don't Tell policy is a firsthand example of the way counterpublic discourse interacts with dominant discourse to change the nature of the discussion and, ultimately, to reshape public policy. It shows the unique way in which counterdiscourses, borrowing from dominant discourses, are used in contexts that reconfigure the very nature of a public debate. They are appropriated, as Frasier suggests, to meet a counterpublic's interests, values, and needs. They represent a rethinking of dominant discourses based on a group's subordinate status. Even more important, however, is the way in which the discourse emanates from apparent silencing, confirming what I have called the theory of post-authorship. By accepting the silencing of certain aspects of language or discourse, counterpublics are able to make their voices heard in the public sphere. The groups—deploying both subordinate and, arguably, more dominant discourses (e.g., *The New York Times*) that agree with the subordinated voices—make silence speak. They are the hallmark of post-authorship theory.

CALIFORNIA'S PROPOSITION 8

The discourse surrounding the campaign for—and ultimate passage of—Proposition 8, the initiative invalidating marriage between same-sex couples in California, shows the way dominant discourse can sometimes be counterproductive when deployed by members of a dominant group. Indeed, some of the tactics used by straight allies of LGBT groups may reveal another unexpected element of counterpublic discourse: it can turn out to be more successful than the dominant discourses used by dominant groups. For example, in the aftermath of a commercial based on his speech about Proposition 8 and on what he considered the inevitability of gay marriage, former San Francisco Mayor Gavin Newsome stated, "This door's wide open now. It's going to happen, whether you like it or not." After the commercial appeared on television, polls showed support widening in favor of the anti-gay-marriage Proposition 8.

In a similar move, then-California Attorney General Jerry Brown changed the title and wording of the initiative, originally titled the "California Marriage Protection Act," to read "Eliminates Rights of Same-Sex Couples to Marry. Initiative Constitutional Amendment," and the ballot summary stated, "Changes the California Constitution to eliminate the right of same-sex couples to marry in California." The wording not only adopted the language of equal rights but challenged the discourse of the majority ("Eliminates Rights") by focusing on the change to the California Constitution. While the discourse surrounding the Don't Ask, Don't Tell initiative showed both dominant and counterdiscourses using a form of dominant discourse that yielded productive results, with California's Proposition 8, we see virtually the opposite happening—ultimately resulting in a far less salutary outcome.

With respect to Proposition 8, supportive heterosexual groups in the fight against the measure used language assiduously avoided by their counterpublic colleagues, that is, members of the gay and lesbian community. In this instance, the dominant discourse amounted to a challenge to the values and assumptions put forth by Proposition 8 supporters. Instead of using the type of counterdiscourses that might resonate with others, especially those ostensibly straight voters who might have been persuaded to oppose Proposition 8 the language attempts to apply majority discourse *against* the majority. It does so by using metaphors of battle (e.g., "the door's wide open"; "It's going to happen, whether you like it or not") and words emphasizing the language of equal rights (e.g., "Eliminates Rights of Same-Sex Couples to Marry"), highlighting what proponents of the measure were trying to take away. Despite the failure of a subsequent court challenge led by Proposition 8, proponents who argued the new language was "so inflammatory that it will unduly prejudice voters against the measure," I submit that the lack of counterpublic discourse is likely part of what led to Proposition 8's ultimate passage. In other words, the anti-gay marriage initiative arguably won because of its failure to incorporate counterdiscourse strategies prior to the general election.

On appeal, the U.S. Supreme Court's decision in *Hollingsworth v. Perry*, which upheld a federal district court's overturning of Proposition 8, was decided on the basis of standing, a procedural argument having to do with the rights of certain parties to appear in court, rather than the merits of the argument itself. Despite the basis of the Court's decision, it is instructive to turn to amicus briefs filed in the case to get a sense of the strategies various groups used consistent with counterpublic discourse and postauthorship theory. First, it is important to acknowledge that many amicus briefs—in line with the federal district court's decision—did, in fact, rely on equality, due process, diversity, or fairness as the principal basis of their argument. However, it is equally significant that several amicus briefs relied on alternative approaches.

One of the *amici curiae*, for example, comes from social conservatives, who state that they hold a "broad spectrum of socially and politically conservative, moderate, and libertarian views" (Mehlman, et al. 2). Their brief opposing Proposition 8 and supporting gay marriage states that "when the government does act in ways that affect individual freedom in matters of family and child-rearing, it should promote family-supportive values like responsibility, fidelity, commitment, and stability" (2). What seems instructive in this instance is the brief's borrowing from discourse identical to that opposing same-sex marriage. Hence, using terms like "family-supportive values" and "child-rearing," when combined with the connotations of abstract nouns like "responsibility," "fidelity," and "commitment," produces a specific effect. As Warner suggests, "The address of public speech is both personal and impersonal" (76), highlighting the importance of counterdiscourses that address multiple, and sometimes unintended, publics. Warner argues that speech or discourse is important not when it focuses on identity but when it is intended to reach strangers belonging to various publics or groups:

> With public speech ... we might recognize ourselves as addressees but it is equally important that we remember that the speech was addressed to indefinite others, that in singling us out it does so not on the basis of our concrete identity but by virtue of our participation in the discourse alone and therefore in common with strangers. (77–78)

Warner's comments about the nature of persuasive public speech are reflected in the discourse of the nonprofit, volunteer group Marriage Equality USA, which is committed, according to the amicus brief it filed in the *Hollingsworth* case, to leading "nonpartisan, community-based educational efforts to secure the freedom to marry for all loving, committed couples without regard to sexual orientation or gender identity" (1). Marriage Equality USA states its argument, in part, as follows:

> Millions of lesbian and gay Americans share the same hopes and dreams of other Americans, including finding a special person to marry, building a family and life together, and growing old with each other. When gay people find that special person, they want to have the same freedom to be able to stand before their friends and family and vow to be there for one another for better or for worse, in sickness and in health, and to love, honor, and cherish for always. Like other loving and committed couples, same-sex couples seek the opportunity to fulfill their dreams and make a lifetime commitment in marriage. (2)

Here, Marriage Equality USA suggests that its discourse is "addressed to indefinite others," in Warner's words, and that it seeks to persuade, as Warner says, "not on the basis of our concrete identity but by virtue of our participation in the discourse alone and therefore in common with strangers" (78). When groups like Marriage Equality USA base their argument on a traditional discourse of marriage and family values, anchored in the discourse of freedom, it seems that identity arguments have been relegated to the background. Indeed, the dominant strategies used by opponents of Proposition 8, without regard to broader groups of strangers, failed at the initiative level. Perhaps that is why the sound of silence, expressed as the adoption of a mixed discourse in some of the amicus briefs, appears there as an alternative strategy.

DOMA

The decision in *United States v. Windsor*, which ruled unconstitutional section 3 of the Defense of Marriage Act, is based on the Fifth Amendment's equal protection and due process clauses. Before it was struck down by the Court, section 3 of DOMA defined marriage as "only a legal union between one man and one woman as husband and wife, and the word 'spouse' refers only to a person of the opposite sex who is a husband or a wife." What is remarkable in the Court overturning Section 3 of DOMA is the way in which Justice Anthony Kennedy's majority opinion, based on the constitutional ideals of equal protection, nonetheless eschews language of equality or equal protection and instead adopts a discourse based on principles of deference to states' sovereignty, the institution of marriage, and the "dignity," "protection," and "freedom and choice" accompanying that institution. In *Windsor*, Kennedy states the reason for the statute's lack of constitutionality: "DOMA rejects the long-established precept that the incidents, benefits, and obligations of marriage are uniform for all married couples within each State, though they may vary, subject to constitutional guarantees, from one State to the next" (18).

Here, Kennedy relies on the discourse of a dominant public, that is, the public that has embraced the institution of marriage. While DOMA sought to highlight the differences between traditional and same-sex marriage, Kennedy chooses to erase those differences by focusing on words that define the institution through a common discourse. He tries to bring same-sex marriage and traditional marriage closer together first by saying they both involve "benefits" and "responsibilities" and then by depicting the way DOMA treats same-sex marriage as unusual (note his use of the word "deviation" in the following): "DOMA's unusual *deviation* from the usual tradition of recognizing and accepting state definitions of marriage here operates to deprive same-sex couples of the benefits and responsibilities that come with the federal recognition of their marriage" (20; emphasis added).

In analyzing how discourse was used to achieve specific effects in *Windsor*, it is useful to turn to Warner, who states that a public is "the social space created by the reflexive circulation of discourse" (90). The idea that the "public" the *Windsor* decision addresses emerges from a confluence of circulating discourses becomes clear when Warner writes:

> No single text can create a public. Nor can a single voice, a single genre, even a single medium. All are insufficient to create the kind of reflexivity that we call a public, since a public is understood to be an ongoing space of encounter for discourse. No texts themselves create publics, but the concatenation of texts through time. (90)

The idea that discourse circulates reflexively is echoed in Fraser, Foucault, Glenn, and others. What seems clear is that *Windsor* is a result of what Warner calls the concatenation of texts through time. It comes from various discourses circulating, pushing against one other, and constructing the text of the Court's opinion. Along the way, the discourse becomes, as Warner suggests, a "social space" that includes multiple encounters with dominant and counterdiscourses.

What is also striking here is that this very notion of discourse is anticipated in Barthes's "The Death of the Author," where he states that the writer's "only power is to mix writings, to counter the ones with the others, in such a way as to never rest on any one of them" (146). Barthes suggests a true flexibility, which manifests itself in the *Windsor* decision through the use of discourses that draw on past writing, such as the landmark decision in *Lawrence v. Texas*, quoted in the *Windsor* case, when the Court writes, "Private, consensual sexual intimacy between two adult persons of the same sex may not be punished by the State, and it can form '*but one element in a personal bond that is more enduring*'" (19, emphasis added). It seems clear that the decision refers to a mix of past and present discourses that circulate and mix, rather than a single, omnipotent discourse. The shift shows how unnamed, silent, even "underground" counterdiscourses work together to shape what ultimately emerges.

CONCLUSION

As Foucault, Glenn, and others have shown, discourse can be used to marginalize members of alternative, minority, or otherwise subordinated communities. The result can be the exclusion of these individuals from full participation in language and culture. In that regard, Foucault and Glenn point out the exclusionary power of silence—and silencing. While silence can be seen in the apparent invisibility of counterpublics and counterdiscourses, however, I contend there is another side to examine. Discourses that seem to go unnoticed can have a substantial impact, and evidence for that assertion can be found in the repeal of Don't Ask, Don't Tell, in the overturning of California's Proposition 8 in the *Hollingsworth* case, and of section 3 of the Defense of Marriage Act in the *Windsor* decision. I argue that the discussion of laws against same-sex marriage and the former DADT policy are not being seen for all they signify. I suggest that the real debate is one about discourse and the way it has been co-opted by marginalized groups to achieve specific aims. Thus, while Foucault says that "none may enter into discourse on a specific subject unless he has satisfied certain conditions or if he is not, from the outset, qualified to do so" (224–25), this apparent restriction comes with important caveats.

When Foucault says that "not all areas of discourse are equally open and penetrable; some are forbidden territory" (225), the evidence suggests that may be true. However, the actions of counterpublics favoring same-sex marriage and a repeal of Don't Ask, Don't Tell show that groups and individuals have found a way to make incursions into this forbidden territory. The groups have circumvented what amounts to a kind of disenfranchisement by essentially redeploying the discourse of dominant groups. It is important to note that this strategy is different from those attempted in the past by marginalized groups. Historically, for instance, the gay community drew attention to itself by empowering discourse; specifically, words like "invert," "queer," and "AIDS" became not only a form of identity, but a call to action, a display of solidarity against an attempt to silence. During the AIDS crisis, groups like ACT-UP (the AIDS Coalition to Unleash Power) took actions that called attention to the difference, identity, and lack of equality of members of the gay community.

The actions taken to reverse Proposition 8 and DOMA and to repeal the DADT policy show a new strategy at work. Instead of adopting the pejorative terms used to label them as subordinate (e.g., "invert") or of proclaiming their difference and unequal treatment through confrontational activism (e.g., ACT-UP) the gay community chose a strategy of inclusion and assimilation. By co-opting the discourse of the dominant group, and making that discourse its own, the community emphasized similarities in values and lifestyles and the shared ideals that unite rather than separate groups and individuals. At the heart of this strategy, however, there are still differences and opposition. The process of transforming a clash of ideas into a discourse shared by opposing groups is what I have called post-authorship theory. The concept implies a blending of dominant publics and counterpublics, of discourses and counterdiscourses, and, in the words of Roland Barthes, of "mix[ing] writings, to counter the ones with the others" (146).

The successful strategies used by marginalized groups seeking to repeal DADT and to overturn Proposition 8 and DOMA may represent a perfect example of *kairos* at work. Indeed, the outcomes show these groups took advantage of opportune moments and measures to achieve their ends. Perhaps the real question going forward, however, lies in how to give new significations to discourse, so that the limitations faced by counterpublics are brought to the surface and exposed, allowing inclusive new meanings to emerge. While the groups involved here may have found a way to let silence speak, what would it mean if it were not necessary to overcome silence in the first place?

WORKS CITED

Bakhtin, M. M. *The Dialogic Imagination*. Michael Holquist (ed.) Trans. Caryl Emerson and Michael Holquist. Austin: U of Texas P, 1981.
Barthes, Roland. "The Death of the Author." *Image-Music-Text*. Stephen Heath (Ed. and trans.) New York: Hill and Wang, 1977: 142–48.
Belkin, Aaron. "Obama To Fire His First Gay Arabic Linguist." *Huffington Post* 7 June 2009. Web. 14 July 2014.
Brief for Marriage Equality USA as Amicus Curiae. Hollingsworth v. Perry. 570 U.S.
———. 133 S.Ct. 2652. Supreme Court of the US. 2013. Web. 12 July 2014.
Brief for Mehlman, et al. as Amicus Curiae. Hollingsworth v. Perry. 570 U.S.
———. 133 S.Ct. 2652. Supreme Court of the US. 2013. Web. 12 July 2014.
Choi, Dan. *The Rachel Maddow Show*. MSNBC. YouTube 20 Mar. 2009. Web. 15 March 2012.
Defense of Marriage Act. 110 Stat. 2419. 28 U.S.C. § 1738C. 104th U.S. Congress. 1996.
Department of Defense. "Report of the Comprehensive Review of the Issues Associated with a Repeal of 'Don't Ask, Don't Tell.'" 30 Nov. 2010. Web. 10 Dec. 2014.
"Don't Ask, Don't Tell." Pub.L. 103–160. 10 U.S.C. § 654. 1993.
"Ending 'Don't Ask, Don't Tell.'" Editorial. *New York Times* 28 Jan. 2010. Web. 17 June 2012.
Foucault, Michel. *The Archaeology of Knowledge and the Discourse on Language*. Trans. A.M. Sheridan Smith. New York: Pantheon, 1972.
Frank, Nathaniel. "Battle Lines." *The New Republic*. 12 May 2009. Web. 9 June 2013.
———. *Unfriendly Fire: How the Gay Ban Undermines the Military and Weakens America*. New York: St. Martin's Griffin/Thomas Dunne, 2009.
Frasier, Nancy. "Rethinking the Public Sphere: A Contribution to the Critique of Actually Existing Democracy." *Social Text* 25/26 (1990): 56–80.
Fulton, Brenda Sue. "Outserve: An Underground Network Stands Up." *Journal of Homosexuality* 60 (2013): 219–31.
Glenn, Cheryl. *Unspoken: A Rhetoric of Silence*. Carbondale: Southern Illinois UP, 2004.
Hollingsworth v. Perry. 570 U.S.
———. 133 S.Ct. 2652. Supreme Court of the US. 2013. Web. 12 July 2014.
Lawrence v. Texas. 539 US 558. Supreme Court of the US. 2003.
Log Cabin Republicans v. United States. 658 F.3d 1162 (9th Cir. 2011). Supreme Court of the US. 2011.
Perry, Kristin. "Scotusblog on Camera: Decision Day (26 Jun 13) Perry, et al." Online video clip. *YouTube*. YouTube, 26 June 2013. Web. 7 Sept. 2013.
Proposition 8. CA Const. Art. 1, § 7.5. 2008.
Somashekhar, Sandhya. "Voices from the 'Don't Ask, Don't Tell' Report of Troops Who Oppose Repeal." *Washington Post* 30 Sept. 2010. Web. 14 Aug. 2014.

United States v. Windsor. 570 U.S.
———. 133 S.Ct. 2675; 186 L.Ed.2d 808. Supreme Court of the US. 2013. Web. 12 July 2014.
Warner, Michael. *Publics and Counterpublics*. New York: Zone, 2005.
Windsor, Edith. "Watch Edith Windsor's Remarks on DOMA Ruling." Online video clip. *PBS Newshour*. YouTube, 26 June 2013. Web. 7 Sept. 2013.

9 The Emotional Contests of Peer Review

Amy E. Robillard

> Peers monitor the flow of people and ideas through the various gates of the academic community.
>
> Michèle Lamont, *How Professors Think*

"The biggest problem with this manuscript, which has nearly sucked the will to live out of me, is the terrible writing style." In this anonymous comment addressed to the author of an article under consideration at the journal *Environmental Microbiology* and reproduced under the heading "Jeer Review" in the May, 2011, issue of *Harper's Magazine*, we first notice, of course, the liberty afforded by anonymity in the double-blind peer review process. Most of us could only write such a scathing comment secure in the knowledge that our identity would never be revealed. Indeed, in the scholarly literature on peer review, the most pressing critique of the double-blind process is the incivility that such anonymity seems to encourage (Selfe and Hawisher; Souder; Wheeler). In this chapter, I want to suggest that perhaps what we've come to recognize as incivility in anonymous peer review is the effect of a more complicated emotional logic predicated on the relative lack of formal structures by which the work of a peer reviewer is recognized as the work of writing. I am not arguing that this lack of recognition is the only or even the primary cause of incivility in anonymous peer review; indeed, scholars have pointed to a number of possible reasons for uncivil critiques such as rivalry; friendship; prestige of author, author's institution, or recognizable name; ideological, methodological, or aesthetic bias (Weller; Shatz). My focus on the relative lack of recognition afforded reviewers is designed to point to a problem that is frequently mentioned (see below) but rarely theorized as a potential impulse for contesting others' authorship.

I want to call attention to two closely related forms of contested authorship at work in the peer review process. Because peer reviewers themselves are denied recognition for their work as the work of writing, their authorship is denied. This is the first form of contested authorship and leads to the second, the denial of authorship of those whose work the reviewer rejects. I want to suggest that the incivility with which we are all familiar is a result of the first and a symptom of the second. A result of both forms of contested authorship is a dearth of disciplinary knowledge about the work of reviewing as *writing*, and I think this is because the peer review process elides what Stuart P. Green calls the norm of attribution.

In his article, "Plagiarism, Norms, and the Limits of Theft Law," legal scholar Stuart P. Green explains that the norm of attribution begins from

> the proposition that people generally value the esteem of others, particularly their peers. Among the ways one can earn the esteem of one's peers is by being recognized for one's originality, creativity, insight, knowledge and technical skill. This is particularly so among writers, artists, and scholars, who, in addition to achieving satisfaction through the creative act itself, generally wish to see those acts recognized by others. (174)

The norm of attribution, then, is a result of this desire for the esteem of others, a practice we internalize as we write and as we read, as we cite the work of others. "Words and ideas may be copied if and only if the copier attributes them to their original author," according to this norm (174). One who refuses the norm of attribution is most often characterized as a plagiarist, and Green makes a convincing case that what a plagiarist "steals," if he or she steals anything, is *credit* rather than words or ideas. And the deprivation of credit is "permanent and ongoing" (222). In "Pass It On: Revising the *Plagiarism is Theft* Metaphor," I drew on Green's work to suggest that a reconceptualization of plagiarism as the theft not of words and ideas but of *credit* could move us closer to an understanding of citation as a metaphorical *passing on* to others. In this chapter, though, I want to zero in on Green's dual points that "people generally value the esteem of others, particularly their peers" and that the deprivation of credit when an author is not given recognition is "permanent and ongoing." These two points play an important part in my argument that the lack of recognition afforded peer reviewers is a contributing factor that drives them (us) to deny would-be authors the recognition that comes with being published. For until the peer reviewers have their say, it is not quite as simple as Green makes it out to be when he writes that "An author offers her work to the world by publishing it in a book or magazine" (218). At least it's not so simple in the world of scholarly publishing.

Beth Mole, in her *Chronicle of Higher Education* piece, "The Future of Peer Review in the Humanities is Wide Open," characterizes peer review as a "crucial yet thankless task," echoing Gail Hawisher and Cynthia Selfe's observation about the "general lack of professional recognition for this labor in systems of tenure review" (682). In his article, "Peer Review: Recent Experience and Future Directions," Mark Ware suggests that "recognition for peer reviewers appears something of a two-edged sword," pointing to reviewers' simultaneous desire to receive recognition for their work and to remain anonymous to the manuscript's author (28). As an editor herself, Bonnie Wheeler confesses to feeling "chagrin tinged with guilt when I request double-anonymous peer reviews, knowing that the reviewer will rarely be credited, either in print or in profit, for a penetrating, helpful review." Additionally, Wheeler notes that reviewers themselves are increasingly unwilling to "provide peer review, precisely because it is 'unrewarded activity'" (314). Lawrence Souder makes the same point, noting that "since referees are unpaid volunteers, their only practical reward is a mark for service in tenure and promotion procedures. However, if peer review is anonymous, even this reward is not available" (63). Souder also suggests that "stakeholders of peer-review systems ... should not be miserly" (57); Robin Derricourt characterizes peer reviewers as "those scholars who are motivated to keep abreast of their field by reading and adjudging new work before it is published" (138). Ware notes that self-reports by peer reviewers indicate that they engage in this unrecognized labor "because they appreciate the benefits they receive as authors" and are motivated by "being able to see work ahead of publication" (27); it is clear that the norm of attribution leaves its mark not only on work that has been published, but also on work that goes on behind the scenes. Peer reviewers, like any other writers, crave the esteem of others. As Michèle Lamont explains in *How Professsors Think*, scholars are often interested in performing their work in "contexts where they can be appreciated, that is, where they can sustain—and ideally, enhance—their identities as highly respected experts whose opinions matter" (5).

This desire for the esteem of others should be understood as crucial, for recognition in the form of credit or attribution constitutes a significant means—if not *the* means—by which authors maintain their identities as authors. Indeed, Green acknowledges as much when he acknowledges that citation of one's work

> can contribute, directly or indirectly, not only to psychic rewards (the satisfaction that comes from being esteemed by one's peers) but also to monetary rewards, including grants and scholarships, tenure and promotion, and other forms of career advancement and compensation. One who is denied the recognition to which he is entitled suffers a potentially serious harm. Indeed, it may be helpful to think of plagiarism as, in some sense, the flip side of defamation. Whereas defamation involves damage to a person's reputation through some affirmative act (a defamatory statement), plagiarism involves damage to a person's reputation through an omission (namely, the failure to attribute). (188–9)

What Green refers to as a "potentially serious harm" I would characterize instead as a fundamental, identity-threatening harm. For those who form their identities primarily as academic authors, the lack of recognition stemming from any kind of lack of attribution can be traumatic. In his article, "Healing Trauma, Preventing Violence: A Radical Agenda for Literary Study," Mark Bracher draws on the work of Heinz Lichtenstein to argue that "maintaining one's identity is the most basic human need and thus the deep motive underlying all human behavior," (519) and on Erik

Erikson to assert that recognition "is the single most important factor in the construction and maintenance of identity" (520). Bracher cites Todorov to articulate the singular importance of recognition as a motivation in itself: "there is no price we are not prepared to pay to obtain it ... The need to be acknowledged is not just one human motivation among others; it is the truth behind all other needs" (qtd. in Bracher 520). When we abide by the social norm of attribution as authors, we attach our name to a piece with the understanding that those who draw from it will acknowledge our labor by giving us credit. Likewise, when we abide by the social norm of attribution when drawing on the work of others, we do so not—as so many undergraduate students have been taught—to protect ourselves from charges of plagiarism, but rather to give recognition to authors whose work informs our own. But the anonymous peer review process, with its relative lack of institutional recognition for peer reviewers, cannot abide by the social norm of attribution. Peer reviewers must seek recognition for their writing in other ways.

To maintain her sense of identity as an author with the credentials to recommend for or against the publication of an anonymous manuscript, the peer reviewer, I want to suggest, works to assert her ability to recognize good scholarship when she sees it. A reviewer who can recognize good scholarship[1] knows how to

Identify the extent to which an author situates her work within a larger scholarly conversation, citing the right work in ways that demonstrate not just that she is part of the field but that she respects the work that came before her.

> *Positive:* I think the author's familiarity with and effort to acknowledge previous scholarship on the subject so as to contextualize his/her argument is the greatest strength of the article. (Recommendation: reject)
>
> *Negative:* This essay is written with no acknowledgement of the considerable dialogue on the subject in contemporary professional literature, which further encrypts the piece as a what-I-did-in-my-class rather than as a voice in the ongoing dialogue by writers, teachers, critics. (Recommendation: reject)

Identify an argument that makes a contribution to existing scholarship.

> *Positive:* Although scholarly citation is integral to our work as publishing writers, we haven't had much critical discourse on citing students' writing. The author makes us think critically about how we cite students' writing. (Recommendation: accept)

> *Negative:* Surely, as a profession, we have more to contribute to contemporary thinking about plagiarism than saying that it generates feelings of anger, guilt, and shame. (Recommendation: reject)

Determine the extent to which a manuscript will appeal to non-specialists.

> *Positive:* Several features of the essay will make it accessible to non-specialist readers: its distinctive voice, its smooth sentence structure, and its accessible diction—all of which are particularly consistent with the essays' subject. To say that the essay is "easy to read" does not mean it lacks rigor; indeed, one strength of the piece in terms of the *College English* audience is that the essay tackles difficult topics in an engaging style. (Recommendation: accept)
>
> *Negative:* Even as I enjoyed this piece, however, I couldn't help but question its overall relevance for *JAC*'s more general readership. (Recommendation: accept)

Recognize good writing.

> *Positive:* Both times [I read this article] I found the essay's argument to be intriguing and its prose invitingly crisp. (Recommendation: accept)
>
> *Negative:* p.5: At the top of this page, things were starting to get a little predictable. (Recommendation: reject)

Identify problems with the argument and offer suggestions for improvement.

> *Positive:* I think these particular choices would seem less arbitrary if we understood from the beginning the specific value each one provided for discussion of this topic. In fact, I suspect an opening discussion of this kind would be more effective than immediate reference to Gilmore. (Recommendation: accept)
>
> *Negative:* Do you listen to what you are saying? Where's your voice? (Recommendation: reject)

At the same time that a peer reviewer's ability to recognize these standard scholarly moves reinforces her own identity as a scholar who knows good work when she sees it, responses like these, even when particularly negative, affirm the would-be scholar's identity as a writer who knows something about the kinds of moves she is expected to make.

When the peer reviewer feels—consciously or unconsciously—that her identity as a scholar who knows a few things about the work of her field is threatened by a manuscript's claims, I want to suggest that one way she works to re-establish her disciplinary identity is by calling attention to the manuscript's faults in ways that refuse recognition and, as such, esteem. James Gilligan, in *Violence: Reflections on a National Epidemic*, argues that "Crime and punishment are reciprocal systems for the symbolic exchange of honor and shame. The currency of these emotional, symbolic, and violent exchanges is the currency of honor and shame" (144). And while I am not suggesting that the system of anonymous peer review is akin to the system of crime and punishment in the most obvious ways that would then categorize writers and reviewers as criminals, I do believe that the system functions as a means of symbolic exchange of acknowledgement and shame. In her editorial letter to me regarding an article's acceptance in *JAC*, Lynn Worsham writes, "I tend to think that recognition is our most basic value and social need, which makes the act of withholding recognition a powerful strategy for damaging social bonds, for regulating the distribution of esteem" (1). And in her study of peer review, Lamont writes that peers "determine the allocation of scarce resources, whether these be prestige and honors, fellowships and grants to support research, tenured positions that provide identifiable status and job security, or access to high-status publications" (2). Peer review is a process by which the distribution of resources that contribute to esteem is regulated, and this regulation is, I suggest, one way by which peer reviewers maintain their identities as authors.

On top of the already minimal recognition afforded peer reviewers by institutional means, the threat to one's disciplinary identity from an unknown author prompts a reliance on what I'll call recognition-seeking criteria for publishable work. The peer reviewer judges a manuscript based on the extent to which it

Matches the peer reviewer's current preoccupations. In response to a manuscript analyzing the rhetorical work of angry responses to plagiarism, a reviewer writes:

> How has technology both made it easier to plagiarize and easier to detect plagiarism? Is this a sign that technology is changing the very nature of writing? (Recommendation: reject)

Matches the peer reviewer's experience. In response to a manuscript analyzing the *plagiarism is theft* metaphor, a reviewer writes:

> As an aside, I suspect that there are many writing teachers out there—and I count myself among them—who do indeed contextualize the issue of plagiarism, not by proposing that their students are criminals, but rather by stressing the value of citation for readers wishing to know more about the topic. (Recommendation: reject)

In addition to employing such recognition-seeking criteria, peer reviewers may respond to a manuscript in much harsher ways that could easily be characterized as arrogant, superior, and self-important. There is one review that I've received that fits this description, remarking that its writer read my paper with "mounting annoyance." In response to an essay exploring the value of teaching the personal essay in a writing course, the reviewer goes far beyond the standard scholarly criteria to the point of dripping sarcasm. For instance, the reviewer writes, "What do you mean by 'the personal essay. ... teaches us how to live?' Are you using Strayed's[2] promiscuous sex, betrayal of her husband, honoring of her dead mother over her living, devoted husband as an example of how to live?" And later, "In using honesty as a criterion for an aesthetic judgment, what are you teaching your students—that the more egregious the behavior and lack of judgment they acknowledge/confess to, the better their writing will be? If students write about the Ds—divorce, dysfunction, disaster, disease, death—do you give them greater trust, better grades than if they tackle, say the Bs—best friends, blueberries, blue skies ...?" It's true that this is the harshest review I've ever received, and I've often said of it that had it been my first, I likely would have quit the profession then and there. I felt so much shame. I wanted to lash right back out at that writer, to tell him that he doesn't get it, that even if he thought my essay was unpublishable, he didn't have to be so *mean* about it. And until I began thinking more seriously about the role of recognition in our responses to one another, I hadn't considered the ways in which this reviewer's response to my manuscript could be read as an attempt at identity maintenance. Again, I turn to Gilligan, who writes

> Attitudes such as arrogance, superiority, and self-importance, to which the term "narcissism" is often attached, and which are so often misunderstood to be the genuine attitudes of the people who hold them, are actually defenses against, or attempts to ward off or undo, the opposite set of feelings: namely, underlying feelings of personal insignificance and worthlessness. (183)

The reviewer's refusal to recognize me as a writer with something to say allowed him to ward off feelings of insignificance produced, at least in part, by a peer review system that grants little to no recognition to its reviewers.

Perhaps the biggest difference between the kind of reviews that afford recognition to a would-be author and the kind of reviews that withhold such recognition is that the former responds to the argument, the writing, the work itself, while the latter responds to the *writer*: a peer reviewer attacks the perceived character of the would-be author in order to shore up her own identity as a writer who can identify those who qualify as authors and those who do not.

None of this is to say that anonymity is the primary problem. Indeed, as Bonnie Wheeler reminds us in her essay, "Scholarly Journals and the Place of Peer Review," anonymity of both author and reader "began with high idealism as an attempt to put an end to the Old Boy system that denied access to women and minorities" (313). And anonymity surely works to protect young scholars from any kind of retribution from authors whose work they recommend against publication. What I'm arguing, instead, is that an unintended consequence of anonymity is a lack of recognition of the work of peer review as the work of writing, the crucial and laborious task of *responding* to writing. And a consequence of this lack of recognition of the peer reviewer as a writer leads to the kind of incivility often attributed to anonymity alone.

Just as there is considerable work pointing to the fact that peer reviewers receive very little to no recognition for their labor, there are plenty of suggestions for how to remedy this problem. Selfe and Hawisher reference Katherine Fitzpatrick's recommendation encouraging "departments to recognize peer review as a scholarly contribution that should be recorded on faculty curriculum vitae and recognized at tenure and promotion time" (682). More specifically, Beth Mole, in her *Chronicle* piece references Nicolas Espinoza's suggestion, in the context of open online peer review, that "editors could achieve quality control by rewarding reviewers for good reports with scores that reflected the helpfulness of their comments—like online karma" (2). And Wheeler points out that "most universities offer some stipend when they approach you for tenure and promotion reviews; most presses reward you for manuscript reviews. But for peer review of *essay* submissions in the humanities, we have traditionally depended upon the open-handed generosity of others" (315). Finally, Mark Ware writes that one way to improve the peer review process is by "providing recognition and reward to reviewers (e.g., publishing a list of reviewers; inviting to an annual reception; awards for best reviewer of the year; certificates they can show to their employer; even token payments)" (34). It is beyond the scope of my argument to determine the extent to which any of these practices would provide the kind of recognition that peer reviewers depend upon to maintain their identities as writers. But I will venture to say that any practice that reduces the temptation to incivility in anonymous peer review will go a long way toward preventing the kind of injury that we all know words can inflict. Although not a scholar of language, Gilligan, comparing the effects of physical and verbal abuse, writes that "Words alone can shame and reject, insult and humiliate, dishonor and disgrace, tear down self-esteem, and murder the soul" (49). And in *Impersonal Passion: Language as Affect*, Denise Riley notes the way in which "injurious speech echoes relentlessly, years after the occasion of its utterance, in the mind of the one at whom it was aimed: the bad word, splinterlike, pierces to lodge" (9). She points out, too, that the injurious word stays with the victim for far longer than with the accuser, noting that "the tendency of malignant speech is to ingrow like a toenail, embedding itself in its hearer until it's no longer felt to come 'from the outside'" (11). Writing teachers and scholars know this. Indeed, this is why we have taken so much care as a field to understand the rhetorical effects of the kinds of comments we write on students' papers.

Can I ever forget the insult from that one reviewer who read my work "with mounting annoyance"? Probably not. But I can come to understand that it wasn't necessarily directed at *me* but instead may have been the reviewer's attempt to maintain his identity as a person who knows a thing or two about teaching writing. But then again, will I ever forget that Linda Brodkey wrote a review of my very first *College English* submission and wrote at the bottom, "Let me repeat. Publish." This line stays with me in a different way; it recognizes my work as publishable and therefore likely to make an impact. Brodkey acknowledges me as an author. But Brodkey's name was revealed to me only after the journal editor specifically asked Brodkey's permission. The editor knew how much it would mean to me.

Perhaps much of this chapter could be read as my own attempt to maintain my identity in the face of a number of reviewers' attempts to contest my status as an author with something to say. As I consider this possibility, I can't help but think, too, about the role of the journal editor in all of this. If the norm of attribution cannot survive the peer review process because the author and the reviewers remain unknown to one another, the journal editor's participation in the process highlights his or her significance in ensuring that all parties are recognized for their contributions. Maybe public recognition in the form of a certificate or a nominal fee isn't the answer. Maybe instead it's the extent to which the editor recognizes the reviewers' contributions as the work of writing in his or her responses to reviewers; perhaps it's the extent to which the editor contextualizes those same reviewers' comments to the manuscript's author in ways that provide the recognition necessary for the author to maintain her identity as an author. The editor as middle(wo)man can affirm each author's status as author.

A review that contests a manuscript author's identity as an author can be contextualized in a couple of ways. The editor can allow the review to speak for itself, as one editor of *College Composition and Communication* did when she simply wrote that "the reviewers offered constructive feedback, and I have enclosed the more helpful of the two." This "more helpful" review indicated that the reviewer either had not read my submission or was so preoccupied with his/her own interest in technology that my failure to address technology's impact on plagiarism rendered my work unpublishable. Or the editor can contextualize the review in ways that allow the manuscript author to save face, to maintain a sense of having something important to say. He can suggest further revision strategies and other outlets for publication. He can express gratitude for the opportunity to have read your work. "Whatever you choose to do now, I remain grateful for the opportunity to consider this particular submission, and of course I look forward to reading any other work you care to offer us," writes a former editor of *College English*. He can claim that he rejects your manuscript with reluctance. The editor is the primary person in contact with both parties during the peer review process; he or she is, therefore, the vehicle by which the norm of attribution might survive the process.

When I was a kid, I began writing a book on a thick pile of construction paper that I then hid inside one of my mom's old pocketbooks which I then stuffed into the back of the bottom drawer of the dresser in my bedroom. The book was about a little old woman who lived alone in the woods. This woman, feared by so many of the neighborhood children, was kind to my protagonist, Becky, and for that reason, Becky did not fear her. Not an original story by any stretch of the imagination. But what strikes me as I recall the child hiding her writing where nobody would think to look (inside of a pocketbook!) is her understanding that authorship was something to be hidden because it was something that could and would be judged. On some level she knows that her authorship is contestable, and she protects herself from that contestation to the extent that she can.

I hope that this chapter will not be read as a call for reviewers to write condescendingly positive comments. My goal instead is to call attention to our relative ignorance about a significant part of the work we do for one another and to recognize that what we say to other writers has longer lasting effects than we might imagine. When we guard the gates of our discipline with our fears and insecurities, we contest the authorship of those who might otherwise be influenced by our careful and thoughtful reviews of their work. Perhaps the norm of attribution does survive the peer review process in ways we haven't yet considered. One implication of this chapter is that we need a better understanding of the work of journal editors for it, too, is the work of writing. The biggest question I'm left with is how editors conceptualize their own roles in offering recognition in ways that allow all parties to maintain their identities as authors. We have an impressive body of scholarship devoted to the ins and outs and the hows and whats of responding to other people's writing; what we don't have yet are journal editors' insights and perspectives on the ways in which the norm of attribution affects peer review.

NOTES

1. As a rhetoric and composition specialist, I draw my data from reader reports provided to me from journals such as *College English*, *College Composition and Communication*, *Composition Studies*, and *JAC*. I do not profess to speak for all scholarship in the humanities, although I do believe that readers will find a great deal of overlap between my discipline and others.
2. This is a reference to Cheryl Strayed's essay, "The Love of My Life."

WORKS CITED

Bracher, Mark. "Healing Trauma, Preventing Violence: A Radical Agenda for Literary Study." *JAC* 24.3 (2004): 515–61.

Derricourt, Robin. "Peer Review: Fetishes, Fallacies, and Perceptions." *Journal of Scholarly Publishing*. January 2012: 137–47.

Gilligan, James, M.D. *Violence: Reflections on a National Epidemic*. New York: Random House, 1996.

Green, Stuart P. "Plagiarism, Norms, and the Limits of Theft Law: Some Observations on the Use of Criminal Sanctions in Enforcing Intellectual Property Rights." *Hastings Law Journal* 54 (2002): 167–242.

"Jeer Review." *Harper's Magazine*. May 2011: 25.

Lamont, Michèle. *How Professors Think: Inside the Curious World of Academic Judgment*. Cambridge: Harvard UP, 2009.

Mole, Beth. "The Future of Peer Review in the Humanities Is Wide Open." *Chronicle of Higher Education* 58.44 (2012).

Riley, Denise. *Impersonal Passion: Language as Affect*. Durham: Duke UP, 2005.

Rose, Mark. "The Author in Court: *Pope v. Curll* (1741)." *The Construction of Authorship*. Martha Woodmansee and Peter Jaszi (eds.). Durham: Duke UP, 1994.

Selfe, Cynthia, and Gail E. Hawisher. "Methodologies of Peer and Editorial Review: Changing Practices." *College English* 63.4 (2012): 672–98.

Shatz, David. *Peer Review: A Critical Inquiry*. New York: Rowman & Littlefield, 2004.

Souder, Lawrence. "The Ethics of Scholarly Peer Review: A Review of the Literature." *Learned Publishing* 24.1 (2011): 55–74.

Ware, Mark. "Peer Review: Recent Experience and Future Directions." *New Review of Information Networking* 16 (2011): 23–53.

Weller, Ann C. *Editorial Peer Review: Its Strengths and Weaknesses*. Medford, NJ: American Society for Information Science and Technology, 2001.

Wheeler, Bonnie. "The Ontology of the Scholarly Journal and the Place of Peer Review." *Journal of Scholarly Publishing* April 2011: 307–22.

Worsham, Lynn. Letter to the author. September 2, 2009.

Part IV
Nascent Authorship

10 "I Feel Like This Is Fake"

Spontaneous Mediocrity and Studied Genius

Val Perry Rendel

My childhood love for Laura Ingalls Wilder's *Little House on the Prairie* books led me to devour everything I could find that was connected with them in any way, including Wilder's letters and collection of columns in the *Missouri Ruralist*. I recall being struck, even then, by the stark contrast between the terse, factual accounts of daily farm life and the lyrical beauty of the books, which not even the difference in genre could account for completely. Secretly I formulated another hypothesis: Perhaps her editor had done with her manuscripts what my English teacher did with my essays—kept giving them back with corrections until she eventually worked them into something more interesting. Years later, this was precisely the same analogy I heard from one of the directors of the Herbert Hoover Presidential Library and Museum, during one of my research trips there to work with the Wilder-Lane papers. Despite the collection of manuscripts and correspondence laid out on the cart between us, she nonetheless had clearly not accepted the evidence of dual authorship, let alone the derogatory term "ghostwriting." "The student does the work," she told me, "and the teacher corrects it. But it remains the student's work."

Perceptions of the textual and cultural legitimacy of written works are primarily based on two factors: the erasure/exposure of the "trail" behind the work's creation and the genre(s) into which the reader places the work. Genre plays a key role in shaping the expectations and perceptions of the audience, particularly with regard to collaborative authorship and revision. This chapter examines the ways in which genre theory and the study of process can complicate and lead us to reconsider concepts of authorship, invention, and ownership. Often, as far as general readers are concerned, the author's personal ethos is sufficient to establish the legitimacy of a text … or lack thereof. Specific "canonical" authors—such as Shakespeare, Anne Frank, and Martin Luther King, Jr.—serve as more than names of individual writers. Each functions as a synecdoche for a set of ideas, prestige, the broader discourse that surrounds his or her work. In a strange inverse of Locke's labor theory of value, however, authorial ethos *itself* may depend on a perceived minimization of labor and process. I invited my upper-level class to examine this complication using case studies of real-life "erased" process and cases of plagiarism and how these cases affected their assumptions and beliefs about the textual and cultural legitimacy of a given work. In my upper-level and first-year courses at Lewis University, I have designed activities "that actively seek to address, as fiction writer Eve Shelnutt puts it, the issue that 'the myth that works of the imagination and full consciousness are anti-thetical'" (Welch 167).

Since "belief in the value of a work" is "necessary to the production of a cultural work and recognition of a cultural work as such" (Robillard and Fortune 189), this value often begins with—and in some cases rests exclusively on—the "direct producer" of the work: the author. Janet Emig, in her landmark 1964 article "The Uses of the Unconscious in Composing," cites Stephen Spender's division of artists into two basic categories, "Mozartians" and "Beethovians":

> The Mozartian is one who can instantaneously arrange encounters with his [sic] unconscious; he is one in whom the creative self leads a constant and uninterrupted life of its own, serene to surface disturbances, oblivious of full upper activity—coach-riding, concert-giving, bill-paying. The Mozartian can "plunge" the greatest depths of his own experience by the tremendous effort of a moment and surface every time with a finished pearl.
>
> (qtd. in Welch 137)

And so it has been presented to the public, this "Amadeus Myth" of perfect conception and production that students bring with them into the writing classrooms: "Good" writers always get it right the first time, with no need to struggle or revise (Shermer 33). Fictionalized and fact-based *künstlerromane* start building this concept in early childhood, and the "classic" literary canon reinforces it: Anne Frank never struggled with process; Laura Ingalls Wilder picked up a pen one day at the age of sixty and produced the bestselling *Little House* series of children's books based solely on her personal memories, etc. Heming and Condell said of Shakespeare, in their preface to the First Folio, that "what he thought, he uttered with that easiness, that we have scarce received from him a blot in his papers."

Because students are likely to be familiar with these authors already, these are among the readings I select for the focus on class activities that ask students to challenge their own assumptions about the ethos-dependent value of a text and/or author. This conceptualization of "good" or "real" writing as unfiltered and spontaneous is hardly unique to twenty-first century audiences, but has roots in the Enlightenment ideal of literal muse-inspired authorship. The same mythologizing of spontaneous creation that made Coleridge hide the Crewe Manuscript draft of *Kubla Khan* also leads bloggers and Facebook users to look with disfavor on overuse of the "edit" function. Thus any indication of labor or revision somehow lessens the authenticity of a work.

EXPOSED PROCESS IN TWO GENRES, OR THE DOUBLE-EDGED SWORD OF DOCUMENTARY ANALYSIS

In my 300-level Editing for Publishing course for English majors, students work with selections from *The Diary of Anne Frank: The Critical Edition*. This compilation by the Netherlands State Institute for War Documentation lays out the text of Anne's original diary as she wrote it between June, 1942 and March 1944 (Version A) alongside the text of the entries she revised with the intent of publication (Version B) and the final text as edited by her father, published in 1947. So, for example, the original text of the entry for July 8, 1944, the day on which the Frank family realizes they must go into hiding sooner than planned, is as follows:

> [Version A] *I still have a whole lot to write in my diary, on Sunday Hello came over to our place, on Saturday we went out with Fredie Weiss, and over to oasis of course. On Sunday morning Hello and I lay on our balcony in the sun, on Sunday afternoon he was going to come back, but at about 3 o'clock a policeman arrived and called from the door downstairs Miss Margot Frank. Mummy went down and the policeman gave her a card which said that Margot Frank has to report to the S.S.* (CE 206)

Compare the above passage with the revised version (B), which Anne rewrote between May and August, 1944, after Bolkestein's address and which her father preserved in the published version (C) with only minor punctuation corrections:

> [Versions B-C]*Dear Kitty,*
> *Years seem to have passed between Sunday and now, so much has happened, it is as if the whole world had turned upside down, but I am still alive, Kitty, and that is the main thing, Daddy says. ... At three o'clock (Hello had just gone, but was coming back later) someone rang the front doorbell. ... A bit later, Margot appeared at the kitchen door, looking very excited. "The S.S. have sent a call-up notice for Daddy," she whispered. ... When we were alone together in our bedroom, Margot told me that the call-up was not for Daddy, but for her. I was more frightened than ever, and began to cry. Margot is 16; would they really take girls of that age away alone?* (CE 206–208)

In attempting to reconcile the streamlined backstory and heightened dramatic tension of the B-C text with the original, which reflects Anne's fragmented state of mind after a sudden and severe emotional trauma, students struggle to determine which is the "real" version. At least one student was dismayed at the revelation that the diary is not a pristine original document, but one that has undergone extensive editing. "I feel like this one is fake," she told me, referring—interestingly—to the Version B text revised by Anne herself. Both passages were written by Anne, I pointed out; each exists in her own handwriting, part of a collection of loose papers and office account ledgers and a small cloth-bound book that together comprise "the diary of Anne Frank." Yet it's clear that, as far as they (and many popular readers) are concerned, genuineness equals immediacy, a spontaneous and unrehearsed communiqué from author to reader. In other words, the students valued the text more highly when they perceived a relatively low amount of labor involved in its production—that Anne's *sprezzatura* had allowed her to simply transcribe her experiences and feelings effortlessly—and devalued both the credibility and the labor value of the diary when presented with documentary evidence of its process.

This initial suspicion of how "neat" Anne's diary appears has long been a point of contention for Holocaust deniers and others who dispute the credibility of the diary. Arthur Butz, a notorious Holocaust denier, sums up a common misunderstanding meant to undercut the ethos of both the author and the text itself:

> The question of the authenticity of the diary is not considered important enough to examine here; I will only remark that I have looked it over and don't believe it. For example, already on page 2 one is reading an essay on why a 13-year-old girl would start a diary, and then page 3 gives a short history of the Frank family and then quickly reviews the specific anti-Jewish measures that followed the German occupation in 1940. The rest of the book is in the same historical spirit.
> (Barnouw and van der Stroom 92)

Butz makes the mistake of conflating the medium of composition with the medium of delivery; he assumes that the bound and printed product he holds in his hands is a materially faithful reproduction of the text produced by the hand of the author alone. This assumption reflects a popular ignorance and even suspicion of process/labor as somehow inherently dishonest or inauthentic when applied to "personal" genres such as memoir. It is significant to note that challenges to the diary's authenticity are rebutted through documentary analysis of the physical manuscripts themselves; attempts to understand on an artistic level the meaning and value of the labor-intensive processes of revision, transcription, and translation behind it are largely ignored.

WHAT'S IN A NAME? AUTHOR(SHIP) AS VALUE

Since we are accustomed to using materiality to find "documentary clues" about the authenticity of a text (Robillard and Fortune 192), it is all too easy to fall into the reverse assumption as well: A lack of "evidence" of the author's process means that there was no process! Thus, when the students work with producing their own editions of selected scenes from Shakespeare's plays, they must not only grapple with questions of whether to favor the Quarto(s) or Folio, but with the lack of ur-texts or other manuscripts that might provide direction about authorial process, labor, and intent. Complicating the issue is the source material that directly influenced many of Shakespeare's plays and poems ... in some cases, too directly for my students' comfort, leading to the perception that (in their words) the Bard "plagiarized" from earlier works. This perception, incidentally, is also prevalent in popular media, with no less a personage than the most cited legal scholar of the twentieth century calling Shakespeare "a formidable plagiarist in the broad sense" (though acknowledging that in many cases "he improved upon the original") (Posner).

While the class eventually comes to a better understanding of literary traditions of mimesis, modern privileging of originality, historic reverence for textual authority, and the artistic ethos gained by showcasing one's ability to reference and reframe classical texts, the charges still seem to stick: if they paralleled outside sources this closely, so one argument goes, they'd be slapped with a violation of the Academic Integrity Policy. It is not enough to attempt to exonerate Shakespeare of these charges simply by claiming that the concept of plagiarism did not exist in his time, as "there are extant seventeenth-century references to 'plagiaries'—that is, people who misappropriate texts" (Thomas 277). These, however, seem much more concerned with the wholesale lifting of plays and poems by "piratical printers" and "textual thieves" (278). But there are indicators that it was the name of the author that carried even more value than the work itself: The printer William Jaggard (later one of the publishers of the First Folio, as well as the notorious 1619 "False Folio") issued *The Passionate Pilgrim* in 1599–1600, a collection of poems by various authors, including some of Shakespeare's sonnets. "W. Shakespeare" was, however, the only name given on the title page.

The fact that the volume included numerous poems on the same theme as one of Shakespeare's long poems, *Venus and Adonis*, suggests that Jaggard was attempting to boost sales by slapping a famous name on his publication. The poet and playwright Thomas Heywood, whose work also appeared in the volume, took issue with this attribution, though for reasons that scholars still puzzle over: One reading sees Heywood concerned that his own authorial reputation would be jeopardized by the perception that he had illicitly appropriated Shakespeare's work, while another claims an even more complicated objection by Heywood to the accuracy of Jaggard's printing, with "the question of 'authorship' ... contextualized as a question of 'workmanship' ... Thus the driving force ... is an efficient market, and the result is not so much anxiety about intellectual theft as of product duplication" (Thomas 280–84).

Students who are grounded in twenty-first century readiness to read appropriation as *mis*appropriation readily equate misappropriation with "*unoriginality*, and therefore as theft" (Thomas 283). Complicating the problem of anachronistic perception is the popular lionization of Shakespeare's genius—and geniuses, of course, are always originally inspired. When presented with evidence of Shakespeare's at-times-heavy reliance on Lily's *Grammar* and Holinshed's *Chronicles*, you can almost hear the air sucked out of the room as they reevaluate their perceptions of his Kantian naturalistic genius. They struggle with the authorship/workmanship divide as they examine the near-identical plotlines and character patterning (including many of the names) between *Othello* and Cinthio's *Gli Hecatommithi*, *Hamlet* and the twelfth-century *Gesta Danorum* of Saxo Grammaticus, as well as between Brooks's *Tragicall Historye of Romeus and Juliet* and the canonical text they read in high school.

Ultimately, though, Shakespeare-as-author does not suffer a loss of ethos in their eyes, though this seems only partially related to the value of his work itself (the most frequent rebuttal to modernist claims of derivation). What it comes down to for them is the power of the name itself—the same commodity Jaggard recognized to be so valuable; Shakespeare cannot be dethroned from his position, simply by reason of the fact that he *is* Shakespeare. This is, in a way, the inverse of the trite argument that is sometimes misguidedly offered to refute the nonsensical claims of Shakespeare denialists ("They are wonderful works—does it really matter *who* wrote them?"). We will see this privileged valuing of authorial name over production of work in the next section and again in the case studies unit, though with a darker twist.

NAMING THE GHOST: LAURA INGALLS WILDER, ROSE WILDER LANE, AND AUTHORSHIP OF *LITTLE HOUSE*

William Holtz's biography of Rose Wilder Lane, who ghostwrote the bestselling *Little House* series for which her mother Laura Ingalls Wilder is best known, averages three stars in Amazon.com user reviews. This is remarkably low, especially for a subject with such an enthusiastic popular following; even the driest of Wilder's works (*Little House in the Ozarks*, the collection of Wilder's newspaper columns that I found so disappointing years ago) averages four and a half stars. The reason for this low rating becomes clear from a quick analysis of the reviews, many of which object strenuously to the very idea that Wilder was not the sole author of the series, or indeed that the books are anything other than a literal recounting of unvarnished biographical facts and events, free of any artistic license. Readers find such a suggestion threatening, as if the "truth" of a series of children's books (officially classified as fiction) is compromised by a collaborative and ideologically driven writing process. Reviewers of Holtz's book are preoccupied with refuting the *Little House* collaboration (an event spanning less than two decades in Lane's eighty-two years of life) and are almost universally hostile toward any challenge to the claim of Wilder's sole authorship.

Wilder's daughter, Rose Wilder Lane, was herself a successful journalist and author of several prizewinning short stories and novels, many of which were autobiographical in nature or based on her parents' experiences of pioneer life. The assumption—often claimed in Wilder's biographies and at tourist meccas—is that Wilder's writing style directly influenced Lane's. In fact, the manuscript evidence overwhelmingly supports the opposite conclusion: that Lane's private work on her mother's manuscripts is far less—or far more—than a collaboration of equals.

Mother and daughter also maintained a regular correspondence about the progress of the books; in Lane's letter of February 16, 1931, she reassures her mother: "I have said nothing about having run the manuscript through my own typewriter, because the changes I made, as you will see, are so slight that they could not even properly be called editing" (Holtz 224). Yet in a private letter dating from this same period, Lane refers to her work on her "mother's goddamn juvenile" in a manner that makes clear she understood the true nature of what she was doing: "This kind of work is called 'ghosting,' and no writer of my reputation ever does it" (Holtz 385). In numerous places in her journals, Lane notes that she is suspending her own professional writing, sometimes for weeks at a time, to "work on" her mother's manuscripts—at one point even using the word "rewriting" (July 31, 1930).

The popular mythology surrounding Wilder, to a large extent, depends on this very mythologizing of her work and talent as unrehearsed and free of process. The exposure of the collaborative process of Laura Ingalls Wilder (through documentary examination of manuscripts) results in a decrease of both textual and cultural capital—her work is presumed to be less "true" as a memoir of her pioneer childhood. Yet the books themselves are categorized as fiction, not memoir. A few key passages in the *Little House* books themselves support a carefully constructed view of her as a Mozartian, able to dash off great writing with hardly a second thought and with no formal training. "Reading Mrs. Wilder's contributions," wrote the *Ruralist*, "most folks doubtless have decided that she is a college graduate. But as she informs us, 'I was never graduated from anything and only attended high school two terms'" (Case 23). A scene from *These Happy Golden Years* in which Laura, the author-heroine, must write and recite a composition on "ambition," serves a similar function:

> Laura had no idea how to begin. ... The only thought in her head was that she was going to fail in a class that she had always led. She must not fail; she wouldn't. She could not. But how did one write a composition? Only five minutes were left. She found herself staring at the yellow leather cover of the dictionary. ... her fingers were chilly as she hurriedly turned the A pages, but the definition was interesting. Back at her desk, she wrote as fast as she could, and kept on writing desperately while the school was called to order. Miserably she felt that

her composition was not good, but there was no time to add anything more. ... (97)

Unsurprisingly, after Laura has read her 96-word composition (complete with a Shakespeare quote), the reaction from the teacher is as satisfyingly dramatic as only fiction can be: "I would not have believed that anyone could do so well the first time. ... there are no corrections. It grades one hundred" (98).

It is this mythos of authorship that enthralls the *Little House* fan base, and that they will go to great lengths to maintain even in the face of documentary evidence to the contrary. "Since 1932, a large body of Wilder's readers ... has invested heavily in the idea of a woman in her sixties and seventies, an untutored 'natural' writer, independently recording the story of her frontier childhood and adolescence. ... However, as critics and biographers of the past twenty years have begun to show, the authorship of the Little House series is more interesting and more culturally complex than this fans' version" (Romines 13–14).

"Invested heavily" is, if anything, an understatement, if the Amazon reviewers of Holtz's book are at all indicative of popular assumptions about textual authenticity. This is the myth that serves as the rock upon which *Little House* fandom is based, and its supporters do not react well to any suggestion that it is not 100% literally true. Historic sites, fan clubs, and websites dedicated to Wilder and the *Little House* series seldom refer to Lane at any length, and the Laura Ingalls Wilder Home and Museum in Mansfield, Missouri, maintains no permanent exhibition on Lane. Holtz himself observes laconically "You will not find my book for sale in Mansfield." The conviction at work here is that, if Wilder did not solely conceive, write, and edit the books herself, they can no longer stand either as historical/biographical documents (which they were never intended to be) or as fiction/memoir.

This resistance to the very idea of such a collaboration reflects a perceived weakening of authorial and textual credibility; the books themselves suffer a severe loss of value (both in terms of authorial ethos and of commodity) when the name of the author is changed from Wilder to Lane. In order for the series to effectively convey the independent pioneer ethos they celebrate, the audience *needs* Wilder to be the sole hand behind the books' creation. The lopsided collaboration between Wilder and Lane, while widely accepted by critics and biographers, is usually dismissed by apologists as merely "editing," "proofreading," or "correcting"—though if a student in any of my classes "corrected" another's work to the extent reflected in the Wilder-Lane partnership, she would undoubtedly face some serious questioning and possibly charges of academic dishonesty. Students often come to equate their own writing with "real" authorship only after great difficulty; for some of them, discovering the struggles and "shortcuts" of other authors is a liberating realization. For others, this discovery comes as the unwelcome exploding of a myth, the dashing of the hope that one day they might finally ascend to the heights of "real" authors who never have to struggle.

ON TRIAL: CASE STUDIES AND ETHOS-BASED REACTIONS TO PLAGIARISM

In real life "case studies" of authors who have had the authorship and/or legitimacy of their work contested, students examine issues of (mis)appropriation and (dis)honesty in professional and scholarly writing. This exercise is framed by the many facets of "plagiarism" outlined in the department's Academic Integrity Policy, including plagiarism (defined as misappropriation of others' texts, whether with a willing participant or not), patchwriting (closely paraphrasing original material without proper citation), cheating, multiple submission, collusion, fabrication, and solicitation. They work in pairs to research the circumstances of each case; one plays the role of prosecutor, arguing that there has been a breach of integrity by the author, while the other acts as the defense, either refuting the charge or persuading the rest of the class (which serves as jury) to be lenient in sentencing. The verdict is decided by majority vote; no unanimous consensus is required in this system.

The clearest-cut cases are Janet Cooke, former journalist at *The Washington Post*, whose 1981 Pulitzer Prize was revoked upon the discovery that her feature article "Jimmy's World" about an 8-year-old heroin addict was a fabrication. Also Southern Illinois University president Glenn Poshard, who was found by a faculty investigative committee to have lifted substantial portions of his dissertation without attribution 20 years previously, is quickly found guilty. Yet even these votes are not unanimous; Cooke garners some sympathy for being a genuinely talented writer with good intentions, and the class accepts her statement that her story was a composite of genuine addicts meant to help raise awareness of the lives of those trapped in poverty and addiction. The social ethics of "Jimmy's World" at least partially redeem Cooke's transgression in their eyes, though her own ethos is further tainted by her claims to hold a degree and professional experience that she did not actually have.

Poshard's circumstances seem to be more personally relatable to them: "I would never offer it up as an excuse but at that point in my life, I had a family. I worked two jobs. I was running for the Illinois State Senate. I was trying to get my dissertation finished" (Wilson and Crawford). The pathos of Poshard's reasoning does not quite override their concerns about authorial ethos or professional ethics, though the class generally concurs with the real-life penalty of simply requiring Poshard to rewrite the contested passages with correct attribution. SIU professor Gerald Nelms summed up the decision with "The world can withstand a few unprosecuted citation infractions" (Powers). In both of these cases, contested authorship seems worth pursuing only when some specific commodity—power, prestige, funding—is at risk. As Thomas observes, "The driving force [of contesting authorship] ... is an efficient market, and the result is not so much anxiety about intellectual theft as of product duplication" (Thomas 280).

The two middle-ground "defendants" demonstrate that, while the intellectual marketplace may overlap with the economic, the latter is perceived as "higher stakes." Charges of intellectual theft and loss of ethos are less severe than charges that there has been damage to specific monetary or power structures—a clear illustration of postindustrial society's commodification of intellectual property. Even now, historians Stephen Ambrose and Doris Kearns Goodwin have their apologists for what can be read as inadvertent patchwriting and miscoding of research notes (respectively). "It can happen to anyone," a student explains, and indeed it can; that's the point.

It is important to note that none of the case study "defendants" in this exercise is named; students receive detailed summaries of the circumstances of each contested authorship situation, and only after both prosecution and defense rest is the identity of each author revealed, just before issuing the verdict. The reason for this approach becomes clear when assessing our final "defendant," the case of a young divinity scholar who, 36 years after receiving his doctorate and continuing on to a brilliant career of scholarship and public service, is found to have plagiarized substantial portions of his dissertation. The class, who demonstrated such sympathy for Poshard's circumstances, is firmly persuaded by the "prosecuting" student's case, which includes a quote from an investigatory panel comprised of scholars and former colleagues who state their admiration for the defendant's subsequent career. Nonetheless, they state, "There is no question ... that [the defendant] plagiarized in the dissertation by appropriating material from sources not explicitly credited in notes, or mistakenly credited, or credited generally and at some distance in the text from a close paraphrase or verbatim quotation" ("Boston U").

A quick straw poll before the official vote shows this to be the first—and only—case where the class is in full agreement about the guilt of the author in question ... until the promising young scholar is revealed to be Martin Luther King, Jr. Suddenly perceptions change, and personal ethos, as well as the reverence of the name, is sufficient to trump all other concerns. More than one student articulates this reasoning very clearly on the ballot: "Not guilty, because he's Martin Luther King." They seem unable—or unwilling—to differentiate between the rhetorical situations of twentieth-century academic standards and the "formidable plagiaris[m]" of a sixteenth-century dramatist. One type of "plagiarism" is as excusable as another, and ultimately their reprieve of King is based on his name alone—or is it? Perhaps the recognition of the incalculable value of King's life and work is so synecdochally bound up with his name and ethos that to challenge one is to devalue the other.

By setting up a guilty-or-not-guilty bifurcation along which to divide complex issues of authorship, ownership, frameworks, ethics, and the commodification of texts and ideas, I may have reinforced modernist perceptions of misappropriation and dishonesty rather than complicated them. What first drew me to Wilder's writing style (separate from the books' content) was the idea that she might have been a writer just like me—in other words, imperfect, needing to constantly practice and revise. This idea, which I found reassuring, actually seems to unsettle my students—having sacred cows slaughtered can be unsettling. Thus the journey through which we have followed her and the other authors is even more twisting and shaded than I had anticipated. This is the best lesson I can offer them. I can expand my pedagogy to include examinations of the process behind my own and others' work, as much as an exercise in emotional reassurance as in the analytical study of process. Exposure of the process behind any work, so easily erased in the digital age, is a vital component of writers' growth, and I now require more in-class writing for this very reason. Students need that trail of re-thinking and re-seeing preserved. And I am drawn to reflect, with new perspective and a touch more humility, on the synecdochal function of both the author and the name on a text, the forces that drive and shape the cost/benefit ratio of contesting authorship, and my feelings about a world in which select "infractions" are allowed to go unprosecuted and unpunished ... and perhaps more significantly in some contexts, unrecognized and unrewarded.

WORKS CITED

"Boston U Panel Finds Plagiarism by Dr. King." *The New York Times*. 11 Oct. 1991. 13 Mar. 2013. http://www.nytimes.com/1991/10/11/us/boston-u-panel-finds-plagiarism-by-dr-king.html. Accessed 10 May 2013.

Case, John F. "Let's Visit Mrs. Wilder." *The Missouri Ruralist*, 18 February 1911.

Holtz, William. *The Ghost in the Little House: A Life of Rose Wilder Lane*. Columbia: U Missouri P, 1993.

———. Message to the author. 8 Mar. 1999. Email.

Posner, Richard A. "On Plagiarism." *The Atlantic*. 1 Apr. 2002. 10 May 2013. <http://www.theatlantic.com/magazine/arch:ive/2002/04/on-plagiarism/302469/>. 10 May 2013.

Powers, Elia. "Southern Illinois President Cleared of Plagiarism." *Inside Higher Ed*. 12 Oct. 2007. http://www.insidehighered.com/news/2007/10/12/siu. Accessed 15 May 2013.

Romines, Ann. *Constructing the Little House*. Amherst. MA: U Mass P, 1997.

Shermer, Michael. *The Borderlands of Science*. Oxford UP: 2001.

Thomas, Max W. "Eschewing Credit: Heywood, Shakespeare, and Plagiarism before Copyright." *New Literary History* 31.2 (200): 277–93. Web. 1 May 2013.

Welch, Nancy. *Getting Restless: Rethinking Revision in Writing Instruction*. New York: Boynton/Cook, 1997.

Wilder, Laura Ingalls. *These Happy Golden Years*. New York: Harper/Trophy, 1994.

Wilson, Jordan, and Joe Crawford. "Poshard Defends Dissertation against Plagiarism Charges." *The Daily Egyptian*. 7 Oct. 2007. <http://archives.dailyegyptian.com/siu22/2007/10/8/poshard-defends-dissertation-against-plagiarism-charges.html>. Accessed 15 May 2013.

11 Student Authorship in the Age of Permissions
Fostering a Gift Economy in First-Year Writing Programs

Matt Hollrah

> There is a sense in which our gifts are not fully ours until they have been given away.
>
> —Lewis Hyde, *The Gift*

Plagiarism as a concept has undergone important revision in recent years as scholars like Rebecca Moore Howard and Amy Robillard have helped develop a more coherent theory of plagiarism. One of the most important changes to the concept of plagiarism has been the change of its central guiding metaphor from one of theft to one of fraud. This change in metaphor has also allowed instructors and administrators to make an important distinction between source misuse and outright plagiarism. But this change in metaphor can also help us understand something fundamental about student authorship and how instructors, administrators, and even students themselves contest student authorship.

If plagiarism is more like fraud than it is like theft, it changes the quality of the ethical wrongdoing from taking something that does not belong to the taker, an issue of ownership, to lying about what one has produced in order to achieve some personal or financial gain, an issue of authenticity and fairness. While issues of reproductive control and origination are the primary issues concerning student authorship, academic writing programs and educational systems often couch plagiarism within the language of the market economy, which is an economy I believe our students need to ignore—at least at first—if they are to think of themselves as authors. Stemming from a misunderstanding of the difference between the value and the worth of creative and intellectual artifacts—what we still problematically call *intellectual property*—students, faculty, and administrators treat student work as a commodity rather than a kind of gift. I will make the case that educational systems have not sufficiently drawn upon the metaphor of creative and intellectual work as a gift, especially where student work is concerned. Doing so can help alleviate the confusion for students, faculty, and administrators about what it means to be an author in both practical and theoretical terms and should help prevent the unnecessary contestation of student authorship.

The problem with connecting intellectual work to the market economy before it is connected to what Lewis Hyde calls a "gift economy" is that our students will confuse the market value of their work with its worth. If our students feel that the value of their work lies in its use as a commodity exchanged for grades, which mimics the exchange of goods and services in the market economy, then they will never really think of themselves as authors because authors do not write just to get paid. To the extent that an author is someone who writes because he or she responds to an exigency, and to the extent that authors compose in order to participate in the free exchange of ideas set up by their communities, our students will not think of themselves as authors until they are encouraged to write about what interests them and to share it by participating in this alternative exchange system. Furthermore, when educators and the legal system hamper student participation in this gift economy, they contest student authorship and create an environment where students even contest their own authorship.

Those not already convinced that some of our students (and even some of our administrators) conceive of education in consumerist terms might turn to Kelly Ritter's article on paper mills. In "The Economics of Authorship: Online Paper Mills, Student Writers, and First-Year Composition," Ritter writes about why the consumerist rhetoric of online paper mills is so convincing to our students. The first problem is that students do not see themselves as authors. According to her survey of 247 students, "even though students may recognize that academia produces authors, the responses indicate that only a third of the students considered themselves authors, even though all were in the process of writing an 'academic' paper for English 101" (610). Furthermore, Ritter reports that only 39% of students who responded to the survey viewed "writing material for the Internet (either a personal or business Web site" as a form of authorship (609). Given the fact that papers for sale at paper mill websites are also "authorless" in the sense that usually no name is attached to them, it is easy to see how students might be confused about what it means to be an author. Ritter also found that 45% of the respondents viewed authorship as "writing something for which one may become famous or well-known," but another 58% viewed authorship as "writing anything, whether it is academic or not, published or not" (609). So we might infer from her study that if there is a name attached to the writing, then it was authored, but if not, it isn't authored and thus free for wholesale reuse.

Unfortunately, prominent theories of what it means to be an author, like Foucault's "author function" or Barthes's notion of the death of the author, are not pedagogically useful in a writing classroom. Try motivating students to write by telling them that they fulfill a social function, or worse, that they are dead because the reader holds the real meaning-making power. This is not to say that Foucault's and Barthes's ideas are not important intellectual challenges to how we think about authors, authorship, authoring, and authorizing. The sociolinguistic phenomenon of attaching a name to a text clearly has an impact on how the text will be understood. This is also not to diminish the importance of anticipating the needs, expectations, and potential reactions of an audience or to suggest that authors are the sole creators of textual meaning. Furthermore, students must be good readers of their own work to be effective writers. Nevertheless, these theorists' notions about authorship violate the lived experience of students and the pragmatic concerns of teaching them that they have something worth saying, that they can do so with words and images, and that they must feel that they have the freedom—and the right—to reuse and transform other writers' ideas. The notion of the independent, autonomous, solitary author may be a fiction, but it is a necessary one for anyone who sits down to write, especially students who struggle to take their writing seriously because very few of their readers have. Therefore, we must find ways of helping students understand the important dialectic between the creative reuse of other works and a sense of ownership of their writing. They must also understand that the primary economy for creative intellectual works is not the marketplace but the gift economy. Authorship, then, can be understood as the act of producing textual gifts and having *some* control over where they go. An author not only creates the gift, but she can also decide to whom it will be given, at least at first. After the initial giving, the author loses control over where the gift goes or how it may be reused or transformed, and this giving over of control is also part of the gift because it allows for an increase, an extra benefit associated with the gift. These three fundamental aspects of authorship—the right to transform other authors' work, the audacious and temporary belief that one owns what one writes, and the subsequent giving up of that sense of ownership once the work is finished—are continually contested when students are authors.

Lewis Hyde, author of *The Gift*, perhaps the longest and most influential study of the customs of gifts and giving in a variety of cultural settings and historical periods, has much to teach us about creative pursuits and the economies they participate in. Specifically, he describes his project as first establishing a theory of gift exchange and second "an attempt to apply the language of that theory to the life of the artist" (xxii). The word *gift* obviously has several meanings and applications, but what Hyde sees in common among them is the idea that "a gift is a thing we do not get by our own efforts" (xvi). Hyde's book-length analysis of gift exchange is remarkably complex, and I cannot reproduce all of its nuances here. Nevertheless, three aspects of Hyde's work are particularly relevant to teaching student writers how to think like authors: the difference between gift and market economies and the problem of usury; the notion that art is a gift; and the notion that academic communities are versions of gift economies.

GIFT AND MARKET ECONOMIES AND THE PROBLEM OF USURY

Gift exchange happens within a gift economy, which Hyde distinguishes from a market economy where the dominant form of exchange is characterized by the trading of goods and services for money. This form of exchange is largely symbolic because money represents the value of the commodity bought or sold. Gift economies, however, are different. Hyde writes that "a commodity has value and a gift does not. A gift has worth" (77–78). The distinction is important because "worth" refers to those things that we cannot put a price on. Therefore, gifts are not given or exchanged for symbols of their worth because, while the item itself might be sold in the marketplace, one cannot put a price on the relationship that giving establishes. Hyde explains, "It is the cardinal difference between gift and commodity exchange that a gift establishes a feeling-bond between two people, while the sale of a commodity leaves no necessary connection" (72). A market economy is impersonal in that no other relationship necessarily follows from the exchange. If I buy something from Target, there is no obligation to buy anything from Target ever again. But if I accept a gift, there is an expectation that I will reciprocate in some way. The gift may not be given with the intention of receiving something in return, but gift exchange tends to die out when the receiving party chooses not to participate over time in the gift economy.

Hyde also explains that the increase in worth that gifts provide through the bonds they establish is different from the increase in value that commodities take on. With the sale of commodities, the seller's increase is only in money, and the buyer's increase is only the thing bought. But with a gift, the recipient's increase is the object plus the bond the generosity of giving establishes. The one who gives also receives the establishment of this bond, which increases the likelihood that he or she will receive something in return (72–77).

Because gift economies rely on the tangible gift and the intangible bond established by the gift, usury looks to be a particularly nasty threat to gift economies because it exploits this increase. Hyde explains that usury used to refer to any sort of interest charged on a loan but today refers to especially high interest. Ancient understandings of usury are also illuminating. Drawing upon the work of Marcel Mauss, Hyde explains that in Maori culture the customs of gift-giving require recipients to make a return gift that is at least equivalent and probably superior in worth to the original gift. He writes, "The superior value that the 'users' of a gift return or pass along is the 'use-ance' or 'use-ury' of the gift. In this sense, ancient usury is synonymous with the increase that comes to the gift when it is used up, eaten, and consumed, and by the ethics of a gift society this usance is neither reckoned nor charged, it is passed along as a gift" (143–44). This idea introduces a third kind of increase that goes beyond the gift object and the bond. Some gifts have to be consumed in order to be gifts, like food. The increase comes in what food does to one's body after it is consumed. Or take, for instance, education. What one learns, even if one pays for it, will often be used in ways that benefit more people than just the person who learned it. Even for the individual learner, one subject might shed light on another so that attention given to ecology might inform an understanding of environmental law. Luckily, students do not have to pay for this "increase" in understanding or any other personal benefits that stem from it. The increase of education is that part of learning that gets used, extended, or perpetuated after the courses are over. The cliché of the gift that "keeps on giving" is a way of describing this increase.

Ancient usury—that extra benefit that comes from gift exchange—got corrupted by the idea that one could charge for this benefit. As Hyde puts it, "Wherever there is the potential for wealth to increase over time, an interest-free loan amounts to a gift of the increase" (143). But today, these kinds of loans only seem to be given for items, like automobiles, that decline in value over time. Even student loans charge interest. At any rate, to charge for the increase that a gift creates is one way to turn a gift economy into a market economy and thereby ruin the bond created by it. The Koran, The Old Testament, and numerous indigenous cultures prohibit this kind of usury, especially when conducted among members of the same tribe. Some usury is permitted, however, with strangers, which further illustrates how gift economies establish and maintain bonds among participants (146, 148–49).

As will become clear later in this chapter, the forced use of plagiarism detection software, like Turnitin.com, is one way educational systems destroy the bond created between students and teachers because they assume students' intellectual creations are automatically suspect—that they might not be the authors of the work they submit for evaluation and that they do not deserve to be in control of where their work goes. Furthermore, since Turnitin.com receives student work for free, and because it is a for-profit company, the increase they receive from the creative reuse of student work, from these students' gifts, starts to look a lot like usury when weighed against what students get in return.

ART AS GIFT

I am not saying that one's intellectual gifts should never enter the marketplace. Hyde's analysis of gifts recognizes that they may start out in a gift economy and move into a market economy. In particular, he suggests that art and creative works generally may exist in both economies simultaneously. Obviously, a painting, a song, a story, an essay, etc., can be sold and become part of the market economy. The money one makes from the sale can also be used to fund the creation of more artworks. However, he argues that creative works are unique in that they are never made with the market economy as their primary concern. If one makes something primarily for the marketplace, according to Hyde, it ceases to be art (xvi). Interestingly, someone who trades in his or her artistic principles for success in the marketplace is called a *sellout*, not a *giveout*.

Hyde identifies three aspects of creative artifacts that make them gifts. The first is "the initial gift bestowed upon the self," essentially the "unrefined materials of experience and imagination" (248). In other words, artists' experiences, either of the world or of their own imaginations, are gifts because they seem just to arrive on their own. Writers have described moments of inspiration for centuries as "just happening." We often do not know exactly where our ideas come from, and because of this Hyde calls the raw material of art a gift. Second is "the ability to do the labor" necessary to transform the raw material into something else (248). In other places in the book, Hyde relies on Coleridge's notion of the esemplastic power of the imagination, the ability of the mind to unify ideas by molding them to a common purpose. Hyde writes, "An artist who wishes to exercise the esemplastic power of the imagination must submit himself to what I shall be calling a 'gifted state'" (195). This is the sense of gift as talent, but it is more specifically the talent of achieving the state of mind necessary to transform the raw material of art into an artwork. The third aspect is the artwork itself, which represents the increase resulting from the effort exerted on the raw materials. What the artist creates is greater than the sum of its parts and thus represents the increase of the first two gifts. When Stephen Dedalus says at the end of *A Portrait of the Artist as a Young Man*, "I go to encounter for the millionth time the reality of experience and to forge in the smithy of my soul the uncreated conscience of my race" he is describing something of the second aspect of art as gift (252–53). However, only if readers actually do receive his art as some form of human conscience that did not exist previously do they experience the artwork itself as the gift, as the transformation of the raw material that the community provides that establishes the bond between artist and community. In other words, the gift economy is a cycle. Creative works return to their communities as the experiences, insights, feelings, and ways of being of the community that have been transformed by the artist in order to be understood more profoundly or even just differently by that community.

ACADEMIA AS A GIFT ECONOMY

It may seem a stretch to compare student writing to art. Some of it is, and most of it is not. (Most scholarly work is not art either.) Nevertheless, student work is the product of a mind responding to the raw materials of experience and culture. To the extent that student authors can learn to make certain moves during the writing process that shape the raw materials of their experiences into an imaginative product that was not there before—that bubbled up out of the community of the classroom or rhetorical situation they find themselves in—I believe the comparison is useful. Hyde writes, "it is when art acts as an agent of transformation that we may correctly speak of it as a gift" (59). He goes on to say, "with gifts that are agents of change, it is only when the gift has worked in us, only when we have come up to its level, as it were, that we can give it away again. Passing the gift along is the act of gratitude that finishes the labor" (60). This idea of passing the gift along is the promise of scholarship, research, and academia generally. The idea of coming up to the gift's level before it can be given away is connected to the academic standards we hold our students to. We know this, but how do we enact this, especially in writing programs? How do we keep the gifts of the writing classroom, in all their forms, moving?

If writers develop their gifts through the processes of transforming the raw materials of experience and imagination into artifacts that come back to the community, then authorship is contested to the extent that a writer's ability to participate in this gift economy is contested. Even though multiple colleges and universities have made great strides toward open access to faculty scholarship through establishing organizations like the Coalition of Open Access Policy Institutions (COAPI), signing the Berlin Declaration of Open Access, and encouraging Creative Commons licensing of faculty intellectual property, writing programs could do more to help students participate in the gift economy upon which academia's free exchange of ideas depends.

Unfortunately, several forces combine to limit students' participation in the craft that has long depended upon the circulation and creative reuse of preexisting material that happens within a gift economy. In recent years, even though academic understandings of plagiarism have moved away from metaphors of theft, scholarship, research, publications, and inventions developed at academic institutions continue to be called *intellectual property*, suggesting that they can be stolen and thus must be protected through an increased use of Institutional Review Board (IRB) restrictions. Furthermore, an increasingly permissions-based market economy has also maintained the theft or piracy metaphor where reuse of creative artifacts is concerned in the public sphere, even when these artifacts are digital and copies of them do not permanently remove them from their original locations. (The loss of revenue that occurs when a copied digital artifact is given away rather than sold is another matter.) The development of COAPI may be evidence of the pressure felt in higher education of the increasingly commercialized nature of academic research. Creative Commons licensing was developed as a reaction to increasingly restrictive copyright law. Both problems come from denying intellectual creations as gifts. If they are treated as gifts, then anyone can reuse them to suit their own purposes.

Academia's key advantage over the dictates of the market economy lies in its dedication to the gift economy. We have the power of giving away what we value most in order to perpetuate our community's free exchange of ideas. Nevertheless, writing programs could do more to foster the belief in student writers that they not only have the right to transform other authors' works, but that doing so is a fundamental aspect of what it means to be an author. Thus, with transformation comes authorship and a sense of owning what one has made through transformation. Paradoxically, one of the best ways to encourage students to feel they own what they make may be to ask them to transform texts they did not make and then encourage them to give their transformations away. In doing so, they establish the bond of the gift that comes through participation in the gift economy, a bond that every author establishes with his or her audience.

JONATHAN LETHEM AND NECESSARY PLAGIARISM

By way of example of what I mean by authorship being inextricably linked to the process of transforming the texts and ideas of other authors, let me offer the example of Jonathan Lethem. In February, 2007, Lethem published an essay in *Harper's Magazine* called "The Ecstasy of Influence: A Plagiarism." The title is an obvious response to Harold Bloom's famous work *The Anxiety of Influence* in which Bloom proposes a theory of how new poets respond to and are made by the literary influences of their precursors. Lethem's revision to Bloom's theory does not challenge its central premise—that influence happens. Rather it challenges the notion that this influence creates anxiety in the emerging author, leading to a kind of Oedipal desire to usurp the status of the established father-like author in order to attain access to the mother-like muse. Lethem argues instead that authors experience more joy, even ecstasy, in looking to their literary and artistic precursors than they do anxiety. In other words, using others' works to create one's own work can bring an author great satisfaction.

What is most interesting about Lethem's essay, however, in the context of discussions about contested authorship, is that he labels it a plagiarism. He does so because it at first appears to be merely a cribbing of approximately thirty sources that Lethem weaves together without adding much, if any, new material. The sources all deal in one way or another with the issues of creative reuse, plagiarism, copyright, the notion of "the commons," and piracy. He combines these sources through a kind of continuous, sequenced set of synthesizing paraphrase to make his argument about the value of not asking for permission to use other authors' ideas and sometimes even their words. At the end of the essay, however, he provides a key to the sources, which identifies them and their authors. He states that "Nearly every sentence I culled I also revised, at least slightly—for necessities of space, in order to produce a more consistent tone, or simply because I felt like it" (11). Therefore, Lethem's essay simultaneously calls into question and ultimately supports the old notion that an author is someone who originates something. His essay demonstrates once again that repurposing existing material, in the vein of Modernist collage and pastiche or Jorge Luis Borge's wonderful Pierre Menard, is a kind of authorship in itself because no one until Lethem had ever put these thirty sources together exactly in the way he had.

In terms of plagiarism, Lethem's essay raises questions not just about the meaning of the term but what it means to own ideas and exchange creative property, more specifically, texts. His reinvestigation of these concepts, ones so fundamental to the administration of writing programs and to the teaching of writing, led me back to Hyde's quotation offered in the epigraph at the beginning of the chapter: "There is a sense in which our gifts are not fully ours until they have been given away" (364). Ownership has been a god-term in composition for decades, but in our increasingly permissions-based culture, what our students actually own or do not own of their writing would appear never to be more important to figure out. And just as important is the attitude that allows Lethem and other writers before him to believe he can use others' works and make them his own. It is not an attitude we spend enough time helping our students understand. Instead, we focus much of our time scaring students into thinking that they are plagiarizing when they integrate others' ideas so thoroughly with their own that they come to believe the ideas now belong to them just as much as to their sources. The one thing that students should own of their work is the ability to give it away, but writing programs go about this in the wrong way when they require student work to be submitted to plagiarism detection services or when they discourage students from playing with and adapting prior texts.

So is Lethem's work really a plagiarism, or is he just using the term figuratively? By the definition outlined in the Council of Writing Program Administrator's "Defining and Avoiding Plagiarism: The WPA Statement on Best Practices," it could be misuse. The statement indicates that "In an instructional setting, plagiarism occurs when a writer deliberately uses someone else's language, ideas, or other original (not common knowledge) material without acknowledging its source." Clearly, Lethem's use of a key at the end of his essay acknowledges its sources, so that is not the problem. However, just after the definition of plagiarism, the "Best Practices" section goes on to make an important distinction between plagiarism and "the misuse of sources." The distinction is one between "submitting someone else's text as one's own or attempting to blur the line between one's own ideas or words and those borrowed from another source," which would be plagiarism, and "carelessly or inadequately citing ideas and words borrowed from another source," which would be source misuse ("Defining and Avoiding Plagiarism"). After reading his essay, it does seem that part of his project is to blur the line between his ideas and those borrowed from his sources, at least until we get to the key. But more than this, one of the explicit points of an essay that is a tapestry of other sources is that its ideas *are* the ideas of the sources, reshaped for a new context. Lethem appears not just to want to blur the lines but to erase them, and this does seem to push back against how the WPA distinguishes intentional and unintentional plagiarism. If we hold students to this definition of plagiarism, then we need to think about how to avoid its potential to shut down the kind of creative reuse Lethem exhibits in his writing. I will discuss some potential options at the end of this chapter.

No one, as far as I know, has ever contested Lethem's authorship of this patchwork essay. If we use the great arbiter of originality foisted upon our students, Turnitin.com, to check Lethem's work it comes back 100% Lethem. It cannot identify the sources from which Lethem creates his essay. Furthermore, the essay won him an invitation to debate Judge Richard Posner on the subject of plagiarism for a segment on C-SPAN's Book TV.

(Judge Posner, a prominent conservative legal expert and justice on the U.S. Court of Appeals Seventh Circuit, had at the time just published his own book called *The Little Book of Plagiarism*.) Lethem's essay went on to become the title piece of his 2012 National Book Critics Circle Award winning collection of criticism, and even though it is an amalgamation of the thoughts and language of others, it is copyrighted and rightfully so. It is his essay. He enjoys all the rights and responsibilities of its authorship.

I mention Jonathan Lethem because his work as a source-based work of non-fiction, however experimental it may be, is not that different from the sort of writing we ask our students to produce. What seems fundamentally different is his attitude toward transforming other authors' texts, which I attribute to his deeper understanding of what it means to participate in a gift economy, a notion to which Lethem clearly subscribes because Hyde's book was one of the sources Lethem "plagiarized." In fact, Lethem provided a blurb for the back cover of the 25th Anniversary Edition of Hyde's book. It should also be acknowledged that Lethem writes novels and other essays that do not rely so extensively on this kind of creative reuse. Nevertheless, if our students were to turn in an essay that did what Lethem did, it would almost certainly be called a plagiarism, or in Rebecca Moore Howard's terminology, a piece of "patchwriting." Depending upon the attitude of the instructor toward plagiarism, students could fail the assignment, the course, and have their names tracked by a central monitoring system for the rest of their time enrolled at a particular school. The attitude that allows Lethem to try such an audacious article for *Harper's* is the same attitude all authors must have to some degree, but we deny this attitude to our students, and we do so, ironically, in the name of protecting them and their work from plagiarism.

A.V., ET AL., V. IPARADIGMS

To see how a misunderstanding about authorship and the gift economy can go horribly awry in a variety of ways, we only need to turn to *A.V. et al., v. iParadigms*. Roughly a year after Lethem published his essay in *Harper's*, four high school students, two in Virginia and two in Arizona, sued iParadigms, the parent company for Turnitin.com, for $900,000 for copyright infringement and duress. The plaintiffs argued that iParadigms used copies of their essays without their permission and forced them into a contract against their will via the "Clickwrap" user agreement. iParadigms countersued, alleging that A.V., one of the high school students, had committed trespass to chattels and had violated the Computer Fraud and Abuse Act as well as the Virginia Computer Crimes Act. The judge dismissed the case after a motion for summary judgment by both sides, and the reasons for dismissal are intriguing where student authorship is concerned.

First, the court ruled that there was no claim to duress against iParadigms because it was not iParadigms that required that students submit their work to Turnitin. Rather, it was the school systems that required students to submit their work. Thus, the court ruled that the claim of duress ought to be aimed at the school systems. Because each plaintiff had agreed to the terms of the limited liability clause of the user agreement by clicking on the "I agree" button when registering to use the website, the terms of the agreement preclude holding iParadigms liable for "damages arising out of or in any way connected with the use of this website ... or otherwise arising out of the use of this website" (qtd. in *A.V. et al., v. iParadigms* 3). Even though students argued they had no choice but to submit their work or else they would have received a zero for their papers, the judge wrote that "Schools have a right to decide how to monitor and address plagiarism in their schools and may employ companies like iParadigms to help do so" (11). Furthermore, there is apparently no precedent in Virginia law, where the trial took place, for the invalidation of a contract because of third party duress. So even if the school system did coerce the students into submitting their work to Turnitin, the court ruled that it does not invalidate the user agreement.

The remaining issue, then, was whether or not iParadigms had violated the fair use part of copyright law. The court outlined four factors in determining fair use:

1 the purpose and character of the use, including whether such use is of commercial nature or is for non-profit educational purposes;
2 the nature of the copyrighted work;
3 the amount and substantiality of the portion used in relation to the copyrighted work as a whole; and
4 the effect of the use on the potential market for or value of the copyrighted work. (12)

Judge Claude Hilton addressed each factor in his opinion and ruled that iParadigm's use of the students' papers constituted fair use. In terms of purpose, he ruled that iParadigm's use of the student work was "highly transformative" because it used the work for a different and new purpose. This factor is important because the more transformative a use the more likely the original work's copyright has not been violated. Citing *Perfect 10, Inc. v. Google, Inc.* the court ruled that digital copies stored in databases can be considered transformative use of the original work when the purpose of the database is to do something new with the original work. Google had won its lawsuit because it effectively argued that storing the Perfect 10 logo in its database was a transformative use of the logo because it was being used as a reference within Google's search engine and, according to the judge in that trial, Google's search service "provides a social benefit" through the new use. Judge Hilton ruled the situation with the students' essays was essentially the same because the stored copies of the students' works were being used comparatively to check for originality, which counted as a new use and benefited students and school systems by protecting student work from plagiarism. Judge Hilton wrote that iParadigms achieved its transformative use of student work "by archiving the students' works as digital code" and by making "no use of any work's expressive or creative content beyond the limited use of comparison with other works" (13–14). In other words, since iParadigms does not want to use student work to say what the students say, unlike the situation with Lethem and his sources, it is being transformative and has fulfilled the first criterion of fair use.

Briefly, his ruling on the other factors is as follows. In terms of the nature of the work, which relates to creative expression and diminished incentive for future creativity, Judge Hilton ruled that since iParadigms' use of student work does not make use of any creative aspect of the student work, it is a fair use. Factor three relates to the amount of the work used, which in the students' case was the entire work. Judge Hilton ruled based on precedent that using an entire work does not immediately constitute violation of fair use. The Google case was cited again as well as a U.S. Supreme Court case between Sony Corporation and Universal Studios concerning the recording of entire television episodes for the purpose of watching them at a different time, which was determined to be a fair use. Since teachers can only see a student paper stored in the database upon the triggering of similarity on the originality report, and since this use is transformative, using the entire student essay was determined to be a fair use. Finally, concerning the last factor, which deals with the market value of the work, interestingly identified as the most important factor in determining fair use, Judge Hilton ruled that iParadigms' use of student work in no way negatively affected its market value because the essays are not publicly available or accessible. He went further and stated that iParadigms actually protects student work from loss of market value by "preventing others from using student works as their own and protecting the marketability of Plaintiffs' works" (17).

In an interesting footnote in Hilton's opinion, he wrote that the plaintiffs argued in their pleadings that submitting their work to Turnitin would make it impossible to sell their papers to websites like www.ibuytermpapers.com but had stated in their depositions that none of them would ever do this because they saw it as a form of cheating (17). The judge ruled that, despite the possible damage to this market value, the plaintiffs' argument was unpersuasive because ruling in favor of infringement in this instance would damage the benefit of the Copyright Act, which aims to protect the originality of student work and which was the very act that enabled students to mount their lawsuit in the first place (17).

One of the interesting things about this ruling is that it is clear that creative works can flow easily from a gift economy into the market economy but not as easily from the market economy into a gift economy. One needs only to look at the extreme rigidity of iParadigms' user agreement to see how willing they are to let anyone use their service for a transformative purpose. Yet, copyright law and the ruling in this case clearly permit a range of options for reusing existing works that were created with no market value in mind to become part of the marketplace. I don't object to this practice necessarily. Lawrence Lessig has written eloquently about the history of innovative piracy—the reuse of creative artifacts without permission—in the marketplace that has given rise to an amazing variety of creative works ranging from Mickey Mouse to cable television. In his book, *Free Culture*, Lessig cites several examples of twentieth century technological innovation that depended upon some form of piracy. The recorded music industry was pirated by radio when stations began broadcasting recorded music. The recording artists who perform this music have only recently been compensated for radio broadcasts of their performances—unlike the composers of the music—because they were seen as benefiting from the free distribution of their work. Broadcast television was pirated by cable television to bring television to areas that could not receive the broadcast signals. *Steamboat Bill, Jr.*, an early Buster Keaton film, was pirated by a then little-known animated filmmaker named Walt Disney in order to make *Steamboat Willy*, which featured a mouse who would become Mickey Mouse. The tape deck and VCR were initially viewed by the recording industry as technologies that enabled the piracy of music, film, and TV. And, of course, we now have the Internet through which peer-to-peer (P2P) file sharing makes it possible to send copies of digital files to virtually anyone anywhere (Lessig 21–23, 58–61).

Beyond Lessig's examples, there is the ubiquitous Google. When anyone performs a Google search, what gets searched is a copy of the Internet at a moment in time, which is stored on approximately one hundred thousand servers that Google owns. In essence, then, Google pirates the content of every text available on the Internet by copying it without permission in order to be able to search it. It does this innumerable times each day. Lessig makes the argument that this kind of piracy was allowed in the past and continues to be allowed (though in fewer and fewer cases) because the innovations that depended upon it were largely beneficial to American culture. We have music on the radio, wider access to TV broadcasts, various other forms of creativity like photography, collage, remix, pastiche, etc., and a searchable Internet because creative people have been allowed to freely use pre-existing works to create new ones. Imagine if Google or Yahoo or Microsoft had to acquire permission from every maker of every text that the search engines search.

So it is not necessarily a bad thing when an artifact that exists in a gift economy finds its way into the market economy or when artifacts already in the marketplace get reused in an innovative and beneficial fashion. That is, after all, what Lethem's work represents. So if some forms of piracy are beneficial to society because they allow for important innovations, why isn't Turnitin (TII) one of those forms of piracy? It is not one of those forms of piracy because it does not give back something of equal worth to what it gets. Students' creative and intellectual works become hoarded commodities. Rather than protecting student work and authorship, I think it is more accurate to call what iParadigms does a form of usury. It takes the student work generated in a gift economy and uses it to make a profit by selling originality reports back to the institutions whose students make the content the reports are about. TII's search functionality is proprietary. They charge universities roughly $1 per student per year for their service. Students "give" their work to TII, and in 2012, according to the *San Francisco Business Times*, iParadigms made $50 million off the service that depends upon this student work to function properly. If students freely gave their work to TII because they felt the service was worth their gift that would be one thing. Instead, iParadigms sells the increase they receive from students' intellectual gifts. And think of what kind of gift it would be to composition scholars all over the world to have access to the millions of student papers TII has collected in order to analyze them for something potentially more meaningful than their textual similarities. If it wanted to, TII could provide the educational community with the biggest corpus of student papers ever collected.

And herein lies another paradox. Had the students won the case, whereby their "intellectual property" would appear to have been protected, it would have violated the very exchange system out of which their writing was produced because the decision would have limited fair use and further turned their writing into a commodity that anyone would then have to ask permission to reuse. This is why the gift economy is so important. Student work must be gifts to the academic community first and potential moneymakers second. Andrea Lunsford and Susan West warned us of the implications of treating intellectual work as property in the late 1990s. In "Intellectual Property and Composition Studies," published in CCC in 1996, Lunsford and West write the following:

> The academy's nearly compulsive scholarly and teacherly attention to hypercitation and endless listing of sources are driven, for the most part, by the need to own intellectual property and to turn it into commodities that can be traded like tangible property, a process of alienation that is at the heart of copyright doctrine based on the abstract concept of "work." This process is self-perpetuating, of course, when we cite others with the expectation that our own "intellectual property" will be acknowledged similarly elsewhere. (397)

We cannot protect student authorship by thinking about student work as property.

The students and lawyers involved in the iParadigms case claim that the suit was not about monetary compensation for creative property but rather permission and the ability to control their work (even though they were asking for $900,000 for violating copyright law) (Glod). This is probably the greatest evidence that we are not teaching students about the gift economies they participate in while in school. Estimating the monetary value of student work is absurd. Furthermore, students know that they would not have written these papers had it not been for the class and that they don't really have much of a choice in whether to hand them in or not if they want to get a passing grade. Students necessarily have to give up some control over their essays in order to participate in a writing class at all.

At the same time, the scholarship of the field depends on student gifts, which should be under their control at least initially but not in a market-based way. Imagine having to compensate every student for the essays we collect for norming sessions and assignment models or for research on error frequency, composing processes, diversity of dialects, and any other inquiry based on student texts. If iParadigms does not have to pay students for their work, we certainly should not have to because we are the ones who encourage and help them make it. If students' names are involved, if their authorship is made public, then asking students for permission to use their work for research, training, and pedagogical purposes is a necessary act of ethical consideration common to the gift economy. Paying students for this work would not only make such research cost-prohibitive for a significant number of writing programs, it would kill the gift economy that academia has relied upon for centuries. This is what worries me about overprotecting student intellectual property—any intellectual property, really. If we allow the market economy to rule the exchange of ideas what would the teaching of writing (or anything for that matter) become? If the gift economy of academic writing programs becomes a market economy, one could imagine that each institution, depending upon resources, would only be able to use writing models to which they have bought access. Students at schools with big endowments would get to imitate, play with, and re-create pretty much any text they wanted. The rest of us would be limited by the textual models we could afford. Student work would become a commodity, and authorship would devolve into the ability to produce and reproduce what the market demands.

The findings of the Citation Project may be another indication that students think about our classrooms in the same way they think about market demand. This multi-institutional research project, headed by Sandra Jamieson and Rebecca Moore Howard, traces the use of sources in student papers across sixteen participating institutions. Some of their initial findings are telling. Of the 174 student papers the team of researchers reviewed, which contained 1911 instances of source use, 41.5% of the instances were direct quotations, and 31.87% were paraphrase. Ninety-six percent of papers worked with two or fewer sentences from each source, and only 6.28% of the instances were summaries (Jamieson and Howard). A couple of things can be inferred from these data. First, students are not working with very much of the sources they select. Second, rather than transform these sources through summary and paraphrase, students prefer to quote, which changes nothing about the original text. The ability to summarize requires a writer to rank key passages of a text for their importance to the overall message of a text and to reword those passages so that a reader can understand the text's message. To summarize effectively, one has to read the whole text as well so that its key sentences can be found. Students know that instructors want papers with x number of sources—that is the market demand—so they put x number of source uses in their papers. They feel like they are delivering the goods. But in terms of being authors who participate in a gift economy, they are really doing a kind of re-gifting. Somehow, instructors are not getting the message across that what they really want is to know what students think about the sources they write with, and that can only happen when students feel they have the right to transform those sources. Is it possible, then, that the reason not more summary takes place is because students are afraid that they will be accused of plagiarizing? Certainly, some of the lack of summary might come from laziness or from not allowing enough time to write the assignment well. But given the messages that educational systems have sent about intellectual property—that every idea that does not originate within a student must have a parenthetical citation after it—it is no wonder students just opt for the quick copy and paste of the direct quotation.

Transformation is one of the criteria of fair use to avoid copyright infringement, and it would appear to be one of the keys to avoiding plagiarism. It also helps students take ownership of a text and feel like authors. Transforming secondary source material, through dialogue with it and interpretation of it, is exactly what our students need to learn how to do because the genres of writing valued by academia, business, and government require it. But students won't ever be successful if they are afraid of violating an academic code of conduct or breaking a law. My long-term fear is not that students we educate for the future will plagiarize on purpose, but that they won't know how to adapt pre-existing sources for new uses because they were either banned from the practice from the start or were too afraid to take the creative and intellectual risks necessary to solve our most important social, environmental, and cultural problems, which will have to happen through reusing, remixing, and rethinking a lot of old texts and ideas. To be the sort of plagiarist Lethem is students must have access to pre-existing texts that can be freely appropriated and then bent not only to a different purpose but into a different form. I am thinking here of David Bartholomae's oft quoted line from "Inventing the University." He says, "The student has to appropriate (or be appropriated by) a specialized discourse" (624). But students can't do this unless they feel safe in doing so. In other words, they must feel that they have as much right to these texts—that they own them, in a sense—as anyone else.

Of course, there are forms of plagiarism that we seem to unanimously dislike, but perhaps not for the reasons that we often say we dislike them. I would argue that what we really don't like about plagiarism is not the supposed damage it does to the original work, which would seem to be minimal if there at all, or the damage to the prior author's ability to reap compensation for the work as a kind of piracy. What we really don't like about it is the lying, the academic and intellectual dishonesty of ignoring how important someone else was to one's own way of thinking. What we really do not like is the violation of the gift economy that takes place when someone refuses to give back something essential to the community of authors. In denying attribution to their influences, students get to deny that they are in a dialogic relationship with other human beings, thereby dehumanizing academic inquiry. Students who buy papers online or who cut and paste without attribution or transformation participate in the gift economy only to get the presents. And yet, if we really believe in the gift economy, we contribute to it because we believe in sharing ideas. When we become too rigid in how we govern the exchange of ideas by forcing students to turn-it-in rather than turn-it-into-something-else, we consequently use students' gifts against them. And a culture that believes every last creative work should be kept under glass, to be seen but never used, except by those who can afford to do so, will necessarily destroy the gift economy that has been so crucial to technological, scientific, and artistic creation in this country as well as the free exchange of ideas that our higher education system is founded upon.

BRINGING STUDENTS INTO THE GIFT ECONOMY

Writing progams likely set up numerous ways of helping students participate in the gift economy, but I will offer three here. First, I recommend some form of textual intervention assignment as part of any first-year composition course. The terminology comes from Rob Pope's book, *Textual Intervention: Critical and Creative Strategies for Literary Studies*. The assignment that I use the most is a variation/adaptation/translation assignment. In this assignment, students choose a short text—it could be a poem, short story, song, skit, scene from a movie, etc.—and create either a variation, a translation (if they know a second language), or an adaptation of it. For instance, students could turn a short story into a skit or a poem into a painting. The variation can either be sincere or parodic. After they have varied, adapted, or translated the precursor text, students must write an accompanying rationale that explains what they changed about the original text and why, what they did not change about the text and why, how what they made reveals an interpretation of the original text, and what they intend their new work to do for readers—what they intend it to say on its own. Student writing about translations will invariably have to explain their choices of words and phrases that do not easily translate.

Students tend to respond well to this assignment, but where they get hung up is exactly where one might expect them to. Often students do not change enough of the original text. A common first move is to make the text do the opposite. If it is a love poem, students will turn it into a hate poem. If the language feels formal and inaccessible, they will want to turn the language into everyday speech or street slang. But when I review these drafts, I always ask why they wanted to do these things, how these changes reflect an interpretation of the original text, and what sort of experience they wanted their work to give to readers. When they cannot answer these questions in sufficient detail, they have to start again, become more audacious, lose their reverence for the text, as Robert Scholes would say, and really mess with it. They become authors.

Another textual intervention assignment I like to give students asks them to make a short play in which the characters of the play are the authors of the scholarly non-fiction we have been reading in class and the lines of dialogue between characters are direct quotations taken from these texts. Often we will have been working with a set of readings on a theme. Students can set the play wherever they wish, and they have total control over what they write in stage directions, but they cannot change a single word of the direct quotations that will become the lines of dialogue. At first, students do not think they can do it, but then gradually, after much rereading of the texts, a conversation emerges between the characters, and even though the whole class has been reading the same texts, not a single play is the same as another. As one might expect, most of the dialogue feels pretty stilted, but some plays have surprisingly natural sounding moments. I ask for volunteers who want to read their plays aloud in class, and again, I ask all students to reflect on what they have done. In particular, I like to ask them what their plays are about, what an audience might take away after seeing the play performed or after reading it. At this point, students' interpretations of the readings begin to reveal themselves in ways they had not when we initially discussed them. They begin to see how one writer responds if not directly then indirectly to the thoughts of another. They start to see that the quotations they chose reveal what they must have thought the most important, or at least the most obvious, connecting ideas of the readings were. Even when the themes of students' plays are similar, we can discuss how different quotations were used to establish the theme. And finally, we talk about adapting the play back into an essay that they could write with a much larger presence of their own voice wherein the conversation they have imagined in the play becomes the basis of their source use. It doesn't always go smoothly, but that is not the point. The point is to show students how they can transform others' ideas to help them express their own.

My last recommendation for helping foster a gift economy in writing programs is one I have only just begun to imagine. Nevertheless, in consultation with the office of research compliance on my campus, I think it is an idea that can be easily implemented. We need to start local versions of the National Archives of Composition and Rhetoric, which is a joint project of the University of Rhode Island, University of New Hampshire, University of Massachusetts Amherst, and the University of Connecticut, on our individual campuses, and part of these archives needs to be devoted exclusively to student work. The idea is to start a repository of student work created on individual campuses that students could contribute to voluntarily, stipulating how their work would be used by potential researchers. As mentioned earlier, one of the great disappointments about Turnitin is that it has archived millions of student essays that composition and rhetoric scholars, not to mention the students who created them, will likely never get to reuse for genuine scholarly purposes. But if we provide an opportunity for students to donate their work to research, not to act as some referent for originality but for the purposes of sharing some of the writing they made as students at a certain moment in history, then students may feel more like they are participating in the gift economy as authors. The archive would be made available for research purposes to anyone, especially those students who contribute to it. Obviously, students would have to sign some kind of informed consent form before donating their work, but the consent form could also include options similar to a Creative Commons license whereby students indicate how they want their writing to be used—e.g., whether it would be anonymous, for how long it would be part of the archive, etc. The essays could be categorized by how their authors have determined they should be used. If such an archive lasts, it would become a tremendous record of the thoughts and concerns of students and their teachers spanning decades. But more than this, it would recognize student writing as a gift and thereby ensure, at least for those students who contribute, that their authorship will not be contested.

I said early in this chapter that authorship depends on believing that one has the right to transform someone else's words or ideas. It is also depends on the irrational belief that people can own words at least for the time it takes to say something worthwhile. As I hope I have made clear, I am not referring to intellectual property. I mean something more ethereal—the idea that some people want their words to be associated with themselves, what they think, and how they see the world. For our students to think of themselves as authors, they must realize that authorship results not from a product that can be bought and sold or exchanged for a grade. Rather, authorship results in a product that can also become a gift, something that can be freely given away because the person who created it feels it is his or hers to give. The longer I teach writing, the more I am convinced that we must create environments where students want what they write to belong to them, to be associated with their minds rather than with an assignment.

But authorship is a paradox. One must feel that one owns the writing before one can give the writing away, which essentially destroys the ownership but protects the gift. It is not just because I made the poem, the essay, the story that I feel it is mine. I write lots of things that I wouldn't want to give to anyone and don't much care about or might even be ashamed to admit I wrote. However, writing becomes more mine the more I want it to be associated with my having made it. And the more I take ownership of it, the better position I am in to give it to someone else, the more I even want to give it to someone else. What do I need it for once it has become so much a part of my own thinking? Let someone else transform it into some other gift.

WORKS CITED

A. V., et al. v. iParadigms. Civil Action No. 07–0293. USDC E.D. Virginia. 2008. Lexology. Web. 18 March 2013.

Barthes, Roland. "The Death of the Author." *The Critical Tradition*. Third Edition. Ed. David H. Richter. Boston: Bedford/St. Martin's, 2007.

Borges, Jorge Luis. "Pierre Menard, Author of Don Quixote." *Ficciones*. New York: Grove Press, 1962.

Council of Writing Program Administrators. "Defining and Avoiding Plagiarism: The WPA Statement on Best Practices." January 2003. 18 March 2013.

Foucault, Michel. "What Is an Author?" *The Critical Tradition*. Third Edition. Ed. David H. Richter. Boston: Bedford/St. Martin's, 2007.

Glod, Maria. "McLean Students Sue Anti-cheating Service." *The Washington Post*. 29 March 2007. 18 March 2013.

Howard, Rebecca Moore. *Standing in the Shadow of Giants: Plagiarists, Authors, Collaborators*. Stamford, CT: Ablex, 1999.

Howard, Rebecca Moore, and Amy Robillard, eds. *Pluralizing Plagiarism*. Portsmouth, NH: Heinemann, 2008.

Hyde, Lewis. *The Gift: Creativity and the Artist in the Modern World*. New York: Vintage, 2007.

Jamieson, Sandra, and Rebecca Moore Howard. "Data Sheet #1: Source Use in the Paper." *The Citation Project*. August 2011.

Joyce, James. *A Portrait of the Artist as a Young Man*. New York: Viking Press, 1964. Print.

Lessig, Lawrence. *Free Culture: How Big Media Uses Technology and the Law to Lock Down Culture and Control Creativity*. New York: Penguin, 2004.

Lethem, Jonathan. "The Ecstasy of Influence: A Plagiarism." *Harper's Magazine*. February 2007: 59–71.

Lunsford, Andrea A., and Susan West. "Intellectual Property and Composition Studies." *CCC* 47.3 (October 1996): 383–411.

Pope, Rob. *Textual Intervention: Critical and Creative Strategies for Literary Studies*. London: Routledge, 1995.

Ritter, Kelly. "The Economics of Authorship: Online Paper Mills, Student Writers, and First-year Composition." *CCC* 56.4 (June 2005): 601–31.

Scholes, Robert. *The Rise and Fall of English*. New Haven, CT: Yale UP, 1998.

12 Authorizing Plagiarism

Joseph Harris

> Socrates: Now I am well aware that none of these ideas can have come from me—I know my own ignorance. The only other possibility, I think, is that I was filled, like an empty jar, by the words of other people streaming through my ears, though I'm so stupid that I've even forgotten where and from whom I've heard them.
>
> (*Phaedrus*, 13–14)

Undergraduates are routinely told to write about their "own ideas" in their "own words." The alternative, it is suggested, is the murky realm of plagiarism and fraud. But what does it mean, exactly, to "own" a word or an idea? A language belongs to all its users, or to none. And few of us of can expect to come up with ideas that no one else has ever thought of before—at least not on a weekly basis over the course of a semester. So what might it mean, then, to say that people have a way of writing that belongs to them, that expresses who they are, that is their own style?

This question becomes even more fraught when asked about the work of student writers. In this essay I look at the work of a group of writers whose claim to authorship is so contested that they are rarely thought of as being authors at all: first-year undergraduates. These are people whose writing is considered, almost by definition, as lacking in interest, originality, or even competence. Students are writers who are usually only asked to produce, in the memorable words of Robert Scholes, "pseudo-non-literature" (1985). That is, they are asked to write themes that imitate the work of their teachers, who themselves only produce non-literature, or commentary on the writing of "real" authors—poets, dramatists, or novelists. So how can someone, a student, who is asked to ventriloquize the work of someone else, a teacher, who merely analyzes the work of yet someone else, an author, possibly hope to make writing seem "his own" or "her own"?

A few years ago I tried to think through these questions with the help of students in two different introductory courses at Duke University—one in Critical Reading (English 90, Fall 2011), the other in Academic Writing (Writing 20, Spring 2012). But rather than ask students to take on some other role as authors—to write apprentice versions of memoir, or fiction, or journalism—I wanted to see if they could claim authorship *as students*, as writers who are asked to work with and comment on the writing of others.

My inspiration for this work was "The Ecstasy of Influence," a remarkable 2007 essay by Jonathan Lethem in which he brings together questions of plagiarism and style. Lethem argues for a view of intellectual work as something to be shared rather than policed and marketed. As he (in a sense) puts it, "The name of the game is Give All" (68). But my parenthesis hints at what is most intriguing about his essay. For Lethem didn't come up with that phrase about give-all himself; the wording is not "his own." Rather, he has lifted it from the letters of Saul Bellow, much as he has lifted each and every line of his essay from some other writer. Indeed, Lethem calls his essay a "plagiarism"—even though he actually names all of his sources in a key at the end of the piece. But his essay works, at least on a first reading, as a kind of trick, a *tour de force*, in which one quotation runs seamlessly into the next. Lethem's originality, his authorship, lies not so much in what he adds to his sources, but in how he tweaks and arranges them into a form of his own devising. My experience in teaching the essay has been that, even though it is subtitled "A Plagiarism," few readers suspect, until he tips his hand at the end, that what they have been reading all along is not Lethem writing in his own voice but an elaborate weave of snippets and near-quotations.

But that is of course precisely Lethem's point—that his "own voice" as a writer emerges from all the other texts he has read, listened to, and watched. "The Ecstasy of Influence" improves with each new reading, because once you know how it has been put together, you hear not just Lethem but the other voices he is writing with and alongside. And while Lethem clearly admires his influences, he also feels free to play with and add to them. As he notes in his key, "Nearly every sentence I culled I also revised, at least slightly—for necessities of space, in order to produce a more consistent tone, or simply because I felt like it" (68). The result is an essay with a distinctive voice of its own, but that also makes a free and open acknowledgment of its influences.

This is of course precisely the sort of piece we want undergraduates to write. It is in many ways a paradoxical task. We ask students to compose essays that are at once sourced and original—to cite authorities but not defer to them, to draw on the work of experts but not plagiarize. Lethem offers a hyperbolic example of how to negotiate such contradictions. And so, as a way of tackling the questions of originality and plagiarism head on, I asked students to read his essay and to take on his approach as a plagiarist. Here's how I phrased the assignment:

> Working in the mode of Jonathan Lethem, construct a brief and original plagiarism of your own. Of course a key part of your task will be to decide just what it means to work in the mode of Lethem. Let me offer two baseline criteria here:

- Your text must in some way remix, appropriate, or tweak several other texts.
- Your text must contain a key to your sources.

I'd also like you to append a brief reflection on your aims as a writer.

Otherwise, the form your plagiarism takes is up to you. You can construct a print, digital, or multimedia text. You can write on any topic or argue any point you like. You can write in prose or verse, and you can work with print, images, audio, or video. Your plagiarism does not need to rival Lethem's in length. A page or two—whatever that means in this context, and not counting your key and reflection—should be fine.

Students in both courses took this assignment and ran with it. They worked hard and enthusiastically, taking their own pieces through several drafts and commenting with care and interest on the work of their classmates. I was especially struck by the attention that many student writers paid to issues of craft—to making the cuts and connections between the texts they were working with as nuanced and precise as they could. I'd like to share several of their pieces here. I think they offer us insights into the nature of authorship in a remix culture, into how writers use old materials to create something new. I also think they suggest ways of talking about plagiarism, not in simply technical but in intellectual terms; they can help us shift from a deadening preoccupation with rules for documenting sources to more engaging questions of use and value.

WRITING AS REMIXING

Usually the work of a plagiarist is meant to be hidden. The aim is to pass off the work of another as your own. But in a plagiarism of Lethem's sort, the influences need to be seen, the voices of others heard in the mix, or otherwise the tension animating the piece will be lost. This creates some interesting challenges for a writer. As Lethem notes, in the key to his essay, about the problems he faced in working with one of his sources:

> … by the time I'd finished, his words were so utterly dissolved within my own that had I been an ordinary cutting-and-pasting journalist it never would have occurred to me to give Dahlen a citation. The effort of preserving another's distinctive phrasings as I worked on this essay was sometimes beyond my capacities; this form of plagiarism was oddly hard work. (70)

In writing a plagiarism, then, you can't simply work like a kidnapper pasting together a ransom note, cutting miscellaneous words and letters from magazines. It has to matter where your texts come from. You have to hear their "distinctive phrasings" within your own argument. But this recognition doesn't have to be immediate. Sometimes, as with Lethem, part of the meaning and pleasure of a piece can stem from a kind of misdirection. For instance, Chinmayi Sharma's "Tigers Awake" (2011) begins with a rather doctrinaire political speech by a character named Revolutionary X.

> We alone, who own the youth, gain the future. I call on my fellow young people, men and women, to go out into the squares and the streets in all of our cities with our millions.
> Go peacefully. Be courageous. ...

And so on. Almost all of us in the class later admitted that we found this speech predictable and dull. The turning point of the essay, what made it stick in all of our minds, comes after a page or so of such familiar exhortations, when Sharma provides the key to her sources. It begins:

The Key

> 1. "He alone, who owns the youth, gains the future" is a quote by Adolf Hitler and was altered to read 'we' instead of 'he' for a sense of universal invitation in this pro-democracy discourse. ... I continued this paragraph with a quote from Gaddafi, from a speech he delivered on Al Rai TV, September 20, 2011. ...
>
> (Sharma 2011)

What had seemed innocuous suddenly became troubling. Learning that what we had been half-listening to as an ordinary stump speech had actually been co-authored by the likes of Hitler and Gaddafi led many of us, as Sharma's readers, to ask how the clichés of our own political discourse could sound so much like the rhetoric of fascism. We began to see her piece, that is, as a critique of the banality and malleability of political speech—of both the right and the left.

I don't feel I need to argue that this insight is especially profound, although I do think Sharma makes her point cleverly and well. What I do want to note, though, is that she makes that point by leading her readers through two experiences of reading—the first seemingly familiar and bland, the second disruptive. We think we know exactly what sort of text we are reading, and then, with a jolt, we are made to realize we do not. Our perspective—on both the writer's materials and the work she is doing with them—suddenly changes.

Several other writers made use, in varied and imaginative ways, of this sort of surprise turn-around. John Hosey, for instance, created a tri-fold brochure, drawing on images and news articles published in both the U.S. and the Middle East, that documented the charitable work done in Palestine by an organization he called Samah. (See figure 12.1) It is only in his key that Hosey reveals that all of the quotations that appear to be about "Samah" are actually about Hamas, the controversial Palestinian

Figure 12.1 Hosey (2012).

political and military organization. While I worried that some readers might be offended by a text that tries to rehabilitate what many consider a terrorist group, I also felt that this concern was itself evidence that Hosey was doing the sort of intellectual work I had asked of him—that he had a real point to make in complicating our view of Hamas. And that he is able to use images and quotations taken directly from not only Middle Eastern sources like *Al Jazeera* but also Western ones like the *LA Times* and *NY Times* lends his perspective some real credibility. Indeed there's a way in which the act of plagiarizing adds to the authority of this text, since it allows Hamas's charitable work to speak, as it were, for itself. Finally, Hosey's decision to use the form of a mock-brochure deeply unsettles how most of us are used to viewing Hamas. As with most such brochures, "Samah" ends not with an analysis but a call to action, a list of ways that readers can "Make a Difference." We thus seem to be asked to consider Samah/Hamas as something more like the United Way than Hezbollah.

Katherine Zhang offers a different sort of surprise in "A 'New' Way to Cheat-Proof Love." (See figure 12.2) On first glance this text seems simply a deft and cute parody of the advice on relationships given to women by fashion magazines in the decades before the feminist movement. But it's actually more than that; Zhang explains in her key that, while all of her images come from old magazines, the actual advice offered in the written text is taken from a mix of articles dating from both the 1940s and

Figure 12.2 Zhang (2011).

the present. In merging these texts from different eras, Zhang suggests that many of the changes brought about by feminism have occurred, almost literally, on a surface level, that while things may now look different, the kinds of problems that young women continue to face in their relationships—and the advice they are given to cope with them—have stayed much the same.

Let me pause here in order to note some ways in which these student writers not only imitate but extend Lethem's approach. They are ambitious in experimenting with genre. Lethem works solidly inside the form of the literary essay, but few of the students I worked with were drawn to that genre. Sharma writes a speech, Hosey a brochure, Zhang an advice column. Others in the class composed poems, letters, children's books, short stories, screenplays, and video and music mash-ups. Students were also adventurous in working with media other than print. The meaning of both Hosey and Zhang's texts depends on the interplay of words and graphics. Other students incorporated video files, mp3s, drawings, handwriting, decorative bindings, and treated paper into their work. In doing so, they added an interest in the materiality of texts to Lethem's overriding concern with influences.

They also differed from Lethem in the stance they took toward their materials. Lethem's aims in "The Ecstasy of Influence" are both expressive and theoretical—to trace how his own voice is composed of many others, and then to suggest that much the same is true for other writers. He uses his sources, that is, to make a general claim about the nature of authorship. But Sharma, Hosey, and Zhang each want to make a point *about their sources*. Their aims are more focused and limited than Lethem's, more critical and interpretive. They want us to look differently at the specific texts they are quoting.

I don't mean to suggest that these writers improved upon Lethem, only that they found ways of changing his approach as they worked with it. Because of that, their texts strike me as original and distinctive—even if they are composed almost entirely of quotations. None of these writers imitates Lethem. The only way in which the form of any of their pieces resembles his essay is that each includes a key—and that was something I required. Rather, each took the idea behind his writing and used it to construct a different sort of text.

It might be useful to distinguish this sort of work with texts from Kenneth Goldsmith's experimental course in "Uncreative Writing" at the University of Pennsylvania, which he describes in his 2011 book of the same name. Goldsmith is interested in what happens when texts are placed and read in new contexts. He thus assigns students various exercises in copying—to retype five pages of a book, for example, or transcribe an episode of *Project Runway*, or graffiti an old slogan in a public space. Goldsmith's insight is that the very act of cutting and pasting changes the meaning of text. He's right, but it seems to me that his exercises tend to repeat that same point over and over again. I am interested in seeing the different things writers can do with the texts they find and remix.

So let me point to a few other variations on Lethem. A number of writers constructed pieces whose aims were admiring and affectionate. Catherine Wang's "Sparks Fly" is a good example. A fan of romantic comedies, and of the work of Nicholas Sparks in particular, Wang sewed together descriptive passages from Sparks' novels with dialogue from his films (and a few other movie rom-coms) to create a screenplay of her own in which Sam and Mikaela, a handsome yet doomed young couple, meet, flirt, fall in love, bicker, and make up, before one (the girl, of course), tragically, dies. Sam is given to slightly incoherent bursts of philosophizing, Mikaela to sarcastic one-liners. Here's an example:

SAM (stuttering): There's something I want to tell you. After I got shot, you want to know the very first thing that entered my mind? Before I blacked out? Coins. I'm a Coin of the United States Army. I was minted in the year 2009. I've been punched from sheet metal. I've been stamped and cleaned. My edges have been rimmed and beveled. But now I have two small holes in me. I'm no longer in perfect condition.
MIKAELA (quietly, to herself): Then why am I the one lying in this hospital bed? (Wang 2011)

When we read this script together in class, even the guys were eventually reduced to laughter. Wang nails all the goofy excesses of the rom-com genre (how couldn't she, since she's quoting directly from it?), but her aim in doing so seems more appreciative than critical. Her screenplay cheerfully lays bare the conventions of a guilty pleasure.

Mary Nielsen also writes in an appreciative if more elegiac mode in "Thoughts on a Simple Light, A Quiet Glory" (2011), a remarkable poem that in 32 lines fuses the verse of no less than six well-known poets—Milton, Marvell, Wordsworth, Browning, Thomas, and Wilbur—all writing on the theme of life's swift transit. An accomplished poet herself, Nielsen uses Wordsworth's "Tintern Abbey" as both the thematic and metrical spine of her text. In inserting lines from the other poets into this framework, she works to ensure not only that they continue a coherent line of thought but also that they conform to Wordsworth's use of blank verse. Here, for instance, is how she begins her poem:

> And I have felt
> A presence that disturbs me with the joy
> Of elevated thoughts; a sense sublime
> It made no earthly sense, unless to show
> How whatsoever love elects to bless
> Brims to a sweet excess that can without
> Depletion overflow.

And here is how she comments on those lines in her key:

> 2. "Wedding Toast," Richard Wilbur, lines 4–8; I was particularly pleased with how well Wordsworth and Wilbur speak to each other in the first fusing of my lines, especially "It made no earthly sense, unless to show. ..." The first half of the sentence is Wordsworth, and the second is entirely Wilbur with absolutely no additions from me. Yes, I merge the two together, but it's still the chemistry of the two lines that convinces the audience so easily it is but one poet. I switch back to Wordsworth after line 8 and then back to Wilbur in the beginning of the second stanza (lines 24–25). If the two had been alive at the same time, I'm sure they would have had much to talk about as poets.
>
> (Nielsen 2011)

The force of Nielsen's poem has little to do with identifying the *carpe diem* theme in her sources—that is banal. Rather, her key insight is that these disparate poets not only take up similar themes but do so in a similar cadence and idiom that, read together, they really do feel like a single author. As with many other creative plagiarists, Nielsen does not simply point to connections among her sources but rather guides her readers in re-experiencing them. Although she writes in a very different genre, her work thus strikes me as similar in aim and stance to Lethem's, since she both wants us to notice something about how romantic poetry works and places herself as a writer in line of influences. It's a beautiful, finely crafted piece.

Benjamin Schwab makes a similarly admiring and thoughtful use of poetry in "The Shot" (2012). Schwab's aim in this piece is to cross genres, to construct a piece of short fiction out of lines culled from poetry. He works with six contemporary poems about father-son relationships, basically turning each poem into a paragraph. Those six paragraphs then tell a story about a young man growing up, first distancing himself from and then later identifying with his father. Making the transition from verse to prose often required Schwab to change and add to his sources in significant ways. I recall a moment while he was working on his story when he came to ask me if he might be allowed to use some of his own language in the piece—the only time in my career as a writing teacher that I can recall someone feeling the need to ask such permission. (I of course said yes!) But Schwab also worked hard to retain the "distinctive phrasings" of the poems that form the spine of his narrative. Here, for instance, is a paragraph from the middle of his text, in which he recasts Robert Hayden's haunting and lovely short poem, "Those Winter Sundays," to advance both the plot and themes of his own story.

> On the bitter cold Sundays in January, my father would get up early; the struggled thumps of his cane echoed through the house. His curses would fill the crisp morning air as he fought the recalcitrance of the furnace in the basement. The pool table with a lone eight ball became a platter for his tools. He was still waiting to take his shot. After emerging victorious from his extended duel with the furnace, my father would secretly dust off my football trophies, and sigh at his ragged reflection in the golden metal, before returning to bed. The house was always warm when I woke up. No one ever thanked him. What did I know of love's austere and lonely offices?

And here is how Schwab glosses that paragraph in his key:

> Some of the actions stolen from the poem fit naturally to drive my plot, such as the father dusting the football trophies (a parallel of "polishing my good shoes"). This shows that the father is still secretly proud of his son. His problem with his son is not with his son's life, but more a concern that he will not properly turn his son into an adult. The idea of heating the house as a symbol of fatherly protection is also lifted from the poem. I choose to make this a recurring symbol in the death scene. There are only two verbatim quotes:
> "No one ever thanked him."
> "What did I know of love's austere and lonely offices?"
> Despite the lack of much direct plagiarism, this paragraph *is* a very close plagiarism—mostly in theme and symbols. The major deviation arises in the recurrence of the pool game symbolism, when I note the pool table again. It is now clear that the father's "shot" is bringing his

son to adulthood. Appropriately, the father who is still protecting his son by heating the house, is still waiting to pocket the eight ball.
(Schwab 2012)

Part of me chuckles when I read Schwab insisting here that he really *has* plagiarized Hayden. But I also think I understand what he is trying to get at. Schwab wants us to hear the echoes of "Those Winter Sundays" as we read his paragraph—even if he needs to change many of the details of the poem to suit the story he is telling and to make connections with the other poems he is quoting. His insistence that he has written a "plagiarism" springs, I think, from a generous impulse. Schwab wants to give Hayden proper thanks—much as Lethem wants to acknowledge the voices that have helped form his own.

Because, and again much like Lethem, Schwab also wants to claim "The Shot" as his own writing. As he writes in a reflection on his work:

> Manipulating two genres really required me to understand what makes a poem a poem, and a short story a short story. This assignment gave me a lot of sympathy for the narrator in *Old School*. While I certainly put more original work in my short story than the narrator did in his, I do feel like this story is *mine*. I feel like I even own the lines I directly plagiarized. This is probably because I put so much work into bridging the genres, that even verbatim selections had to be considered carefully.
> (Schwab 2012)

(*Old School* is a 2004 novel by Tobias Wolff about a young writer who plagiarizes a short story that we had read together in class.) I am struck here by how Schwab describes earning ownership of his piece through the work of "manipulating" and "bridging" texts and genres. Yes, he has put some "original work" into the story, but what he seems to feel really makes the piece his own is more a process of transformation, of creative reuse. He forges a voice of his own not by trying to separate himself from his influences but by melding his work with theirs.

AUTHORSHIP AS CREATIVE REUSE

In an intriguing 2004 essay, "Something Borrowed," Malcolm Gladwell tells of learning that an article he had written years earlier had been plagiarized as the basis of a play then being performed in London. Gladwell is at first indignant, as one might expect, but his response changes after he reads the play and discovers, to his surprise, that he likes and admires it. As he says,

> I found it breathtaking. ... Instead of feeling that my words had been taken from me, I felt that they had become part of some grander cause. (42)

This sets Gladwell to wondering about the nature of plagiarism. How is it that some borrowings of prior work strike us as imaginative, even revelatory, while others seem derivative or dishonest? What distinguishes, for instance, Kurt Cobain's brilliant reprise of "More Than a Feeling" in "Smells Like Teen Spirit" from the Beach Boys ripping off "Sweet Little Sixteen" in "Surfin' U.S.A"? To some degree, the question answers itself: One use adds value; the other does not. Cobain's rough handling of Boston's power chords serves as a sardonic comment on teen pop culture, while the Beach Boys simply sound like they are trying to sound like Chuck Berry.

The difficulty is that this approach turns a simple technical requirement into a complex question of judgment. Gladwell points to the standard journalistic practice of assigning junior reporters the task of rewriting copy from other news sources. The content of the new piece can be exactly the same as the source—in fact, it is supposed to be the same—but so long as the wording is different, the rewrite is considered original. Gladwell thus observes that

> The ethics of plagiarism have turned into narcissism of small differences: because journalism cannot own up to its own heavily derivative nature, it must enforce originality at the level of the sentence. (47)

The same can obviously be said for academic writing. It's easy to tell students how to avoid plagiarism at the sentence level: Cite your sources, change how they're worded when you can, use quotation marks when you can't. But it is hard (and exciting) to help them write an original essay. Avoiding plagiarism, that is, turns out to be not at all the same thing as becoming an author. Indeed it seems to me that many writing assignments actually direct students to plagiarize on a grand scale—since the task they set is for them to write something that looks and sounds as much like a generic academic article as they can. They are asked, that is, to imitate a form at the level of the essay but to avoid plagiarism at the level of the sentence.

I tried to turn this situation on its head with the Lethem assignment. Since I was asking students to work with found texts, it was almost impossible for them to claim originality at the level of the sentence. They had to look for it—make it—elsewhere. A side effect was to turn questions of authorship and creativity into the obsessive focus of everyone in the class. When students asked what they should write in their reflections on their plagiarisms, I told them: Tell me what makes this piece yours, what you're adding to your sources. It strikes me, in retrospect, that this is a good question to ask the writer of any piece.

In 2010 David Shields published *Reality Hunger: A Manifesto*—an elaborate collage of texts that is in some ways a book-length version of "The Ecstasy of Influence" (it features a blurb from Lethem on the back cover). But Shields strikes me as far more grudging in his acknowledgment of his influences than Lethem. Near the end of his book, he informs us, somewhat churlishly, that "Random House lawyers determined that it was necessary for me to provide a complete list of citations" of the works he has recycled. But before meeting this legal obligation, Shields offers this disclaimer:

> If you would like to restore this book to the form in which I intended it to be read, simply grab a sharp pair of scissors or a razor blade or box cutter and remove pages 210–218. ... Who owns the words? ... Stop, don't read any farther. (209)

In short, he would like every voice in the book to be merged into a single, totalizing discourse—that of David Shields. But this hope was turned nicely on its head when Shields was interviewed on the *Colbert Report* (April 14, 2010). For upon learning that Shields would like the citations cut out of his book, Colbert grabs a conveniently placed pair of scissors and does exactly that. *But then he tosses Shields' own text aside*, and tucks the eight pages of citations back between the jacket covers of the book, with a winking promise to read the now much-reduced volume.

With his usual acumen, Colbert cuts to the quick of the matter. There is an author, there are sources. What matters is their interplay. Shields' book without its references is as of little interest as the list of references alone. The book is just longer. Indeed, I was struck, in reading both Lethem and the work students did with him, that the most provocative and personal part of a plagiarism is often not its main body but its *key*, that part of the text in which a writer comments on the work he or she is doing with sources.

The lesson here seems to me plain: If we want to help students to not only avoid plagiarism but also become authors, we need to ask them to do two things: 1) be as transparent as they can about who their influences are, and 2) show what they are doing with those influences. In all the courses I teach, then, I ask students to add notes of acknowledgement to the final versions of their essays in which they not only thank the people who have helped them in writing but also discuss the authors who have informed their work. These notes are often witty, personal, and charming. But of course the real work needs to go on inside the piece itself, and the question we need to ask students over and over is: What do you want to do with this text? What uses are you making of it? A mediocre answer to such questions is: Summarizing its main idea. A good answer is almost anything else: forwarding, countering, reworking, recontextualizing, parodying.

But there is another lesson to be learned here, I think, that has to do with the difference between asking students to imitate a form and to take on an approach. As I mentioned earlier, few of the students I worked with were drawn to the literary essay as a form. Rather, most took up Lethem's approach, his way of working with texts, and adapted it for work in another genre (speech, brochure, advice column, screenplay, poem, short story) and/or other media (audio, video, digital). Indeed much of the originality and interest of their work sprang out of this process of adaptation. They were not only doing things with their materials, they were doing things with Lethem. The result was a set of pieces that varied widely in structure and genre but that attempted a similar sort of intellectual work with texts.

This contrasts with the familiar sort of academic essay that, while perhaps not plagiarized, is nonetheless derivative, in which a student carefully documents her or his sources but has little to say about or add to them. Our ambitions, our demands, for student writing should be higher. Recent years have seen a marked surge of interest in genre in rhetoric and composition. To some degree I share this interest, so long as it includes how writers can surprise as well as meet the expectations of their readers. But I find the teaching of set forms stultifying. Our focus needs to be on the intellectual work a text does, not the structure or form it follows. The kind of writing I want to teach hinges on a responsiveness to the work of others. If writers are doing that sort of critical work, if they are adding something new to the conversation, then it seems to me their writing can only grow more interesting as its form grows more unexpected, nuanced, and idiosyncratic. All of us have the words of other people streaming through our ears. The trick to becoming an author is to learn how to respond to those voices and make them part of your own.

Perhaps the defining characteristic of composition as a subfield of English studies is its interest in the writing of ordinary people: students, workers, and community members. But as soon as you begin to look closely at the work of such writers, you see that it is often not so ordinary at all. What composition contests, then, is a division of the universe of discourse into authors and non-authors. What it allows is an appreciation of the things we can all do with texts, of how we can use the materials of our cultures to our own ends.

ACKNOWLEDGMENTS

I'd like to thank the students whose work I discuss in this essay for giving me permission to quote their writing. But I also want to thank all the students in English 90 and Writing 20. They did remarkable work, and I wish I were able to quote more of their pieces. My view of authorship and plagiarism changed as a result of the work we did together. Readers can access the materials for English 90 and Writing 20 by clicking on the links for those courses at josephharris.me.

WORKS CITED

Colbert, Stephen. Interview with David Shields. *The Colbert Report.* Apr 14, 2010. http://www.colbertnation.com/the-colbert-report-videos/270740/april-14-2010/david-shields. Accessed 15 September 2013.

Gladwell, Malcolm. "Something Borrowed." *The New Yorker* (Nov 22, 2004.): 40–48.

Goldsmith, Kenneth. *Uncreative Writing.* New York: Columbia University Press, 2011.

Hosey, John. "Samah: A Force for Good in Palestine." Durham: Duke University, 2012.

Lethem, Jonathan. "The Ecstasy of Influence: A Plagiarism." *Harper's* (Feb. 2007): 59–71.

Nielsen, Mary. "Thoughts on a Simple Light, a Quiet Glory." Durham: Duke University, 2011.

Schwab, Benjamin. "The Shot." Durham: Duke University, 2012.

Scholes, Robert. *Textual Power*. New Haven: Yale UP, 1986.

Sharma, Chinmayi. "Tigers Awake." Durham: Duke University, 2011.

Shields, David. *Reality Hunger: A Manifesto*. New York: Knopf, 2010.

Wang, Catherine. "Sparks Fly." Durham: Duke University, 2011.

Wolff, Tobias. *Old School*. New York: Vintage, 2004.

Zhang, Katherine. "A 'New' Way to Cheat-Proof Love." Durham: Duke University, 2011.

Contributors

Paul Butler is Associate Professor of English at the University of Houston, where he teaches undergraduate courses in writing and graduate courses in the doctoral concentration, Rhetoric, Composition, and Pedagogy. He is the author of *Out of Style*, *Style in Rhetoric and Composition*, and *The Writer's Style*, forthcoming from Oxford University Press. His articles appear in *JAC, Rhetoric Review*, WPA, and other venues.

Ron Fortune is Professor Emeritus of English at Illinois State University. His research and teaching interests have focused on the relationship between textual scholarship and writing studies. Subsidiary interests involve the role of computers in exploring this relationship, the effects of manuscript studies on the development of critical reading and critical writing abilities, and textual forgery as a form of writing. His published scholarship has appeared in various academic journals and essay collections, and the National Endowment for the Humanities has funded a number of manuscript-focused projects that he has directed.

Erin A. Frost is an Assistant Professor at East Carolina University. She specializes in technical and professional communication, rhetoric and composition, and women's and gender studies.

Joseph Harris is an English professor at the University of Delaware, where he directs the writing program and teaches academic writing, critical reading, creative non-fiction, and digital writing. Previously, he was the founding director of the Thompson Writing Program at Duke University. His books include *A Teaching Subject: Composition Since 1966* (updated 2012), *Teaching with Student Texts* (2010), *Rewriting: How To Do Things With Texts* (2006), and *Media Journal* (1998). He served as editor of the CCC journal from 1994–99 and of the SWR book series from 2007–12. He is currently at work on *Dead Poets and Wonder Boys*, a book on how the teaching of writing has been depicted in film and fiction. To learn more, visit josephharris.me.

Matt Hollrah is an Associate Professor of English and the Director of Composition at the University of Central Oklahoma. His academic work has appeared in the *Minnesota Review* and *READER*. He is also the author of two online composition textbooks entitled *So What?* and *Now What?* He lives with his wife, Julie, and their two children, Sadie and Simon, in Edmond, Oklahoma.

Rebecca Moore Howard is a graduate of West Virginia University who has taught at Texas Christian, Cornell, Colgate, and Binghamton Universities and is now Professor of Writing and Rhetoric at Syracuse University. She has written and edited a number of scholarly and pedagogical books and essays, including *Standing in the Shadow of Giants: Plagiarists, Authors, Collaborators* (1999) and (with Amy E. Robillard) *Pluralizing Plagiarism: Identities, Contexts, Pedagogies* (2008). With Sandra Jamieson, she is a principal researcher in the Citation Project <citationproject.net>, a collaborative, multi-site, data-based study of college students' use of research sources.

Kyle Jensen is an Assistant Professor of English at the University of North Texas, where he teaches courses in rhetorical theory and writing studies. He is the author of *Reimagining Process: Online Writing Archives and the Future of Writing Studies* (2014), and his essays have appeared in *JAC* and *Rhetoric Review*.

Seth Kahn is a Professor of English at West Chester University of PA, where he teaches courses in writing and activist rhetoric, and serves as Mobilization Chair for his faculty union local. He is currently serving as Co-Chair of the CCCC Committee on Part-Time, Adjunct, or Contingent Labor. Recent publications include a co-edited (with Sharon Henry and Amy Lynch-Biniek) special issue of *Open Words* on contingent labor and educational access, the chapter "What Is a Union?" in *A Rhetoric for Writing Program Administrators*, and the co-edited (with Jong Hwa Lee) collection *Activism and Rhetoric: Theories and Contexts for Political Engagement*.

Kevin Mahoney is an Associate Professor of Composition and Rhetoric at Kutztown University of PA. He teaches courses in writing, rhetorics of advocacy, and activist media. He has been active in his faculty union leadership since he arrived on campus in 2002. In 2011, Mahoney founded Raging Chicken Press–a progressive, activist media site–to help build a progressive media network in Pennsylvania. His recent publications include *Democracies to Come: Rhetorical Action, Neoliberalism, and Communities of Resistance*, co-authored by Rachel Riedner of The George Washington University and "Viral Advocacy: Networking Labor Organizing in Higher Education," in *Reflections: A Journal of Public Rhetoric, Civic Writing, and Service Learning*.

Rachel Parish currently teaches Rhetoric and Composition at Southeastern Illinois College, John A. Logan College, and Shawnee Community College. When she's not teaching, Rachel works as a freelance writer and artist and helps her family maintain their herd of Hereford show cattle and raise Pembroke Welsh Corgis.

Val Perry Rendel is known as The Writing Doctor. She spent 18 years teaching in and directing college writing programs before leaping from the ivory tower to embrace her alter ego as a freelance copywriter. Now she works with businesses and entrepreneurs to provide the writing services they need, and teaches MOOCs on writing and literature through a variety of platforms.

Amy E. Robillard is Associate Professor of Rhetoric and Composition at Illinois State University, where she teaches undergraduate and graduate courses in composition, rhetorical theory, authorship studies, and life writing. She is the editor, with Rebecca Moore Howard, of *Pluralizing Plagiarism: Identities, Contexts, Pedagogies*. Her work has appeared in *College English*, *JAC*, and *Life Writing*, as well as several edited collections.

Kellie Sharp-Hoskins is Assistant Professor of English at New Mexico State University. Her research investigates and theorizes rhetorical imagination, especially as it manages possibilities for relationships among language and bodies.

Julia Marie Smith is a Marion L. Brittain Postdoctoral Fellow at Georgia Institute of Technology. She completed her PhD at the University of Illinois, Urbana-Champaign, with a concentration in Writing Studies. Her specializations include history of rhetoric, especially concerning issues of collaboration and the use of text technologies.

James Zebroski is the senior composition faculty person at University of Houston. The focus of his scholarship over the last thirty-five years has been critical theory and writing. This work has centered on many forms of unauthorized writing. In nearly fifty published essays, he has widely explored a variety of related topics including Vygotsky, social class, alternative histories of rhetoric and composition, ethnographic writing, and Post-Stonewall gay literature. His book, *Thinking through Theory: Vygotskian Perspectives on the Teaching of Writing*, published in 1994, is still in print. It is the first and only book-length treatment of the work of Lev Vygotsky in rhetoric and composition. He put into place a new PhD program in Rhetoric, Composition and Pedagogy at University of Houston.

Index

A Very Natural Thing 131, 132n, 133
abduction 30, 52
activism 89, 97, 100, 123, 145, 208
al Omaril, Amina Abdallah Arraf 9, 21, 23, 37
anonymity 33, 35, 37n, 38, 39, 49, 112, 148, 154–55
Aristotle 22, 37, 75, 88
attribution, norm of 2, 7, 8, 10, 13, 47, 51, 71, 76, 77, 90, 148, 149, 150, 151, 156–57, 165, 169, 188
authenticity 8, 23–25, 29, 32–34, 36, 57–59, 64–65, 71–72, 79, 162, 164, 168, 172
authorless 37n, 72, 78, 81–83, 85, 173
authorship and anxiety 8–9, 40–45, 52, 73, 165, 170, 179; and gender ix, 5–6, 9, 12, 17, 24, 27, 33–35, 38, 78, 86n, 93, 142; and technology 6–7, 17, 38, 48, 53, 85n, 86, 88, 107, 108, 153, 156, 158, 191; automated 2, 9, 40–49, 51, 54; collaborative 3, 5, 10, 12, 17, 37n, 76, 83–84, 100–102, 104, 161, 166–67; contrived 7–9; distributed 7, 10–11; excluded 7, 12, 14; formalist 122; gay 9, 13, 21–25, 27–33, 35, 37n, 121–32, 135, 138–142, 145–46; multiple xii, 2, 10, 12, 22, 36n; nascent 7, 14; post-authorship-theory 13, 137–38, 140, 145; romantic 2, 4, 10, 57–58, 198–199; sexual practices 126, 130, 131; solitary 2, 10, 36n, 174; student ix–x, 3–4, 7, 14–15, 57, 83, 99, 125–26, 151, 153–55, 161–65, 168–71, 172–178, 180–90, 192–194, 197–198, 202–204

Barthes, Roland xi–xii, 49, 74–75, 105, 137, 173; "Death of the Author" xi, 109, 137, 144–145

Bergman, David 121–28
Black, Rebecca 107–08, 112–13
Bourdieu, Pierre ix
Bracher, Mark 150–51
Bram, Christopher 121–29
Butler, Judith 75

Chatterton, Thomas 10, 56, 58–59, 62
class 1, 5, 12, 27, 55, 89, 105, 126, 128, 131, 151
Colbert, Stephen 203
commodity 15, 166, 168, 170, 172–73, 175, 185–86
composition studies 3, 14, 71–72, 85, 185
copyright 4–5, 12, 35, 73–74, 77, 83, 108–10, 112–113, 178–79, 181–83, 185, 187
counterculture 121–22, 128–29, 131–32
counterpublic 136–38, 139–41, 144–45
Crafts, Hannah 1, 5, 12; *The Bondwoman's Narrative* 1, 5
credibility 23–25, 28, 32–34, 36, 37n, 73–76, 80–81, 104, 164, 168, 196

Defense of Marriage Act (DOMA) 13, 135–37, 138, 143, 145
Don't Ask, Don't Tell (DADT) 13, 135–36, 138–41, 145

ethos 9–10, 15, 21–25, 27–28, 30–37, 37n, 56, 72, 74–83, 93, 104, 122, 161–62, 164–66, 168–70

fan fiction 2, 11–12, 107–16
forgery 2, 9–10, 55–56, 58–68, 71

Index

Foucault, Michel xi–xii, 8, 12, 36n, 40, 47–53, 72, 74, 76–77, 105, 135–36, 138, 144–45, 173; author function xi, 8, 10, 48–49, 51, 72–74, 79, 105, 173; "What Is an Author?" xi, 36, 51–53
Frank, Anne 161–64

Gates, Jr. Henry Louis 1–2, 5
Gay Girl in Damascus, A 9, 21–23, 25, 27–31, 33, 35, 37n
gift economy 15, 173–78, 181, 183–90
Gilligan, James 153–55
Gladwell, Malcolm 201–2
Glenn, Cheryl 135–37, 144

Hollingsworth v. Perry 135, 141–42, 145
Howard, Rebecca Moore 4, 8, 14, 73, 78, 172, 181, 186
Hyde, Lewis 172–77, 179, 181

identity maintenance 154
intellectual property ix, 3, 12, 15, 77, 170, 172, 178, 185–87, 190
iParadigms 15, 181–86

Johnson, Samuel 58

kairos 11, 89, 95, 105, 145
King, Jr., Martin Luther 15, 162, 170
Kinneavy, James x–xii
Knights Out 138–39

Lane, Rose Wilder 166–67
legitimacy 64, 71–74, 79, 161–62, 169
Lessig, Lawrence 184
Lethem, Jonathan 15, 179–81, 183–84, 187, 193–95, 197–99, 201–04
Longfellow, Henry Wadsworth 60–61

MacMaster, Tom 9, 21–22, 24, 30–37, 37n
Macpherson, James 10, 56–59, 62
Marriage Equality USA 142–43

Obama, Barack 100–01, 128, 139–40
Occupational Safety and Health Administration 79–80
Occupy Wall Street 11, 89–96, 101, 103–04
One Wisconsin 90

originality 4, 15, 72–74, 78–79, 95, 104, 149, 165–66, 180, 182–83, 185, 190, 192–93, 202–03
ownership 3–4, 11–12, 15, 36n, 73, 77, 95, 104, 107, 109, 161, 170, 173–74, 179, 187, 190, 201

patchwriting 4, 14, 169–170
peer review 13, 108, 113, 148–57; and recognition 13, 148–51, 153–57; role of editor 149, 155–57, 162; scholarly 149, 151–52, 154, 155
Perry, Kristin 135, 141
plagiarism i, 192x, 2–4, 14–15, 21, 31–32, 37n, 71–73, 78, 85n, 149–53, 156, 161, 165, 169–70, 172, 176, 178–83, 187, 192–94, 200–04
Poe, Edgar Allen 10, 60, 62–63, 65–67; "Leonainie" 60, 63–64, 66–67
Proposition 8, California 135–38, 140–43, 145
Pugh, Sheenagh 107, 109, 113–15

Raging Chicken Press 11, 89–90, 96, 98, 102, 104
rhetorical chorus 9, 22–23, 25–27, 29–36
Riley, James Whitcomb 10, 60, 63
Ritter, Kelly 173
Rowley, Thomas 58–59

Scholes, Robert 189, 192
Shakespeare, William 15, 108, 162, 165–66, 168
Shields, David 202–03
social media 32, 92, 96–97, 102–03, 107–08, 112
source use 4, 6, 15, 23, 28, 37n, 41–42, 81, 101, 111–112, 165, 170, 172, 179–81, 183, 185–87, 189, 193–200, 202–04
Steward, Sam 13, 122, 125–28, 132n
Stonewall 13, 121–22, 124–32, 132n

technology 6–7, 48, 85n, 86n, 107–08, 153, 156
text/textual xi, 6–7, 15, 22, 48, 55, 57–58, 67, 71–72, 76–79, 81–82, 112, 161–62, 165, 167–68, 174, 185, 186, 188, -89
textual poaching 109

United States v. Windsor 136, 143–45

Violet Quill Writing Group 121–23, 125, 128

Warner, Michael 137, 142–43, 144
Wilder, Laura Ingalls 161–62, 166–68, 171
Wisconsin Uprising 89
Woodmansee, Martha 2, 36n

Worsham, Lynn 73, 153
WPA council 180
writing algorithmic 9, 44, 46, 48; and rhetorical studies x–xii; creative writer ideology 13, 122; digital 36, 36n; software 40–48, 51, 83, 176; teaching of 156; technical 78, 83; transitive 49, 51